IL MORO

Ellis Heywood's Dialogue
in Memory of Thomas More

IL MORO

Ellis Heywood's Dialogue in Memory of Thomas More

EDITED AND TRANSLATED WITH AN

INTRODUCTION BY ROGER LEE DEAKINS

Harvard University Press   Cambridge, Massachusetts   1972

Publication of this book has been aided by a grant
from the Hyder Edward Rollins Fund

Library of Congress Catalog Card Number 75–184107

SBN 674–58735–9

Printed in the United States of America

ACKNOWLEDGMENTS

I would like to thank Professor Elizabeth Blackburn of Wisconsin State University for her kind assistance, and Professor Thomas G. Bergin of Yale University for letting me consult both his own translation of *Il Moro* and some manuscript notes on Ellis Heywood compiled by the late Professor R. C. Bald.

The Italian text of *Il Moro* has been reproduced from a copy in the Harvard College Library.

CONTENTS

INTRODUCTION

Ellis Heywood

Il Moro is the record of a debate between Sir Thomas More and six friends about the ultimate goal of human activity ("true happiness"). Laurence, a merchant, argues for riches; Charles, for honor; Peter, for love; and Alexander, for knowledge. After these alternatives are dismissed, Leonard argues that happiness is relative to the individual, and Paul holds forth on the theme that seeking for happiness is the worst kind of vanity. Then Sir Thomas More steps in to reconcile these antagonistic views from the standpoint of a Christian humanist. Happiness, says More, is to be found in the control of appetite by reason, that divine faculty in man which uses the things of this world as instruments for working out the full implications of our relation to God.

Ellis Heywood's principal intention in "recording" this debate about happiness seems to have been to provide posterity with a loving memorial of England's greatest humanist (also his granduncle). The More who speaks in *Il Moro* is the More who wrote *Utopia* (1516), the exponent of a tolerant, humanistic culture and an internationally renowned man of letters, not the fierce anti-Lutheran polemicist of the 1520's or the Catholic martyr of the 1530's. *Il Moro* is, in fact, superbly indifferent to the pressing political and religious concerns of the time in which the dialogue supposedly took place. The two crucial events of the period for More were his retirement from the Lord Chancellorship (1532) and his execution (1535). Both events were due to More's unwillingness to accept Henry VIII's claim to supreme headship of the Church, yet Heywood attributes the retirement to More's lack of ambition and he reserves mention of the execution until the very last sentence of his dialogue.

The More of *Il Moro* not only speaks well of happiness, but also leads a happy life. He has enough wealth to be able to put his house at the disposal of his friends; he has the honor of his friends, who revere him as the wisest of their circle; he has love, that "affinity of souls" that unites human beings in the most trustworthy of all bonds; and the fact that he has true knowledge is the burden of the entire dialogue. More in *Il Moro* is a "speaking picture" of a man who has realized perfection in the active life as Lord Chancellor and is now about to achieve perfect realization of the contemplative life by confronting the vision of God.

The serenity with which More cultivates his philosophical garden in *Il Moro* is less surprising when we consider the author of the dialogue and the time in which he wrote. Ellis Heywood (1530–1578) was born into a prominent London family that contributed in diverse ways to the literary culture of England during the Counter-Reformation. Ellis' father, John Heywood, wrote plays for Henry VIII's court, as well as epigrams and epic poems; Ellis' younger brother, Jasper, was the first translator of Seneca's tragedies into English; a grandfather and an uncle were prominent London printers and editors. The most notable of Ellis' relatives, however, were Sir Thomas More, his granduncle, and John Donne, his nephew.[1]

Like many less prominent but no less resolute English Catholic families, the Heywoods walked carefully during the confusions of political and religious reformation. Only after the death of Queen Mary (1558) did the Heywoods abandon their property and flee to the Continent. In the 1530's and 1540's, when Ellis and Jasper were studying at Oxford, their father wrote a series of plays that seem to crystallize what must have been the mood of many thoughtful English Catholics forced by the times to defend threatened institutions.

The structure of most of John Heywood's plays is the same: a debate in which the characters engage in order to assert their superiority over others. The specific debate may be about who has the greatest pleasure in love, or who can tell the biggest lie, or whether the weather should be hot all year round. Whatever the subject, the message is always the same: find contentment in the good that God bestowed on you and do not envy others their good. Accept your place as a finite will in a hierarchical universe where the hierarchy manifests itself primarily as contradiction. In the world of John Heywood's plays, when the wills of individual characters conflict, "reason" degenerates into "cunning" or "wit," thereby reversing hierarchical order. Will becomes the master and reason the

---

[1] For the few facts known about the life of Ellis Heywood, see the entry prepared by Thompson Cooper for the *Dictionary of National Biography*, s.v. "Heywood, Ellis." Cooper's assumptions that Heywood was on the Continent for several years preceding the publication of *Il Moro* and that he was in Florence in 1556 may be incorrect, for Heywood was presented with the prebend of Eccleshall in the Cathedral Church of Lichfield in 1554. See Thomas Harwood, *History and Antiquities of the Church and City of Lichfield* (Gloucester, 1806), p. 228. Additional information on several members of the Heywood family can be found in A. W. Reed, *Early Tudor Drama* (London: Methuen, 1926).

servant. John Heywood's solution for the inversion of proper relationship is not to assert the fundamental rationality of the universe (as in *Utopia* and *Il Moro*) but rather to assert the necessity to suppress and chastise the will in the name of social order.

Chastisement of the will for the sake of order is the formula that John Heywood offered to resolve complex social and political issues. When he applied that formula to the troubled institutional life of early Reformation England, it was apt to sound like a kind of genial know-nothingism. Here, for instance, is how the Peddler in *The Four PP's* answers those who are skeptical of miraculous saints' relics:

> But where ye dout the truthe nat knowynge
> Beleuynge the beste good may be growynge
> In iudgynge the beste no harme at the leste
> In iudgynge the worste no good at the beste
> But beste in these thynges it semeth to me
> To take no iudgement vpon ye
> But as the churche doth iudge or take them
> So do ye receyue or forsake them[2]

What the Peddler advocates here undoubtedly made excellent practical sense to perplexed Catholics in the latter years of Henry VIII's reign, but if we extrapolate the basic formula from its specifically religious context (which Heywood encourages us to do by applying it himself to a deliciously Chaucerian variety of amorous and clerical situations), we see that Heywood tells us to find contentment in irrational acceptance of the contradictoriness and refractoriness of things as they are.

Heywood's tone was not, of course, the only one adopted toward Henry's policies. When the King executed Sir Thomas More in 1535, Catholics everywhere were shocked. Henry's cousin, Reginald Pole (to whom *Il Moro* is dedicated) called More's execution the "blood drinking" of "wild beasts," and it precipitated his long and emotional defense of papal supremacy, *Pro unitatis ecclesiasticae defensione*. Pole's book depicted More as "the greatest of the English" and his execution as the act of a madman bent on asserting his own authority at the expense of all law, positive, natural, and divine. When thinking of More's "murder," wrote Pole, "the involuntary tears that fill my eyes prevent me from writing further, and tear drops dissolve whatever letters I manage to set

---

[2] John Heywood, *The Play Called the Four P. P.*, quoted from R. de la Bère, *John Heywood, Entertainer* (London: George Allen & Unwin, 1937), p. 229.

down on the page."[3] The unrestrained emotional stance of Pole's rhetoric culminates in parallels of More to Socrates and to Christ—all perfect models of martyrdom to the fury and ignorance of those for whose welfare they were working.

The More whose loss Pole laments (the same More that Heywood describes in the opening pages of *Il Moro*) is the humanist scholar whose learning "might have adorned every branch of knowledge" and the "sweet spirit" whose "urbanity and refinement of wit devoid of impertinence" revealed a nature that "would harbor anything before maliciousness." Devoid of personal ambition, More had abandoned the Chancellorship when it became impossible for him to work for the welfare of the people within the institutional framework. But even retirement was not enough; the cause of true religion demanded that he give up his very life, and this he did courageously, with, like Christ, a prayer on his lips for the conversion of his enemies. "O beloved country, O England," cried Pole, "surely no widow ever had more cause to beweep the loss of her only son, nor any army the loss of its beloved commander, than you have cause to bewail, in grief unending, this illustrious child, this truly unique son, whose like you have never borne before!"[4]

A generation later, when Ellis Heywood set out to memorialize his granduncle in *Il Moro*, religious conditions had altered drastically. Mary, daughter of Catharine of Aragon and cousin of Charles V, the Holy Roman Emperor, was busy undoing the religious changes initiated by her brother and her father, and she had brought Reginald Pole, now Cardinal Pole, back from the Continent to direct her church policy.

To twenty-four-year-old Ellis Heywood, Mary's appointment of Pole as her Archbishop of Canterbury must have seemed like a progressive move because Pole had taken an active part in the Counter-Reformation. Created Cardinal Pole by the reform-minded Paul III, Pole served as papal legate to, and a prime mover behind, the Council of Trent (1545). Like John Colet, Sir Thomas More, and Erasmus, he was a strong advocate of reforming the ignorance and greed of the clergy. Pole was not esteemed by those members of the Roman Curia who thought his views on justification smacked strongly of Lutheranism—a prejudice that

---

[3] *Reginaldi Poli Cardinalis Britanni, ad Henricū Octauum Britanniae Regem, Pro ecclesiasticae unitatis defensione, libri quatuor* (Rome, 1536), fol. xciiii[v]. [Translation mine.]

[4] *Pro ecclesiasticae unitatis defensione*, fols. xc[v], xci[r], xc[v].

was later reinforced when Pole, who, like More and Erasmus, had little taste for the subtleties of scholastic philosophy, retired from the Council discussions on justification "for reasons of health."

Pole initiated his career as Queen Mary's Archbishop with sermons which, like those of the Edwardian Anglican, Hugh Latimer, stressed reformation of the immorality and ignorance of the clergy. Such themes, and the earlier religious and cultural themes in the illustrious Cardinal's writings, must have had a singular appeal for young Ellis Heywood, who, after taking a B.C.L. at Oxford (1552), held a position as a private secretary in the Cardinal's large continental retinue. The relationship between the two men was not necessarily intimate; the affinities of their scholarly temperaments would have been balanced by large differences in age and social station. To Heywood, when he penned the dedication to *Il Moro*, Pole must have seemed first of all a symbol of England's return to the mainstream of a reformed European Catholic civilization. In Cardinal Pole, the embattled Catholic culture of Ellis Heywood's family had found a firm footing at last.

Another sign of the optimism generated by the succession of Mary to the throne was a revived interest in Sir Thomas More. The Latin text of *Utopia*, translated into English for the first time in 1551, was republished in 1556, and a complete edition of More's English writings was published by William Rastell, Ellis Heywood's uncle, in 1557. Rastell also planned a full-length biography, but that project was apparently abandoned after Mary's sudden death.

To satisfy that renewed interest in More, Ellis Heywood has created in *Il Moro* a figure of myth, not of history, a *figura* of that moral and spiritual idealism that animated Roman Catholic art in its post-Tridentine phase. Heywood's More is a baroque figure who turns easily from abstract discussions of moral philosophy to elaborately self-conscious word plays, and just as easily from puns to the ecstatic contemplation of God.

In Heywood's dialogue, seriousness and lightness are held in perfect suspension, and this juxtaposition of opposed qualities creates the balance that emerges as More's most salient characteristic. More loves life, but he does not value it unduly. The perennial question of moral philosophy, "What is true happiness?" engages him; but, because he is already truly happy, he is also detached from a discussion that provokes strongly ego-involved "position statements" about happiness from each of the other speakers. Thus the relationship of More to the other speakers (expressed in the totality of his words and deeds) is a figural representation of an ideal, yet possible, state of being. This figural representation takes the form of a mock trial with More as judge and the other speakers as persons before the bar. After each has had his say, More defines the problem of happiness and proposes the solution that has evaded the others. They have been concerned only to assert their superiority in argument, while More wants to discover the truth. The others cling tenaciously to partial notions about happiness (each typical of a current in Renaissance moral philosophy) and are unhappy, while More is happy precisely because he has moved beyond these partial insights to a more comprehensive vision of human happiness.

Like other writers and artists of the post-Tridentine phase of the Counter-Reformation, Heywood found the materials for that vision in St. Thomas Aquinas. From St. Thomas comes More's assertion in *Il Moro* of the superiority of the contemplative life over the active. Also from him comes the formula for happiness that More presents at the end of the dialogue: happiness consists in that act of judgment whereby reason checks the will and, at the same time, understands the appropriateness of doing so. Thus More restates, in psychological terms, the hierarchical view of reality that had provided the intellectual framework for pre-Reformation Catholic apologetics. In More's formula for happiness, reason subordinates the will out of a full sense of the justness of doing so, not out of a sense of the futility of doing otherwise. Reason liberates the will from enslavement to itself by bringing men into tune with cosmic order.

If *Il Moro* reflects the optimism of Catholic intellectuals of the 1550's, it reflects an optimism that was not fated to last. Within two years of the publication of Heywood's dialogue, Queen Mary and Cardinal Pole were dead, and Elizabeth had initiated the compromising solutions that spelled the end of the Roman Catholic cause in England. Eight years after the publication of *Il Moro*, in 1564, Ellis Heywood left England for the Continent and joined the Society of Jesus. In England, *Il Moro*, like the Catholic cause it was written to serve, passed into oblivion. An entry in the Stationers *Registers* for 1601 indicates that a London printer intended to publish an English version in 1601. If he did, however, no copy of that edition has survived, and the present edition may fairly claim to be the first since 1556.[5]

[5] See *A Transcript of the Registers of the Company of Stationers of London; 1554–1640 A.D.*, ed. Edward Arber (London, 1894), III, 194, for Nov. 7, 1601: "Entred for his [William Aspley's] Copye vnder the handes of master Doctor BARLOWE and the wardens a booke Called the Englishe Academy A Dialogue betwene Sir Thomas MOORE and others . . . vj^{d}."

The Structure of Il Moro

In *Il Moro*, More and his fellow investigators follow, rather informally, the method of scholastic disputation that Ellis Heywood was familiar with from his Oxford days: a *question* ("What is true happiness?") is proposed; the major term is defined (to distinguish true happiness from false happiness); alternative solutions to the question are proposed, objected to, and dismissed; and, finally, More proposes a solution that meets all the objections and is therefore accepted by all the disputants. The alternative solutions are ably defended, so that, when the discussion is finished, we feel, as always in scholastic disputation, that we understand not only the answers, but, more important, we understand the full meaning of the *question* itself.

The *question* of happiness in *Il Moro*, as all the disputants realize at the conclusion and as More has known all along, concerns the relation of virtue to pleasure. This relation is given explicit intellectual formulation by More at the conclusion of the dialogue; it is also given figural formulation throughout the dialogue by the character of More—his words and deeds; in addition, the same relation is stated narratively when Ellis Heywood introduces Sir Thomas More at the outset of the dialogue: "he did not have that stiff reserve or misanthropy that we see in many people whose disdain brings about two evils: first, they plainly show just how far they have to restrain their wills; and second, they deter others who conclude that virtue must be just as unpleasant on the inside as it is on the outside."

The encomium of the joys of virtue in *Il Moro* accords with More's own writings about the relation of virtue and pleasure. In *Utopia*, More created a race of men who wrestle with the problems of philosophy by reason unaided by revelation. For them, the central problem of virtue is its relation to pleasure. The Utopians, More tells us, are Epicureans, that is, they maintain that the end of all virtuous action is pleasure, which they identify with the undisturbed tranquillity of the soul. For the Utopians, the problem connected with the virtuous life is to distinguish true pleasures from false pleasures.[6]

The relation of virtue to pleasure is also the subject of *The Four Last Things* (c. 1522). In this unfinished tract, More vividly describes the agonizing physical and spiritual consequences of sin. The clear implication

---

[6] More's invocation of the name of Epicurus in *Utopia*, sometimes seriously and sometimes in what might be called an ironic trope, is studied very carefully by Father Edward L. Surtz in *The Praise of Pleasure* (Cambridge, Mass.: Harvard University Press, 1957).

is that "pleasure" (freedom from terrible pains of body and conscience) is to be found only in "virtue." Both of these works, but especially *Utopia*, form part of the story of the re-evaluation of Epicurus as a serious philosopher, which was initiated in the Renaissance by Lorenzo Valla's treatise *De Voluptate* (c. 1431).[7] Epicurus' insistence upon the pleasurableness of virtue made him a convenient dialectical opponent of the neo-Stoics, who insisted upon the necessity and nobility of virtue.

The revival of Epicurus, like the revival of the Stoics, was useful to Christian writers of the Renaissance as a means of examining critically certain divergent tendencies within the Christian tradition. More invokes the name Epicurus in *Utopia* to emphasize his favorite doctrine of the pleasurableness of virtue, but, as More would be the first to point out, this doctrine is not exclusively Epicurean. For proof, we can turn to *Il Moro*, where Ellis Heywood relates the doctrine to the *Summa Theologica* of St. Thomas Aquinas. It was in St. Thomas' discussion of happiness that Heywood found a philosophical formulation for that deeply joyous style of living and writing that has intrigued every generation of Sir Thomas More's biographers.

The pervasive influence of St. Thomas' discussion of happiness in *Il Moro* may be quickly sensed from an analysis of the definition that underlies the discussion in both works. In both, happiness is defined as *contentment of desire*.[8] Scholastic analysis of this definition reveals that it contains two variables: "contentment" and "desire." St. Thomas analyzes both of the variables; the disputants in *Il Moro*, who are not very skilled in scholastic analysis, take the meaning of "contentment" for granted and argue only over the meaning of "desire." Thus the debate over true happiness in *Il Moro* takes the form of a debate over which desire is superior (most worthy of fulfillment). Of the eight alternative "desires" or goals offered in *Il Moro*, six—wealth, honor, fame, power, pleasure, speculative science

[7] The revival of Epicureanism in the Renaissance is treated in a cursory introductory chapter in Thomas Franklin Mayo, *Epicurus in England (1650–1725)* (Dallas: Southwest Press, 1934), pp. xi–xxviii, and in Don Cameron Allen, "The Rehabilitation of Epicurus and his Theory of Pleasure in the Early Renaissance," *Studies in Philology*, XLI (January 1944), 1–15.

[8] St. Thomas Aquinas, *Summa Theologica* [hereafter cited as *ST*], II, i, Q.5, A.3: "Since happiness is a *perfect and sufficient good*, it excludes every evil, and fulfills every desire"; *ST*, II, i, Q.1, A.5: "Since everything desires its own perfection, a man desires for his ultimate end, that which he desires as his perfect and crowning good . . . It is therefore necessary for the last end so to fill man's appetite that nothing is left beside it for man to desire." (All the translations of St. Thomas in the text and notes are from *The "Summa Theologica" of St. Thomas Aquinas literally translated by the Fathers of the English Dominican Province* [London: Burns, Oates & Washbourne, 1914–1929].)

—are discussed, in that order, in the *Summa Theologica*. The result of examining these alternatives is the same in both treatises; none is found to provide true contentment. In *Il Moro*, the disputants must finally agree with Peter: "You know how much more pleasing is the sweet that is mixed with some bitterness. Every pastime in this life is, in fact, none other than a continual change from one thing to its opposite."

St. Thomas, however, turns from his rejection of the possible kinds of "desires" implied in the phrase *contentment of desire* to an analysis of "contentment," which constitutes a major part of the "Treatise on Happiness." Contentment, according to St. Thomas, is the last of three active phases in the soul's attainment of happiness: *the act of recognition*, whereby the rational soul recognizes its good; *the act of concupiscence*, whereby the appetitive faculty, intellectual or sensual, desires the good and moves to obtain it; *the act of enjoyment*, whereby the rational soul finds contentment and pleasure in the fulfillment of its desire.[9] For St. Thomas, then, *contentment of desire* does not mean "cessation of desire"; nor does it imply changing one desire for another. "Contentment" is, rather, a *rational act of enjoyment* of the satisfaction of desire. When More proposes this solution to the original question—"what is true happiness?"—at the end of *Il Moro*, he turns a desultory debate over the "desires" proposed by his friends into a triumphant scholastic analysis of the full significance of the initial definition of happiness.

St. Thomas' formulation of the three phases in the attainment of happiness creates an active relationship between "contentment" and the power of rational choice; it does the same for the relationship between "pleasure" and rational choice. Pleasure, according to St. Thomas, is the delight that the soul takes in its awareness that the will has achieved contentment. Pleasure, so defined, is a necessary concomitant of happiness although not an essential part of it. So defined, pleasure may even be called the greatest of human goods: "Now the greatest good of everything is its last end. And the end . . . is twofold, namely, the thing itself, and the use of that thing. Thus the miser's end is either money, or the possession of money. Accordingly, man's last end may be said to be either God Who is the Supreme Good simply; or the enjoyment of God, which denotes a certain pleasure in the last end. And in this sense, a certain pleasure of man may be said to be the greatest among human goods" (*ST*, II, i, Q.34, A.3).

Thus, St. Thomas relates virtue to pleasure. In this respect, he is like the

[9] *ST*, II, i. Q.3, AA.1,5; II, i, Q.4, AA.2,3,5.

Epicureans, and his formulation satisfies the requirement, shared by all (including More) in *Il Moro*, that happiness be the "highest delight of the soul." But, unlike the Epicureans, St. Thomas does not put the cart before the horse. We are not, as the Epicureans maintain, to seek the good because it is pleasurable; rather, we must seek the good in order to find contentment, and pleasure will inevitably follow.

The discussion of happiness by St. Thomas (and, through St. Thomas, by Aristotle) thus exerted a profound influence on the structure of *Il Moro*, as well as on a host of other Renaissance Italian dialogues. St. Thomas' discussion served as an argumentative skeleton, as it were, upon which Heywood proceeded to hang imaginative elaborations relevant to his purpose. None of the elaboration is, in itself, original, and each can be paralleled by other Renaissance dialogues. As Professor Francesco Tateo wrote of all these dialogues: "In these writings, which deliberately and of necessity make use of commonplaces, we are able to trace the particular solutions proposed [to moral problems], not in their fundamental ideas, but in the turns of the argument and in the importance that this or that traditional motive assumes from one time to the next."[10]

Each of the seven sections that follow attempts to demonstrate the significance that the "traditional motives" assume in the structure of *Il Moro*. The argument will be seen to turn in one direction only: toward an encomium of Sir Thomas More as an ideal Christian humanist. We must remember that in reworking the great moral and philosophical commonplaces Heywood was guided by this encomiastic purpose and not by an intention to give final solutions to the moral and spiritual problems of his own time.[11]

Contentment Is in Riches

The liveliest argument in *Il Moro* is the argument that true contentment is in riches, a proposition put forward with much heat by Laurence, a bumptious and cynical London merchant. Laurence's defense of the "acquisitive spirit" takes the form of a defense of the miser as the happiest of

[10] Francesco Tateo, *Tradizione e realtà nell' Umanesimo italiano* (Bari: Dedalo Libri, 1967), p. 357. [Translation mine.]
[11] Nello Vian cites Heywood's removal of Sir Thomas More from his historical context as evidence that *Il Moro* was originally written in Italian, not English. Nello Vian, "San Tommaso More tra la Saga e il Mito," *Miscellanea Pio Paschini, Studi di Storia Ecclesiastica*, II (1949), 213–222.

men. Laurence, who refuses to give an encomium of the "happiness" he supports, gives instead a speech that follows the logic of the Renaissance genre of the mock encomium, like Erasmus' defense of foolishness and John Donne's praise of baldness.

With a nice sense of the irony that he is a rich man arguing before a group of "poor" humanists, Laurence defends miserliness on the grounds that it is the most "spiritual" ("ascetic") of pleasures. His argument plays humorously with the distinction that St. Thomas makes between carnal and spiritual sins: "Sins of the flesh are those which are consummated in carnal pleasures, while spiritual sins are consummated in pleasures of the spirit without pleasure of the flesh. Such is covetousness; for the covetous man takes pleasure in the consideration of himself as a possessor of riches. Therefore, covetousness is a spiritual sin" (*ST*, II, ii, Q.118, A.6).

The truth of the matter, as Charles is prompt to point out to Laurence, is that miserliness is not based on pleasure at all, but on the pain of insecurity and the fear of poverty. Charles probably took the credibility of his retort for granted, for the association of miserliness and insecurity was a stock theme from Plautus to Molière.

But, whatever Charles may believe about misers from reading about them in books, the Laurence of *Il Moro* is not insecure. He is, in fact, sublimely self-confident about himself and his relation to other men. He exudes the self-assurance of the man who has made his conclusions about human nature. Laurence has but one insight into the nature of man, but it is, as More admits, a powerful one: wealth is the only value that men really respect.

"I could," says Laurence, "show you sixty people, honored now by everybody, who, if you took away their money, would have no reason left for anyone to lift a hat to them any more than to a jackass." He echoes Ben Jonson's Volpone, who says to his gold, "Thou art virtue, fame,/Honor and all things else. Who can get thee,/He shall be noble, valiant, honest, wise . . ." (I, i, 25–27). Both Laurence and Volpone echo the Stoic Stertinius in Horace: "For all things—worth, repute, honour, things divine and human—are slaves to the beauty of wealth, and he who has made his 'pile' will be famous, brave, and just. 'And wise too?' Yes, wise, and a king, and anything else he pleases."[12]

[12] *Ben Jonson*, ed. C. H. Herford and Percy Simpson (11 vols., Oxford: Oxford University Press, 1925–1952), V, 25; Horace *Sat.* II, 3, 94–110, quoted from *Satires, Epistles, Ars Poetica*, trans. H. Rushton Fairclough (Cambridge, Mass.: Harvard University Press, 1961), p. 161.

The paradoxical value of the "acquisitive spirit," according to Laurence, is that it sees reality. The miser's eyes are opened to the infinite hypocrisies and humbuggeries of the world's idealists. The portentous pessimism of Paul's *memento mori,* as well as the effusive Neo-Platonism of Peter—all is grist for the mill of Laurence's reiterated cynicism that man is by nature an acquisitive animal. Laurence has one insight, but he is ultimately too unimaginative to be taken seriously. "Nothing," wrote St. Thomas, quoting Cicero, "is so narrow or little-minded as to love money" (*ST*, II, ii, Q.118, A.5, Obj.1).

In contrast to the self-centered, cynical merchant stands another rich man in *Il Moro:* Sir Thomas More, himself. More ridicules Laurence's acquisitive spirit, but not the possession of wealth itself. The More of *Il Moro* has a "beautiful and commodious home" that graces the river Thames, where five gentlemen as unexpected overnight guests apparently pose no logistical problems. The difference between the cynical Laurence and More is the difference between sterile money and money that has borne fruit in furnishing the conditions under which philosophical investigation, the most characteristic human activity, can take place.

The contrast between Laurence and More is, to borrow St. Thomas' terminology, the contrast between the covetous man and the liberal man. In St. Thomas' analysis, wealth is defined as the medium of exchange of goods, and hence classified among the "useful" things of the world. Men, then, are to be classified, not according to "rich" and "poor," but according to whether they make proper or improper use of whatever wealth they possess. The liberal man gives to proper objects, in proper quantities, at proper times. The covetous man, on the other hand, may be guilty of either improper spending—niggardliness—or of immoral accumulation—"base gain." Accumulation of wealth, as defined by St. Thomas, and thus the acquisitive spirit, is not bad per se. It is only bad if the acquisitor turns to immoral sources of income—"base gain."

Seen within this Thomistic framework, Laurence is a figural representation of the vice of improper spending or niggardliness. All the stories that Laurence tells, and those told at his expense, concern his unwillingness to put his money to use so that others might benefit. The analysis of the acquisitive spirit in *Il Moro,* then, is a Thomistic analysis wherein acquisitiveness is not denounced as "base" or "unworthy" of a human being; instead, it is brought into meaningful relationship with what might be called social responsibility.

Social responsibility, argued on a practical plane between Laurence and

Charles, is argued on a theoretical plane in the debate-within-a-debate between Charles and Alexander over whether it is better ("more liberal") to give material goods to others, or to "give" them spiritual and intellectual aid. In this debate, Ellis Heywood brings a Thomistic analysis of "improper spending" directly to bear on a cherished ideal of those who were reviving the Stoic philosophy in the Renaissance.

St. Thomas had faced the question debated by Charles and Alexander in his discussion of the Christian virtue of almsgiving. He considered almsgiving to be an act of charity, which was the highest of the virtues. A necessary precondition of almsgiving, however, was the possession of riches, and this seemed to conflict with the ideal of evangelical poverty recently enunciated by St. Francis of Assisi. The Franciscans interpreted quite literally Christ's injunction to "give up all you have and follow me." They taught that the God who provided for the lilies of the field would provide for anyone who put his trust in Him. The austere ideal of Franciscan poverty represented one pole of economic thought in the thirteenth-century church; the good steward theory of St. Thomas represented the other.

The good steward theory is a justification for the existence of the rich as well as the poor. God created some poor that He might test the strength of their faith; He created some rich that He might test whether, like the good steward in the parable, they put their money to proper use (*ST*, II, ii, Q.117, A.1). The good steward is truly liberal: he is both just, for he never obtains riches by immoral means; and he is merciful, for he gives to those in need because of a warm affection for them. This liberality can be practiced by poor and rich alike, for, as St. Thomas maintains, what is given must suit the means of the giver.

St. Thomas further distinguishes between corporal alms (goods and money) and spiritual alms (services). In an absolute sense, spiritual alms are superior, but, in particular situations, corporal alms may be superior: "A man in hunger is to be fed rather than instructed, and, as the Philosopher observes (*Top.* iii, 2), for a needy man, *money is better than philosophy*" (*ST*, II, ii, Q.32, A.3).

Professor Hans Baron has demonstrated the alternating popularity of the Franciscan and Thomistic doctrines in Renaissance Italy. Holy poverty, extolled by Dante, was rejected in the fifteenth century when the bourgeoisie entered into the public life of Florence. The humanists who espoused the good steward doctrine hoped that the bourgeoisie would use their capital to benefit society. In the sixteenth century disillusionment with the bourgeoisie caused nationalistic writers like Machiavelli to turn once again to the ideal of poverty, this time the poverty of early republican Rome extolled by Seneca, not the holy poverty of the Apostles.[13] Thus, the idealization of "poverty" was linked to the re-emergence of Stoicism in the Renaissance.

The state of "poverty" extolled by the Stoics was not the beggary of the Franciscans, but rather the healthy simple life lived without any sophisticated luxuries—life lived in accordance with the law of "Nature." This kind of "poverty" was to bestow three Stoic benefits—self-sufficiency, self-awareness, and mental tranquillity—though Ellis Heywood makes Alexander insist only on self-sufficiency, for Heywood's intention at this point in the discussion of riches is to expose a cherished moral ideal of the neo-Stoics as inadequate when measured in terms of the Christian value of social responsibility.

From the viewpoint of the neo-Stoic Alexander, it is better ("more liberal") to "give" spiritual and intellectual aids to others because the Stoic sage must be independent of material circumstance in all his doings. For him, the important part of an act of charity is the inner disposition of the giver. For him, self-cultivation is all. The fact that another person might be aided in the process of self-cultivation is immaterial. The Thomistic position, represented by Charles at this point in *Il Moro*, is more moderate: charity has the dual function of improving both the doer and society. "It is twice blest—/It blesseth him that gives and him that takes."[14] The debate between Charles and Alexander ends inconclusively when the Stoic arguments advanced by Alexander in defense of poverty are exposed as logically indefensible. Charles, who ought to defend the Thomistic position, hesitates uncertainly as to how to defend the necessity of having "some" riches in order to be happy. The defense of that proposition will come only at the end of *Il Moro* when Sir Thomas More finally speaks. Meanwhile, two extreme positions about one of the goods of the world—that money is all (Laurence), and that money is nothing (Alexander)—have both been denied.[15]

[13] Hans Baron, "Franciscan Poverty and Civic Wealth as Factors in the Rise of Humanistic Thought," *Speculum*, XIII (January 1938), 1–37.

[14] *Merch.*, IV, i, 185–186, quoted from *The Complete Works of Shakespeare*, ed. G. L. Kittredge (Boston: Ginn, 1936), p. 282. All future references to Shakespeare are to this edition.

[15] See Alfonso M. Orlich, "L'Uso dei Beni nella Morale di S. Tommaso," *La Scuola Cattolica*, XL (October 1912), 201–223; XL (December 1912), 227–466; XLI (January 1913), 41–60; XLI (March 1913), 390–413; XLI (July 1913), 378–405.

Contentment Is in Honor

The second major division in the argument of *Il Moro* is Charles' argument that happiness is to be found in "honor," which he defines as any form of recognition bestowed by society as a reward for individual "excellence." Charles' definition of "honor" is contrived in such a way as to focus attention on two relevant questions: Can happiness obtained in such a way be depended upon? Is it ever good to seek honors? The first question, had been answered by St. Thomas Aquinas, who, like all who speak on honor in *Il Moro*, defined honor as a "witnessing to a person's excellence" (*ST*, II, ii, Q.103, A.1). Such a witnessing is a good, but it is a "good of fortune" bestowed by society upon worthy and unworthy alike and withheld just as arbitrarily; therefore, no man can be confident of getting or keeping it. "Honour is not in the honoured, but rather in him who honours and who offers deference to the person honoured." St. Thomas concludes that however worthy honor may be in itself, "happiness does not consist in honour" (*ST*, II, v, Q.2, A.2). The Thomistic objections to putting happiness in honor so defined—that honor has no real existence in the person honored, and that its bestowal is at the mercy of fortune—are the same arguments with which Charles is put down in *Il Moro*.

The second question involves the idea of social responsibility, which first emerged in the discussion of liberality, set in the context of sixteenth-century moral philosophy. The point at issue in the debate between Paul and Charles is that the traditional private Christian virtue of humility (defended by Paul) conflicts with the Renaissance social virtue of public recognition for civic achievements (defended by Charles). Such a struggle between the private and public aspects of honors was anticipated by St. Thomas, where both sides were given a full hearing. On the one hand, St. Thomas argued that honors are good, for they are "due to the good and beautiful, that they may be made known," and St. Thomas quotes St. Matthew: "*Neither do men light a candle, and put it under a bushel, but upon a candlestick, that it may shine to all that are in the house*" (*ST* II, ii, Q.103, A.1). On the other hand, St. Thomas strongly opposed an individual ethic of pursuit of glory. To perform virtuous acts for the sake of renown destroys the moral value of an act (*ST*, II, ii, Q.131, A.2). His opinion may be summed up in the terse comment: "It is requisite for man's perfection that he should know himself; but not that he should be known by others, wherefore it is not to be desired in itself" (*ST*, II, ii, Q.132, A.1). Pursuit of honor is allowable only when honor is pursued for an end beyond itself, as when, for instance, getting a reputation for virtue will help a person persevere in goodness; or when winning honors will stimulate others to practice virtue.

Incitement to virtue is the justification for public honors in Sir Thomas More's rational commonwealth in *Utopia*. "They set up in the market-place the images of notable men and of such as have been great and bountiful benefactors to the commonwealth, for the perpetual memory of their good acts, and also that the glory and renown of the ancestors may stir and provoke their posterity to virtue."[16] For the same reason, the Utopians honor those who fulfill a public office justly and give the heads of families special place at the table. Virtuous Utopians are rewarded at death by having their good deeds recounted at special memorial services. The justification of public honors as inciters to virtue also provides a formula for distinguishing true honors from false honors in Utopia. Utopians are not honored for false reasons—riches, family name, or expensive clothes—nor are the marks of respect gaudy or magnificent. The prince is distinguished from a commoner only by a sheaf of grain carried before him; the priest is known only by a wax candle. Vain shows of honor are prohibited, for, "what natural or true pleasure dost thou take of another man's bare head or bowed knees? Will this ease the pain of thy knees or remedy the frenzy of thy head?"[17] True honors (and true pleasures) are only given as rewards for good deeds, and they are given in such a way as to inspire a love of virtue in others.

In the debate with Paul in *Il Moro*, Charles restates the Thomistic justification of public honors that the Utopians had endorsed, but he gives it an emphasis entirely his own. Charles' argument seems to run something like this: All men seek honor; if we glorify public officeholding and the teaching profession, then we will make men seek those things. On the basis of this naïve, if not cynical, psychology, Charles expects to create a socially responsible citizenry with private vices and public virtues.[18]

The argument that Charles has perverted from St. Thomas implies a

---

[16] *Utopia*, trans. Ralph Robinson, quoted from *More's Utopia and A Dialogue of Comfort*, ed. John Warrington (London: J. M. Dent, 1951), p. 103. All future references are to this edition.

[17] *Utopia*, p. 88.

[18] Cf. More's ironic parenthesis on Hythloday's "foolish" narrative of Utopian communism: "by the which thing only all nobility, magnificence, worship, honour, and majesty, the true ornaments and honours, as the common opinion is, of a commonwealth, be utterly overthrown and destroyed" (*Utopia*, p. 135).

double standard: what is bad for an individual may be good for society. The More of *Il Moro* knows that the double standard does not work out in practice. What is bad for an individual is always bad for society. In *Il Moro* More has nothing good to say for honor at all. The only strong language in *Il Moro* is that in which More lashes out at the ambitious princes and vain professors of law and theology whose lust after honors has created political and social chaos in Christian Europe. The princes and the professors fail to see that the criterion of true honor is that it must incite others to virtue. They have failed to see that public ethics and private ethics are identical. A resolution of the apparent conflict between Christian humility and civic recognition is at last suggested in the arguments More draws from St. Thomas: a man may take inward pleasure in bodily and mental excellences God has endowed him with; excellence is to be pursued, not for our own sake, but for God's.[19]

To underline this lesson about the interdependence of public and private morality, Heywood has Charles and Peter debate whether the public acts of princes are subject to the same moral standards that govern the private acts of individual citizens. The accountability of the prince to law was the subject of a vast literature during the Renaissance, including Cardinal Pole's *Pro unitatis ecclesiasticae defensione* and John Milton's *The Tenure of Kings and Magistrates*. Machiavelli, the best-known writer on the topic, discussed it (as do Peter and Charles in *Il Moro*) in terms of the prince's accountability in his public acts to common standards of private morality, a central issue behind the concept of *ragione di stato*. In *The Prince*, Machiavelli, like Charles, argues that the prince may resort to the cunning and force of the fox and the lion in order to win his battles. But in *The Discourses*, Machiavelli, like Peter, distinguishes between deceit and treachery: "Although deceit is detestable in all other things, yet in the conduct of war, it is laudable and honorable," he writes. But, he adds, "I do not confound such deceit with perfidy, which breaks faith and treaties; for although states and kingdoms may at times be won by perfidy, yet will it ever bring dishonor with it."[20]

As Machiavelli's seeming inconsistency shows, this debate has too many ramifications to be decided in two pages of general discussion in *Il Moro*. Its function in the structure of Heywood's dialogue is to continue the elaboration of the fundamental theme of the necessary interconnection of

---

[19] *ST*, II, ii, Q.131, A.1.
[20] Niccolo Macchiavelli, *Discorsi*, III, 40, quoted from *The Prince and the Discourses*, trans. Christian E. Detmold (New York: Modern Library, 1940), p. 526.

public and private morality that began with the discussion of charity and acquisitiveness.

Contentment Is in Love

The third major division in the argument of *Il Moro* is Peter's argument that love is the greatest contentment that life has to offer. He departs from St. Thomas, who was not familiar with love as conceived by Peter. When Peter speaks of love, he means only that attraction felt by a susceptible man for a beautiful woman. For Peter, the ultimate value of this attraction is that it is the unique means of human salvation; by it the enamored human soul frees itself from enslavement to fleshly corruption and unites itself to, first, female beauty; then, to the beauty of humanity; and, finally, to the source of all beauty in the universe, the Godhead itself. In his argument Peter borrows from the Florentine Neoplatonist, Marsilio Ficino. Where Ficino's emphasis was on the beauty of the Godhead, however, Peter's emphasis is on human beauty—the beauty of women, and the beauty of human social intercourse. Though developed in a minor key, Peter's theme is the theme of Pico della Mirandola's great oration on the dignity of man.

Against this enthusiasm for the beauty of humanity (a youthful enthusiasm that Peter shares with Shakespeare's Miranda), is pitted the cynicism of the merchant Laurence. Laurence heaps all the pent-up scorn of a husband who married in order to relieve his sexual needs upon the bachelor Peter's bookish theories about the spirituality of love. But there is more in Laurence's scorn than the scorn of experience for naïveté, for Laurence's is a scorn not only for Peter, but for Ovid, Propertius, Horace, and any other doting lover, "Languishing all night at the door of his Goddess, doubly chilled, by the night air, and by his cold mistress."[21] In this image that Laurence uses for the absurdity of lovers, we get a sudden retrospective glimpse of a baffled schoolboy (Laurence) snickering nervously at Horace's *Odes* in some Tudor Latin grammar class. In age as in youth, we see, Laurence is uncomfortable when faced with manifestations of romantic love. To him, such romanticization, whether in the texts of pagan antiquity or in the texts of Christian Neoplatonism, is a deluded

---

[21] Cp. Ovid *Amores* 1.6,9 and 3.11; Propertius 1.16; Horace *Od*. 1.25 and 3.10. J. C. Nelson, *Renaissance Theory of Love* (New York: Columbia University Press, 1955), pp. 172–173, discusses the similar outburst against the idealization of eroticism in Giordano Bruno's *Eroici Furori*.

attempt to give spiritual value to that very thing that is the badge of our bodily dependency—our sexuality. Behind the debate between Peter and Laurence lie two contrasting images of human nature: the vision of human dignity and freedom of Florentine Neoplatonism, and a "naturalistic" view that analyzes all human behavior as a reflex of physical needs.

Laurence, the exponent of this "naturalistic" view, is presented as the advocate of a particularly brainless kind of hedonism that takes the human body as its standard of what is "natural": romantic love is "unnatural" because it sometimes imposes bodily hardships; cosmetics are "unnatural" because they are applied *to* the body. Fall in love? More natural to eat, drink, and be merry, especially at another's expense. Laurence's simple-minded moral calculus seems unworthy of the space devoted to it until we realize that we are hearing in the English merchant's prejudices against romantic love, love poetry, cosmetics, and feminism the stirrings of the spirit that animates popular Elizabethan moral works like Phillip Stubbes's *Anatomy of Abuses*.

In the intention to contrast these two views of human nature— the Neoplatonic and the "naturalistic"—is to be found the principle behind Peter's selection of arguments from the basic text of Renaissance Neoplatonism, Marsilio Ficino's *Commentary on Plato's Symposium*. Peter finds ready ammunition in Ficino's book to battle the social barbarousness and aesthetic dullness of the money-making classes, and he sets forth five arguments:

(1) The love of a man for a woman is the same as the friendship of a man for a man, and both are the same as that love of God enjoined by the First Commandment. That these three kinds of love are identical is assumed throughout Ficino's *Commentary*. They have different objects, but they spring from the same "root" or primary impulse. Each is but a different aspect of a single experience: the infinite longing of the soul for its own good. Since this desire is infinite, the soul may find temporary satisfaction in union with a woman or, better yet, in friendship, but it will find final and complete satisfaction only in union with God.

From the standpoint of Ficino, Peter commits a fundamental error when he accepts Laurence's distinction between two kinds of love: friendship (love "for the goodness of the soul") and love of women (love "for the beauty of the body"). For Ficino, such a distinction is inadmissible since physical beauty is the means by which goodness makes itself attractive to the soul; thus, goodness and beauty cannot be separated. Should they be separated, beauty would become an end in itself, instead of being, as Ficino held, a means by which the soul throws off the chains of physical existence and regains its true home in the Divine Mind.

Ficino distinguishes three possible kinds of love responses. The highest is the contemplative, in which the soul ascends from contemplation of earthly beauty to divine beauty and is moved to spiritual generation or acts of creative thought and imagination (the celestial Venus). The lowest response is the voluptuous, in which the soul longs to touch and procreate in the flesh (the earthly Venus). Between these two responses is a third, the "practical," in which the soul finds satisfaction in seeing the beloved and having social relations with him.[22] The love that Peter argues for in *Il Moro* is practical in this sense. Peter does not aspire to divinity. If he finds himself "clasped to the heart" of the beautiful woman of his desires, he concludes, "he would have no other desire whatever." The aesthetic emphasis in this cult of graceful femininity is too courtly for the London merchant, Laurence. But it would be far too voluptuous for Marsilio Ficino, to whom a woman's beauty is but a stepping-stone to divinity.

(2) Peter's second argument in favor of love is strictly encomiastic: love is all-powerful. To Peter, the processes of birth and growth manifest love in the vegetable world just as the "tenderness" shown to offspring manifests love in the animal world. It is precisely this anthropomorphic equation between "love" in the physical world and human sexual love that is fundamental to Ficino's *Commentary:* love is the source of all activity in the universe.

It was a commonplace of Renaissance physics that the four elements of the universe are always at war with each other. As Marlowe's Tamburlaine, rationalizing his violence, put it:

> Nature that fram'd vs of foure Elements,
> Warring within our breasts for regiment,
> Doth teach vs all to haue aspyring minds.[23]

[22] *Marsile Ficin Sur le Banquet de Platon ou de l'Amour*, ed. and trans. Raymond Marcel (Paris: Société d'Edition "Les Belles Lettres," 1956), p. 212. All future references to the *Commentary* are to this edition. Cp. Annibale Romei, "Of Human Love": "The second kind, without contaminating chaste thoughts, reioyceth onely in beholding, discoursing, and conuersing with his beloued, as also by her to be mutually affected. This is discrepant, from that in the diuine louer, insomuch as admiring humane beauty, without lifting vp the mind to that from whence she had her beginning, hee meditateth on this beauty humane, not as the Image and representation of Diuinitie, but as if it were most true and essentiall beautie, and reioyceth in this contentment: this is called chaste loue, and is in the second degree of temperance. It seemeth kissing vnto this love, is permitted for a reward." (*The Courtiers Academy*, trans. I. K. [London, 1598], p. 40.)

[23] Christopher Marlowe, *Tamburlaine*, Part One, II, vi, 869–871, quoted from *The Works of Christopher Marlowe*, ed. C. F. Tucker Brooke (Oxford: Oxford University Press, 1910), p. 32.

Ficino, on the other hand, found the natural world filled with images of generative love: "Nor does water put out fire because of hatred for fire, but because the desire of extending its essential cold causes water to conjoin with the body of fire to produce more water. Since every natural desire aims at good, and not at evil, the aim of water cannot be to put fire out, for that would be evil; the aim must be to produce water like itself, and that is good. If water could accomplish its aim without putting fire out, it certainly would do so."[24]

Ficino seems to point toward a truth that underlies all schemes of the physical universe, anthropomorphic or "objective": all such schemes must necessarily reflect the mental disposition of their inventors. Those who feel antagonism and hate in their minds will project it on their models of the universe; those who feel love will do the same. Peter is a Ficinian enthusiast of the heart. He initiates the whole discussion of happiness with his appreciative outburst over the beauty of More's garden, and each detail of his argument for love communicates his aesthetic joy in the universe of created things: plants and animals, children, art, fencing, and a woman's graceful movements.

(3) Peter's third argument is that love is always a desire for beauty. So also does Ficino define love, and it is his—and Peter's—great paradox. To desire a woman, both in the flesh and in the abstract, is to desire her beauty, not to desire relief for a bodily need. Love is a need of the soul, a spiritual incompleteness, not a physical one. Paraphrasing the speech of Diotima to Socrates in the *Symposium*, Ficino enumerates the successive stages by which the soul mounts from union with a particular beauty to universal beauty, to beauty itself, and, finally, to union with the source from which all the lesser beauties emanated, the Divine Mind.

That the beautiful and the good are ultimately identified in the Divine Mind is assumed throughout Ficino's *Commentary*, but Peter, who has agreed to separate love for a woman from love for God, must find more immediate connections between the beautiful and the good.

The foolhardiness of Peter's enterprise becomes apparent when he tries to show that love of beauty is rational. The assumption that love is rational was much disputed in the love literature of the Renaissance, though in general the Neoplatonists held that love-desire is rational in the sense that it is preceded by knowledge; that is, the rational faculty of the soul has knowledge of the goodness of an object before the willing part is attracted by the beauty of that goodness. "Love," wrote Leone Ebreo, "must be

[24] *Marsile Ficin*, ed. Marcel, p. 165 [Translation mine.]; cf. *ST*, I, i, Q.49, A.1.

preceded by knowledge, for we could not love any thing we had not first known as good."[25]

But Peter, presumptuously supposing to answer Laurence with "common sense," tries a short-cut argument to show that love and reason are compatible. Having defined "love" as "desire for a beautiful object," Peter proceeds to argue that love is a kind of knowing (and hence rational), since we can only desire an object that we know to be desirable. But Peter's argument is unacceptable, for it assumes that to know a thing is desirable is to know that it is good—the very assumption that Laurence rejected at the beginning of the discussion.

(4) Peter's fourth argument is that the pains and sorrows of love act as foils to make the pleasures more pleasurable. Discussion in *Il Moro* shifts from the ultimate goals of love to the immediate effects of love on lovers. Like Robert Burton in *The Anatomy of Melancholy*, Laurence maintains that love is a morbid state. It is a headache and a burning in the flesh, and the way to clear up the symptoms is to stop thinking about the cause. In the *Commentary*, Ficino, too, discussed the morbid states of mind and body induced by love and suggested some remedies. But, for Ficino, love causes the morbid state. For Laurence, the reverse is true; the morbid state causes love. Love is a "sickness of the soul caused by surplus desire." Relief comes from getting enough sleep and surrounding oneself with distractions. Laurence's intention is to undercut the notion that romantic love has value, and his remarks seem aimed not only at the classical poets, Ovid, Horace, and Propertius (whom he cites) but also the whole Renaissance school of those who imitated the love poetry of Petrarch. Laurence's images of the lover "off in the forest talking to the birds or languishing all night at the door of his goddess" find many parallels in Renaissance love literature where the lover wanders off by himself "With tears augmenting the fresh morning's dew,/Adding to clouds more clouds with his deep sighs" (*Romeo and Juliet*, I, i, 139–140). To the bourgeois mind, such symptoms were clear violations of nature and common sense. The cure for them was not to get the coy mistress to submit but to banish such dangerous indulgences of romantic sentiment altogether.

But good Petrarchans like Romeo knew that romantic sentiment had its own kind of value. This value, cutting as it does across the grain of middle-class morality, can only express itself in paradoxes that violate common sense. Thus, the Petrarchan sings of "sweet sighs, sweet anxieties, and sweet

[25] Leone Ebreo, *The Philosophy of Love*, trans. F. Friedeberg-Seeley and Jean H. Barnes (London: Soncino Press, 1937), p. 6.

tears." The "sweet tears" the Petrarchan sings of are neither pleasurable nor painful. They represent a psychological state that defies the neat and mechanical pleasure-pain calculus characteristic of the merchant mentality. The Petrarchan paradox is intended to tease the mind out of its habit of recording everything as a debit or a credit.

On Peter, unfortunately, the mantle of Petrarch sits uneasily. Instead of arguing the value of the Petrarchan paradoxes, Peter tries to explain them away. The "tears," he says, are "sweet" because they reinforce by contrast the smiles that succeed them. Thus, lovers are doomed to endless alternations of pleasure and pain. Peter's explanation damages his whole argument for he admits that pursuit of beauty, like all pleasures, grows tiresome in the end. The beauties of the art gallery and the ballroom, apparently, must be taken in small doses.

(5) Peter's final argument is that love can last indefinitely. An obvious objection to positing love as a goal of action is that it is self-defeating; that is, the lover's desire is to put an end to his desire. Therefore, the lover's real end is not love itself, but the further end of putting an end to love. To answer this argument, Peter relies on a purely verbal distinction between "desire" as a "need for a thing not possessed," and "desire" as a "longing to enjoy the thing possessed." But can a lover really long for a thing possessed? The answer lies in our definition of "possession." For Peter, "possession" involves no more than "having in front of the eyes" or, at most, "having in one's arms." For Ficino, to whom love of beauty is love of the good and not simple aesthetic appreciation, "possession" of the beautiful object is a series of "possessions" leading from earth to heaven. Coitus is the lowest form of possession. It is only momentarily satisfactory, for what the lover really wants is to "possess" the object of his desire by becoming the object. The lover must be "born in beauty"; that is, he must destroy his own personality and transform himself into the image of his beloved. Thus does beauty initiate those wondrous transformations of the soul into ever more beauteous forms until, finally, the soul rejoins the source of beauty itself. In Ficino's terms, Peter's notion that a lover can "long for a thing possessed" is superficial since the thing the lover longs for, the "Idea" of beauty, is not possessed until the soul of the lover is reunited with God.

As all, including Peter himself, realize, he is merely juggling with the terms "long" and "possess" and he soon sits down in disarray. Had Peter been gifted with the insight that Sir Thomas More provides at the end of *Il Moro*, he might have fitted the Ficinian theory of love into the framework of the Thomistic quest for happiness, thus effecting, through the medium of St. Thomas, a reconciliation of the Neoplatonists, Plato, and Aristotle.[26] Peter approaches such a synthesis, especially in his last argument, in which he struggles with the definition of "desire." For the distinction Peter tries to make between desire for what we lack and desire for what we possess seems to adumbrate St. Thomas' distinction between the act of concupiscence and the act of enjoyment.

Contentment Is in Knowledge of the Physical World

The next major division of *Il Moro* is Alexander's argument that happiness is to be found in knowledge of the physical world. This section is short; Alexander's sole argument in support of the value of knowledge is that man has a natural desire to understand his world just as he has a natural desire for food. Both proposition and image are drawn from St. Thomas: "Just as in respect of his corporal nature man naturally desires the pleasures of food and sex, so, in respect of his soul, he naturally desires to know some thing: thus the Philosopher observes at the beginning of his *Metaphysics* [I, i]: *All men have a natural desire for knowledge*" (*ST*, II, ii, Q.166, A.2).

Like Alexander's argument, Sir Thomas More's rebuttal of it is drawn directly from St. Thomas. According to St. Thomas, knowledge, like all natural appetites, must be tempered by reason, for inordinate pursuit of knowledge is sinful (*ST*, II, ii, Q.167, A.7). A man pursues knowledge inordinately when he "desires to know the truth about creatures, without referring his knowledge to its due end, namely the knowledge of God. Hence Augustine says that in studying creatures, we must not be moved by empty and perishable curiosity; but we should ever mount towards immortal and abiding things" (*ST*, II, ii, Q.167, A.1).

---

[26] Cf.: "The beautiful is the same as the good, and they differ in aspect only. For since good is what all seek, the notion of good is that which calms the desire; while the notion of the beautiful is that which calms the desire, by being seen or known. Consequently, those senses chiefly regard the beautiful which are the most cognitive, viz., sight and hearing, as ministering to reason; for we speak of beautiful sights and beautiful sounds. But in reference to the other objects of the other senses, we do not use the expression *beautiful* for we do not speak of beautiful tastes, and beautiful odours. Thus it is evident that beauty adds to goodness a relation to the cognitive faculty: so that *good* means that which simply pleases the appetite; while the beautiful is something pleasant to apprehend." (*ST*, II, ii, Q.27, A.2). The attempt of the humanists to reconcile Plato and Aristotle is discussed briefly by Eugenio Garin, *L'Umanesimo italiano* (Bari: Laterza, 1964), pp. 148–153.

The structural function of Alexander's argument and its refutation, taken directly and without any elaboration from St. Thomas, is to focus the reader's attention on the concept of rational control of appetite which is to be the key idea in Sir Thomas More's concluding discussion of the nature of true happiness.

Contentment Is Fulfilled Desire

The theme of the insufficiency of natural appetite as a guide to happiness, introduced in the previous section, is developed more explicitly in Leonard's short argument that happiness is simply the attainment of whatever you desire. St. Thomas offers a similar definition of happiness ("Happy is the man that has all his desires, or whose every wish is fulfilled." [*ST*, II, i, Q.5, A.8]) only to reject it for the same reason that Leonard's definition is rejected in *Il Moro:* "This definition . . . is a good and adequate definition" only "if we understand it simply of all that man desires by the natural appetite." True happiness, however, must be based upon the "apprehension of reason" and reason may have to curb rather than yield to the natural appetite (*ST*, II, i, Q.5, A.8).

There Is No Contentment to Be Found

The last major division of the argument about happiness is that there is no contentment to be found in this life. This is true, argues Paul, for three reasons: the impossibility of satisfying infinite desires with finite means; the will of God that we be unhappy and dissatisfied with this life; and, finally, the ineluctable fact of death. Although each of these arguments is criticized by the other speakers, the most effective criticism is provided by Paul himself. The seriousness of what he says is consistently undercut by his portentous mode of saying it. Paul has an exaggerated sense of his own importance, and he lacks what such people always lack: a sense of humor. When it is his turn to speak, he sits silent and withdrawn until all eyes are focused upon him. Then, before defining happiness, he quarrels with the order of procedure laid down by More. When not quarreling with More, he quarrels with fortune. The Stoic contempt for fortune that he proclaims at every opportunity (pp. 56, 94) seems prompted primarily by a sense that his true worth is going unrecognized by the world at large. Paul, one feels, would applaud loudly the sentiments of Dryden's Aureng-Zebe: "When I consider Life, 'tis all a Cheat!"

Paul is an attitudinizer who has mistaken grimness for seriousness. He reinforces his discourse on death by melodramatically displaying a ring on which is inscribed: *memento mori*. When this theatrical gesture (atypical of Renaissance dialogues not intended for stage presentation) fails to impress upon his audience the seriousness of his theme, Paul strikes a grim posture as though he were playing Death in a morality play.

Our appreciation of the ironies surrounding the presentation of Paul increases when we consider that his "sermon" on death is taken directly from Sir Thomas More's own treatise on death, *The Four Last Things*. It is as though the words of More himself are put into the mouth of Paul for the purpose of ridiculing them.

More left his treatise of *The Four Last Things* unfinished, but the extant fragment is sufficiently developed to stand by itself as a sermon on death. It concerns the four ultimate realities that each man must face: death, judgment, heaven, and hell. The theme throughout the treatise is *memento mori:* "Remember death." More makes his way steadily through a standard catalogue of the deadly sins—pride, envy, wrath, covetousness, gluttony, sloth—showing that a sufficient antidote for each is to remember that we must face eternal judgment. We are all (to use one of More's favorite metaphors in the treatise) prisoners condemned to die. The surest way to stop sinning, says More, is to imagine your own death: "For there seest thou, not only plain grievous sight of the bare bones hanging by the sinews, but thou seest (if thou fantasy thine own death, for so art thou by this counsel advised), thou seest, I say, thyself, if thou die no worse death, yet at the very leastwise lying in thy bed, thy head shooting, thy back aching, thy veins beating, thine heart panting, thy throat rattling, thy flesh trembling, thy mouth gaping, thy nose sharping, thy legs cooling, thy fingers fumbling, thy breath shortening, all thy strength fainting, thy life vanishing, and thy death drawing on."[27] This is the More that Paul hopes to see immortalized by a translation of *The Four Last Things* into Latin, the language of international humanist culture!

If we turn from Paul's summary of *The Four Last Things* to the treatise itself, we discover that Paul has selected from it only those parts that depict man's weakness and helplessness in the face of death. When put back into

[27] Sir Thomas More, "The Four Last Things," quoted from *The English Works of Sir Thomas More*, ed. W. E. Campbell (London: Eyre and Spottiswoode, 1927–1931), I, p. 468.

context, passages such as the one just quoted bear a different emphasis. More's concern is not really with death, but, as in *Utopia*, with the relation of virtue to pleasure. The treatise demonstrates that the deadly sins cause terrible anguish, while virtue bestows mental and physical well-being. The source of this well-being, according to More, is the meditation on the last things, for then repentant sinners feel "so great a pleasure grow thereby that they never felt the like before nor would have supposed that ever they should have felt any such."[28] Meditation on death instructs the living, not the dying: "For well thou wottest, he [Sirach, in Ecclesiasticus] biddeth thee not take neither death, nor doom, nor pain, but only to remember them, and yet the joy of heaven there with to temper them withal."[29] To remember death is not to despair at the possibilities of life, but to learn to distinguish true pleasure from false pleasure.

It is Paul's sentimental harangues on fortune and death that focus our attention, by a negative emphasis, on the source of the strength of More's character in *Il Moro:* his joyous acceptance of the concrete historical conditions under which he has lived his life. More was not, we are told at the outset of *Il Moro*, one of those misanthropes for whom virtue is "as painful on the inside as it is on the outside." It is this elusive quality of joyous acceptance that the dialogue has tried to represent figurally in the humor and irony that More shows when he is, as it were, practically in the jaws of death itself. For More, death is not a crisis that demands a different sort of response from other situations in life. Truly to know how to die, as More wrote in *The Four Last Things*, paraphrasing Socrates, is to know how to live. To remember death in a meaningful way is to live every moment as an existential moment in full awareness that we may be on the brink of death —and on the brink of an even fuller life.

The Nature of True Happiness

The debate stemming from the definition of "happiness" as "contentment of desire" has come full circle. The disputants have canvassed the range of obtainable human goods and found none capable of providing contentment. The disputants in *Il Moro* have done just what Dr. Faustus does in the opening scene of Marlowe's play: dismissed every condition of

[28] *Ibid.*, p. 461.
[29] *Ibid.*, p. 460.

life open to them as unworthy of their limitless desires. Where then, short of black magic, is contentment to be found?

It is at this climactic juncture that Sir Thomas More breaks the impasse by redirecting the inquiry toward the nature of "contentment" itself. Whereas the others had taken the definition of "contentment" for granted, More finds it necessary to distinguish true contentment from false. "We must," says More, "realize that to content oneself within a certain limit consists, not only in not desiring more, for this would be better called not being miserable than being happy, but also in understanding why there is nothing further to be desired beyond that limit."

That contentment consists in *not desiring more* is the false notion of contentment put forward by the Stoic sage: "Rule your passion, for unless it obeys, it gives commands. Check it with a bridle—check it, I pray you, with chains."[30] And, to put it into another Renaissance context, this is the same false notion of contentment that lies behind the idealization of the mean and low estate of the shepherd in pastoral literature. "Sir," brags Corin in *As You Like It*, "I am a true labourer; I earn that I eat, get that I wear; owe no man hate, envy no man's happiness; glad of other men's good, content with my harm; and the greatest of my pride is to see my ewes graze and my lambs suck" (III, ii, 77–81). But this is a contentment of passivity, of subjection to the conditions of life, a contentment, as More points out, suitable to animals and not to human beings endowed with reason.

True contentment is not passive satisfaction: it is *understanding why there is nothing further to be desired beyond that limit.* This is a formula for contentment as a rational act of enjoyment that embraces all three phases in the attainment of happiness outlined by St. Thomas: the act of recognition, the act of concupiscence, and the act of enjoyment. Earthly contentment, for Sir Thomas More as for St. Thomas, is to be found in the activity of the soul deciding upon the proper use of worldly goods. Such an activity is rational because "proper use" depends upon a careful weighing of circumstances in any human situation. The man who penetrates the meaning of More's formula for happiness will not waste time seeking absolute answers to questions such as: "Is it better to be poor or rich?" "Is it better to be honored or not?" "Is it better to be knowledgeable about the physical world or not?" More's formula implies that a man can set a limit on how much wealth, honor, or knowledge he needs only after he has

[30] Horace *Ep.* 1.2. 62–63, quoted from *Satires, Epistles, Ars Poetica*, trans. Fairclough, p. 267.

examined his own status as an animal, rational, and social being. "How much of these goods do I need to maintain my body and the bodies of my dependents?" "How much do I need to maintain the position of my family in society?" "How much do I need to perform the obligations of my social position?" Contentment achieved through such self-analysis involves a state of self-awareness, as well as an affirmation of and a commitment to the social institutions that are the concrete embodiment of divine order. Sir Thomas More solves the question "What is true happiness?" in the scholastic sense that he reveals the full meaning of the original question.

Even closer to the heart of Sir Thomas' ethical system than the formula for use of worldly goods is More's final assertion that true happiness is to be found only in the contemplation of God. More's words are almost those of St. Thomas himself: "Final and perfect happiness can consist in nothing else than the vision of the Divine Essence . . . For perfect happiness the intellect needs to reach the very Essence of the First Cause. And thus it will have its perfection through union with God as that object, in which alone man's happiness consists" (*ST*, II, i, Q.3, A.8). And therefore, says St. Thomas, "a certain participation of happiness can be had in this life, but perfect and true happiness cannot be" (*ST*, II, i, Q.5, A.3).

IL MORO

TRANSLATION

To the Most Illustrious Monsignor

CARDINAL REGINALD POLE

Primate of the Church of England

If I, Most Reverend Lord, like others who dedicate their works to famous men, endeavor to exalt your infinite virtues, I would but rush instantly into two great errors: the first, of praising that which ought rather to be revered; the second, of presuming to reveal to the world what is already clearly evident of itself. It is not because I fear to reveal a lack of awareness that I set out to speak your praises; nothing hinders me from honoring you except that you are too worthy of honor. For if your reputation, like that of other virtuous men, could be besmirched by malice or diminished by envy, perhaps the loving duty of him who set out to defend it would not be amiss. But, since it is thus privileged above all others that up to now there has not appeared a tongue so poisonous that it lacked respect for your fame, nor anyone so envious that he did not proclaim its power, I do not see how my feeble ability can possibly add to the sublimity of your honor without either falling short of the merit or else exceeding the need.

And to whom shall I describe your worth who does not already know it better than I do? Who among the Italians does not know that your life at Rome was acclaimed by everyone a paragon of saintliness and virtue? Who among the French or Germans does not know how much your Christian spirit has labored to resolve the enmities that have plagued Christendom for these many years? Who among the English has not seen how, since returning to your country, you have brought your country back to itself again? Is anyone so new to the affairs of Christendom that he has not heard that in these last few days Our Holy Father, needing your aid in governing the Church, urgently requested you to return to Rome? Your country, on the other hand, moved you to pity its recent wounds and forced you to remain behind, finding your aid as ready as its need. When you are thus requested so warmly by the foremost and, at the same time, by the outermost parts of Christendom, may it not truly be said *quod hic orbis Christianus* (not unlike that universe invented by the astrologers) requires another Pole to sustain it?[1]

---

[1] *quod hic orbis christianus:* "that this Christian world." According to a manuscript note of the late Professor R. C. Bald, this sentence in *Il Moro* is the only record of such a papal request before 1557. Though the title page of *Il Moro* gives the date 1556, Professor Bald suggests that it was perhaps printed later.

But these matters are too lofty, and it would not suit my low style to wish to climb as high as the Pole. A more fitting subject for me, perhaps, would have been to disparage the slightness of this work that humbly betakes itself to your receptive spirit and begs you to accept it. I would have decried this work at length had I not realized that such a diminishing of my book would have increased its size, and that increase would have diminished your receptivity.

I shall say only this about my presenting you with a book of this sort—that I followed the example of those of the villa to whom, poor though they be, custom has granted the privilege of presenting to the great lords nuts, peaches, pears, and other little things of no importance which, the less valuable they are, the more suitable they are both to those who offer and to those who receive. In this sense, it seemed to me that there was some appropriateness in your highness and the lowness of this work.

I fear you will be offended when you see the acute mind of Sir Thomas More speaking in a manner so cold that it does not even correspond to More dead; still, I hope that my complete affection for his reverend name will keep this book from being distasteful to you.

Your Reverend Lordship's

Most Affectionate Servant

Ellis Heywood

BOOK I

Among the many delightful estates that grace the River Thames, there is one, quite close to London, where Sir Thomas More (a man well known for his virtue) had a beautiful and commodious home where it was his custom to withdraw when he tired of the city. The house was so close by and the owner so excellent a man that the rarest and finest intellects of the city gathered there.

At their leisurely meetings they took delight in subtle discussions of the essential concerns of human life, and, since all participants were intelligent and well educated, each derived great benefit and satisfaction. Whenever I think of a company as rare as that one, I feel the need to describe it in order to depict a true and perfect Academy, but I must leave that undertaking to those who, having lived in Chelsea, have greater knowledge of it.[1] I shall describe only one discussion which, if I am not mistaken, will delight and reward those who read it. If, in this discussion, anything should appear less than perfect (as I am certain there will), it is because of the smallness of my understanding or that of those who told me all that I am now preparing to write (for I was not present). No other excuse would be acceptable, for if I tried to transfer the guilt for these defects to him who was the judge in this dispute, those who knew him would not believe me. All of them know his refined judgment could never be satisfied with imperfection.

Well then, Sir Thomas More, having for certain reasons disencumbered himself of one of his offices (he had been the Lord Chancellor of England, an office inferior only to that of the King) after having sought with as much difficulty to abandon the office as others were accustomed to seek it, turned his attention completely to the study of the True Good.[2] In fact,

---

[1] Erasmus described More's home in a letter to John Faber: "You might call it another Platonic Academy. But I wrong his home which I compare to that of the Academy of Plato, in which they used to dispute of numbers and geometric figures, and now and then of moral virtues. With greater justice, you will have called this house the school and gymnasium of Christian religion." (*Opus Epistolarum Des. Erasmi Roterdami*, ed. Percy Stafford Allen [Oxford: Oxford University Press, 1941], X, 139 [Translation mine.]).

[2] The description here of More's voluntary retirement reflects More's own view as expressed in the moving "Epitaph" he wrote during this period: "He, therefore irke and wery of worldly busines, giuing vp his promocions, obtained at last by the incomparable benefite of his most getil prince (if it please god to fauour his enterprise) the thing which from a childe in a maner alway he wished and desired, that he might have some yeres of his life fre, in which he little and little withdrawing himself from the busines of this life, might continually remembre the immortalite of the lyfe to come." (*The Workes of Sir Thomas More*, ed. William Rastell [London, 1557], p. 1421.) The description of More's leisured, philo-

even when he was Lord Chancellor, he had not abandoned his studies. He wrote every day and taught his daughters Greek and Latin letters. Yet he did not neglect his offices, for the number of important suits decided by him testifies that he gave them more attention than anyone who had held them in the past. Freed now from so many burdens, he turned his thought more fixedly to true wisdom. Even when he had abandoned those desires that blind the rest of us, he did not have that stiff reserve or misanthropy that we see in many people whose disdain brings about two evils: first, they plainly show just how hard it is for them to restrain their wills; and, second, they deter others who conclude that virtue must be just as unpleasant on the inside as it appears from the outside.[3] Sir Thomas More was one who obeyed virtue with joy and eagerness, and, when in the company of others, where he liked to be during the hours of dining and others unsuitable for study, he enjoyed turning a doubtful proposition into a useful debate. He knew so well how to make it yield truth that the antagonist whom More could not satisfy completely would have to be very obstinate.

Among those who frequented More's house were six for whom I will give only Christian names since their last names are English and do not translate well into Italian: Leonard, Paul, and Alexander, who had learned about foreign culture and customs by taking a long trip together through the most famous cities outside their own country, and, in addition, two gentlemen named Peter and Charles who were brothers; finally, there was Laurence, a citizen of London who was crude and ignorant in matters of learning but otherwise perspicacious and pleasant.[4] He was a great amasser of money, for which More often laughed at him, showing that his grasping after money was foolishness by arguments so effective they could not be refuted, at which More (as was his custom) took great pleasure.

These gentlemen, as I have said, came to More's house to dine. After the meal they went to walk in a garden that was about two stone's throws from the house. On a small meadow (in the middle of the garden and at the crest of a little hill), they stopped to look around. The spot pleased them greatly, both for its comfort and for its beauty. On one side stood the noble City of London; on the other, the beautiful Thames with green gardens

---

sophical retirement in *Il Moro* stands in contrast to the anxieties and straitened circumstances of More's retirement described in R. W. Chambers, *Thomas More* (New York: Harcourt Brace, 1935), pp. 282–287.

[3] misanthropy: In Heywood's text, this word is quoted in Greek in its adjectival form.

[4] I assume that the friends are fictitious and that the reason given for not translating their last names into Italian is intended to further the joke.

and wooded hills all around. The meadow, beautiful in itself, was almost completely covered with green and flowers in bloom, and tender branches of fruit trees were interwoven in such beautiful order that they seemed, to the guests, to resemble an animated tapestry made by Nature herself. And yet this garden was more noble than any tapestry, which leaves more desirous than content the soul of him who beholds the images painted on cloth.

The garden pleased them all, but Peter became so ardent (congenial spirits generally wax ardent over things that are beautiful) that he could hardly contain himself. After many extravagant commendations, the excitement in his voice rose as he proclaimed the place to be so delightful that simply being there would suffice to make any man happy.

His brother laughed and said, "Tell me, please, how happy you think he would be who found himself here while he had a headache?"

"What I said," answered Peter, "was that the pleasantness of this place is enough for a man, and, in speaking of a man, I mean one in that state in which it is natural for a man to be."

"Well, then," replied Charles, "setting aside the first part of my question, let's consider the rest. What happiness do you think he would find who had to stay here all day, from morning until evening?"

"I have to admit," answered Peter, "that an excess in anything is annoying, but I have set a definite limit to this happiness, knowing well that no one can take continuous delight in any thing, since all pleasures pall in the end."

"I certainly disagree with that," said Laurence, "because I can show you one pleasure that grows no matter how often it is tasted. If you don't believe me, just tell me, please, what man have you ever known who was afflicted by having too many riches? Quite the contrary! The more they have, the more they want. So, among the happinesses of this life, whichever of them Mr. More may find pleasing, I have always held riches to be the greatest."

"Those things that do not satisfy and those things that satiate are equally alien to happiness," answered Peter.

"This way," said Laurence, "no one will ever be happy if that which satisfies and that which fails to satisfy must both be contrary to happiness."

"I did not say that," answered Peter. "Satisfaction and satiety are not, as they seem to you, the same. Satisfaction means an end to desire, while satiety is a kind of annoyance. Between the two extremes of desire and annoyance there has to be a middle, that is, contentment."

"Of these middles and extremes I know nothing," said Laurence, "but I do know that, when it comes to getting rich, everyone applies himself to extremes without any middles. No one is ever content or satiated when it comes to this! So, I see no reason for saying that happiness in this life is anything else but making money."

Everyone grew silent, whereupon Sir Thomas More said, smiling, "Well, gentlemen, shall we let Laurence steal away happily with so many riches without saying a thing to him, or shall we, before he goes off with them, investigate them in the manner of detectives, examining carefully what they are, where he has gotten them, and where he would take them?"

"We are certain," said Paul, "that Laurence will never give us anything purely for the sake of courtesy; therefore it seems best to investigate the whole business minutely in order to stop him short—and not in order to understand its worth; for, in his ignorance of how to *syllogizesthai*, Laurence has put his argument together so illogically that the errors fairly glare out at us.[5] However much we might like to do this, none of us has the courage to undertake it, since we are in the presence of one before whom the authority of lesser judges ceases."

"Go right ahead," said More, "for whatever my authority here might be, I delegate it to you, so that each of you will speak your opinion freely."

"If you are determined," said Alexander, "to delegate this case, putting it into our hands, at least prescribe to us some order by which we should proceed in this examination of happiness."

"The order," said More, "although it is greatly out of order for me to prescribe it to you, shall be this: before you set out to disturb the happiness defended by Laurence, you must first agree upon another definition. In this way you will displace this false happiness and confront it with the true; also, you will provide yourselves and me with a better concept, instead of unwisely taking away one happiness without supplying another, which would leave us unhappy. Once there is agreement about the nature of true happiness, which I am certain you will easily reach, try to persuade Laurence of this and show him how to lift the great burden of money (if you understand it to be contrary to happiness) off his back so that he may be happy."

Laughing skeptically, Laurence said, "Whenever I take a notion to become happy that way, all I have to do is offer myself as prey to thieves; the more forceful their arguments for happiness, the more amenable I shall be to yours. Begin, however, and relieve me of my great fear that you will

---

[5] *syllogizesthai:* "syllogize."

give birth to some monster of happiness with as many heads as you five have."

Then Charles, looking at the others, said, "Gentlemen, to put an end to Laurence's hopes and his fears at one and the same time, let us make public our idea of happiness. Since happiness is the highest delight of the soul, should we not find it in honor, which, as everyone knows, satisfies our souls more than anything else?"

"I shall never agree with you," said Peter, "that honor is the happiness we seek, for it does not have an existence of and for itself in the person honored. To find happiness, we must find a thing so constituted that is really exists in the soul of him who wants to be happy, and, in my opinion, it is that most noble emotion of all, love, which not only dwells in the heart of the lover, but, furthermore, does not let any other emotion enter."

"I do not believe," said Alexander, "that plunging into desire for either honor or love, both of which are disturbances of the soul, is happiness, any more than is a fever in the body, which makes drink that much more pleasant. Since the soul is in itself quite perfect, that which maintains and preserves it in its natural state is, without doubt, our happiness. And who does not know that this is knowledge, the true nourishment of the soul, just as food is the nourishment of the body?"

Leonard, who had listened with interest, said, "I am amazed that all of you, having agreed that happiness is none other than a delight of the soul, have equated it with one single thing, trying to convince us that it is either this good or that good. Our souls are so different that it is difficult to find two that take equal delight in the same thing. Therefore, in my opinion, happiness ought not to be equated with one thing more than with another, but with anything that furnishes delight to the soul."

Only Paul had yet to speak. He remained silent and withdrawn for a while, finally saying, "The law given to us by Sir Thomas is, if I am not mistaken, that each of us shall describe so truly what he believes happiness to be that in every way the rest of us will have to agree. Since it seems to me that no happiness is to be found in this life, I will have to disobey this law in order to obey it. Nevertheless, I will speak freely, since I do not accept as law that which contains an impossibility within itself. It seems to me, then, that happiness (speaking of this life) is not to be found in anything, and that all our life, if you consider it carefully, is nothing but a continual misery, coated, like those bitter pills that doctors give their patients, with a little sugar."

When Paul had spoken, Laurence guffawed and said, "Just look now, was I not a true prophet in predicting the birth of happiness? What a monster she is! Her own parents do not know how to baptize her; one calls her Honor, one Love, a third Knowledge, a fourth Everything, and the last Nothing."

"It is true," said More, "that you have accomplished little. I had confidently expected to find, through you, a true happiness. Instead, thanks to your disagreement, you have brought the matter to such a bad state that I don't see how I can mend it. Therefore, I think it well to leave it completely, lest disturbing ourselves too much about this subtle happiness, we become unhappy." With these words, he prepared to leave the garden. But the other gentlemen, somewhat aroused by the discussion and each thinking his argument most rational, were determined not to end the discussion. They surrounded More and begged him fervently to listen and render a judgment at the end in favor of him whom he thought to have argued most effectively.

They were able to convince him. Turning back, he said, "Here I am, ready to please you in every way I can. Reason as long as you like; I am more willing to listen than you are to ask me to do so. As for a judgment, however, let me say that I will not decide in favor of him who argues most effectively but in favor of him who argues most rationally. If it should happen that I do not find such a one among you, I will leave the controversy undecided, writing on it simply those two letters of the ancients, *n.l.*"

"It would displease me greatly," said Alexander, "if we were to spend so much time pursuing this, only to find ourselves worn out without having accomplished a thing. If you give us those letters *n.l.* for a judgment, Mr. More, each of us will interpret them to mean *non libet* instead of *non liquet.*[6] At least promise that, should you not award any of us the victory, you will explain why, showing us where we have swerved from reason and how we could have done better."

"This," said More, "would be no other than to give you my own opinion about what you are seeking. I am quite willing to do so, but as a litigant, not as a judge—so that I do not give a decision in my own trial, and also so that when I seem to judge you severely you can get even by doing the same to me."

---

[6] *non libet:* "I don't like it"; *non liquet:* "it is not clear." ("In the Roman courts, when any of the judges, after the hearing of a cause, were not satisfied that the case was made clear enough for them to pronounce a verdict, they were privileged to signify this opinion by casting a ballot inscribed with the letters *n.l.*, the abbreviated form of the phrase *non liquet*." (*Black's Law Dictionary*, s.v. *non liquet*.)

"That," said Laurence, "suits me very well, for, to judge by your good will toward my side on other occasions, I can expect more satisfaction in this trial from your revenge than from your justice."

"You are far more concerned than you need to be," answered More. "It appears to me that you have nothing to do with this deliberation since we have already half condemned your money as too light to be weighed with happiness."

"Oh, fine," said Laurence. "You have condemned them as too light without weighing them, or even finding the counterweight against which to weigh them!"

"Let us be good enough not to refuse Laurence the little courtesy of weighing his coins," said Alexander. "After all, he may be interested in exchanging them."

"Certainly not," declared Laurence immediately, "though these coins may not be of good weight, nevertheless, I would not exchange them for any of your happinesses, which, as far as I can see, do not weigh anything at all."

"You see, gentlemen," said More, "what you receive for the courtesy you have extended to Laurence, but, since it pleases you that he too take part in this dispute, let it be so, if it please God. We will give him the first place, proceeding not as rhetoricians but as cloth merchants, who always show their worst goods first. Begin, Laurence, and please use your words about riches just as you are accustomed to use riches themselves—spending no more than necessary."

"In that case," said Laurence laughing, "I would not say a word, for I have never wasted a penny on anything that concerns me so little as this present dispute. But, since it pleases you that the reasoning start with me, I am quite content, even if Mr. More put me before the others in order to drive me behind all. I consider it appropriate that our dispute begin with riches, without which, as far as I can see, nothing begins at all.[7] I could make an unassailable argument out of that, but I prefer to begin with the direct contrary—that is, with the end of our actions. Happiness being the highest contentment of the soul, there is no more direct route to it than to seek the true end of our actions, the attainment of which must necessarily provide full contentment.

"Who, then, having considered carefully, will not admit that our sweat

[7] The argument that "nothing begins without money" anticipates Charles's argument a few pages later.

and labors are endured to grow rich? I think I may safely say, no one. Were I to ask Mr. More himself this question, I think even he would concede this, or, should he deny it, I could force him to admit it. If I put before him one by one every kind of man to be found in the world, I know perfectly well not one of them would have set himself any goal but this. We may leave aside those who live by physical exertion; the end for which they work is only too obvious. Even those who pursue intellectual matters, seemingly for honor only, really practice their trade for money rather than for anything else. Let me say a little about such men, characterizing them in four words. First, I have never seen any professor of the seven so-called Liberal Arts so liberal that he would teach for nothing. Your doctors, too, study how to cure the defects of others solely to cure themselves of the saddest one of all, the defect of money. They never give a dose of syrup to anyone without giving themselves a dose of silver. Not long ago, my doctor gave me a dose of medicine, and, when I asked him if it was sweet, he answered that it was sweet in the drinking, but afterward it would leave a slightly bitter taste. When I had finished drinking, he asked for a half-scudo. Whenever I am sick, I am plagued more by the doctor than by the disease.

"There is no need to say anything about lawyers here. Who does not know how with their *jus suum cuique tribuant nummos suos cuique auferant?*[8]

"Perhaps here you will introduce against me those philosophers of yours whose clever words and sayings against riches you cite so often. But it is plain that they never disparaged money without getting money in return; they were well paid. I often laugh and say to myself, 'What way won't these greed philosophers find to turn up money, if by speaking evil of it they gain such a good?' Many of them became very rich; I remember having heard Mr. More say that Seneca himself, who ridicules rich men more than any other writer, left a legacy of more than eighty thousand gold scudi. The only thing I can say of greedy philosophers, therefore, is that these truly wise men disparage riches in front of others in order to get them more easily themselves. Let us now leave this argument that riches are the end of our actions lest perhaps Mr. More say that I speak endlessly of ends; let us turn instead to speaking of their effects."

"Turn to them, indeed," said More, "for if you do not bring this effect to a better end than you brought that end to an effect, you may be sure that, in the end, I will say that you have, in effect, accomplished nothing."

[8] *jus suum cuique tribuant nummos suos cuique auferant:* "they give their right to whoever brings them cash."

"Now, I ask you," said Laurence, "whether I can ever hope to have justice in this case, when our judge begins to speak about it out of prejudice, before I have even half defended it. I could refuse him as suspect, and I would except that I believe the authority of riches will grow a great deal from a successful defense before an unfavorable judge. But let us now proceed more convincingly in this trial, as he must who is not looked upon too well by the judge. Before I start to speak of the effect of riches, I want, in connection with my argument, to show my adversaries one of their very palpable faults. And what is that, gentlemen? Do you not see that there are ordinarily three things that everyone desires in this life? These are to be honored, to be powerful, and to be rich. Unless one has all three of these goods, he is not content with his life. Since our souls desire all three, how can you expect to find happiness, which you yourselves say is contentment of the soul, in one of these without the other two?"

"You see, Laurence," said Charles, "how, like a desperate man, in avenging yourself on your adversaries you ruin yourself as well. For, having conceded happiness to be that contentment which results from these three goods—honor, power, and riches—does it not seem as reasonable to put it in honor, or power alone, as in riches alone?"

"Not at all," said Laurence, "and just see whether, of the three, riches do not have more right than the others to the name of happiness. Whereas the others in their operation limit themselves to a single good beyond which they work nothing (as honor can cause you to be honored, but cannot make you rich), riches, you see, not only do their own proper office, but also those of the other two. You may bring here any man you like, as long as he is rich, and it will inevitably follow that he will be well known, honored, and powerful, every man his friend. If you deny that these effects follow immediately from riches, I could show you sixty people, honored now by everybody, who, if you took away their money, would have no reason left for anyone to lift a hat to them any more than to a jackass. Riches, then, contain in themselves honor and power; they are not, like the others, particular goods that make a single part of happiness without the other parts, but they are a general good because they contain in themselves all the others. Even if I lacked other means of proving my point, the very name itself would prove it, for where all other goods have only specialized names like 'honor' and 'power,' you see that riches, besides the specific name of 'riches,' have also the general name of 'goods,' as it were, of that general good which in its nature actually contains the others. This is the reason, I think, that the ancients, wanting to signify in a single word that the first age abounded in every good, called it the Golden Age. Therefore, to wind up my argument, I say that our desires are satisfied by three things: the first is to feel oneself preferred above others, which is honor; the second is to be well supplied with friends, which is power; the third is to be supplied with the goods of this world. The first comes from riches since they are greatly honored; the second also comes from riches since they are greatly loved; the third is no other than riches themselves. I conclude, then, in one word that, if you show me a man who is rich, I'll show you a man who is happy."

Laurence stopped speaking. Charles waited a while and then, seeing that no one was preparing to oppose him, said: "Laurence has defended his riches very poorly. If the locks on his chests were as weak as his arguments, he would soon find out, I think, how much greater the pain of losing riches than the pleasure in keeping them safe. Actually, I do not fear for him at all; the rest of you know how well that part of the house in which Laurence keeps his golden happiness is fortified. It is so packed with sheets of metal, nails, locks, and other such arguments that it seems to be made entirely of iron."

Laurence, amused, answered, "And what do you expect? Since we are living in the saddest of all Ages, the Age of Iron, I have to accommodate myself to the times."

"But," said Peter, "you show little respect for the times when you try to preserve not only the Age of Silver but also the Age of Gold by means of so much iron."

"As to this," said Charles, "Laurence can easily defend himself since it is certain that gold and silver are more appropriate to the Age of Iron than iron itself; they, as the poets say, are the cause of it. The Golden Age disappeared as soon as gold began to appear, and, it seems to me (to answer Laurence), it takes its name from gold by *antiphrasin*—as, in the Latin language, 'mountain' gets its name from that which does not move."[9]

"I do not know how to thank you, Charles," said Laurence, "for the industry with which you turn my defense against me. Truly, as an advocate, you are as gallant as was that doctor who, in order to preserve the tooth of a patient, took out one of his eyes. But do not think me so lacking in eyes that I do not see how much more tolerable is a known than a secret enemy. Go ahead and speak against my defense of riches, about which you have

[9] *antiphrasin:* "antiphrasis" ("a figure of speech by which words are used in a sense opposite to their proper meaning" [Oxford English Dictionary]).

spoken such outrageous things. Tell how much worse it is to be rich than to be poor. I do not doubt a bit that I can show they are good."

"You talk like all rich men," said Charles, "who with great ease and on the slightest pretext take offense at poorer men.[10] But, since it pleases you, and only because it pleases you, I will argue against you in our discussion. I will disagree with you in order not to be disagreeable to you. Laurence, if you are going to show us happiness, that is, contentment of the soul, as the end for our actions, you will have to bring forward a final end; only that will satisfy us. These instrumental ends, which must be referred to a further end, contain as much discontent as contentment. Riches are of this sort. We desire them not for themselves, but in order to live more comfortably, and, where this end does not follow, we get little benefit from having acquired them. Riches are, therefore, a means and not a final end. If an end of this sort suffices to show happiness to you, I will show you what the labor of it will be. Everyone who sets out to acquire some power, whether of soul or body, does so in order to be able to exercise it: to work with that power in order to gain, to gain in order to live. In respect to being ends, gaining and working are equal, that is, in respect to their operation they are ends, and in respect to their ends they are means. Speaking properly, we may say that they are means rather than ends. Now then, we see the effect of those riches that Laurence wants us to believe bring us honor and supply us with friends. Not only do they not bring friendship, they often cause continual enmity, which can produce a goodly supply of foes or, even worse, those who hide a drawn dagger under the cloak of friendship. Riches, then, do not give us true friends, but they do keep us from knowing true friends from false. So that I do not show myself to be one of those unamiable friends, I shall concede what I cannot in conscience deny: riches are truly a cause for some happiness. But what do you propose to infer from that? That they are, then, happiness itself? That they are a cause does not help you to prove your point; rather, it hinders the proof. Indeed, to show that riches are not happiness itself I shall look for no clearer argument than that they are an instrument of that; it is never possible for the instrument to a thing to be the thing itself. Therefore, riches, if they are to be the cause of happiness, are no more closely joined to

[10] Charles's charge against rich men is probably not based upon experience, but rather upon the comments of Aristotle in *Rhetoric*, 2. 16. Aristotle's comments on the insolence and pride of the rich man have much in common with Heywood's portrait of Laurence and culminate in the statement that "the character of the rich man is that of a fool favored by fortune." (Aristotle, *The Art of Rhetoric*, trans. John Henry Freese [London: W. Heinemann, 1926], p. 259.)

happiness itself than is the carpenter to the house he builds. You see, then, Laurence, that you have argued unsuccessfully about the end and the effect of riches and, to put the matter shortly, I say that you have not, in my opinion, accomplished a thing in this prolix discourse of yours."

"It is certain," said Peter, "that either he has accomplished nothing, or, if he has, you have demolished it so completely that there is nothing left. I fear greatly that Laurence, leaving *pro derelicto*[11] his riches, comes here now to take from one of us our happiness in exchange for it."

"None of you need have any fears on that score," said Laurence, "and you, Peter, least of all, for it is certain that I would never exchange my happiness for yours unless I had decided to abandon my head *pro derelicto* along with my money. I see you are only too ready to get at the riches abandoned by their owner. To prove that I am not yet ready to give them up, I shall reply to what has been opposed to them, maintaining as I have up to now that, both in end and in effect, they are the happiness for which you seek. I want you to know, however, Charles, that when you speak against the end, saying that they are not an end in themselves but only with respect to some other, and against the effect, saying that this proves them to be rather the instrument of happiness than happiness itself, I deny both charges. Who would be so stupid as to concede that men desire riches for the end of living when we see every day how much more willing men are to keep them than to spend them on the necessities of life? Besides, an end must be that which, once acquired, brings an end to our actions. But that man who finds himself with enough riches to satisfy a thousand persons with the end you speak of does not stop acquiring them. He tries harder than ever. Furthermore, if the end of riches were to give the power to live, it seems to me (for every agent desires always to approach as closely as possible to its end) that, among the kinds of riches, those ought to be desired above all which immediately and *in actu* constitute our livelihood, like grain, wine, beef, and such things. But you see that we always draw away from these things, exchanging them for ready gold, which does not constitute *in actu* one of the things necessary to life, although in potential (as you are accustomed to say, when you philosophize about the Primal Matter) it contains all."[12]

Alexander, laughing at this crude philosophy of Laurence, said, "Who would ever have thought that Laurence would penetrate so far into philo-

[11] *pro derelicto:* "as derelict or abandoned."
[12] *in actu:* "in a state of possibility realized."

sophical matters? Just look how, in these few words about Matter, he has shown himself to be a very materialistic philosopher."

"And would you not expect," answered Laurence, "that, after practicing with you for so many years, I would not end up at least half a philosopher?"

"No more," answered Alexander, "than that we, practicing the same with you, would have become even halfway rich."

"Riches," answered Laurence, "are more difficult to come by than philosophy is. But let that pass, lest these half philosophers and half-rich men make me leave my answer half-furnished, and let me return to the first part of my argument. When, Charles, I called it reasonable to equate happiness with money, since it is that good whose general nature contains all the others, you snapped me up with your logic, arguing that whatever is an instrument to happiness cannot be happiness itself. But I did not say, you see, that money is instrumental in producing honor or power, but that, like a more absolute good, it contains in its own proper nature the other two. And, whereas the instrument and the thing produced are, as you say, separate, money and these two kinds of goods, as I have shown you, are so united that they commence, endure, and die together. It is obvious, then, that money is the cause of honor and power, not in the way that the instrument is cause of the thing produced, *sed ut totum est causa suae partis*.[13] So, to say that money makes us happy by means of honor or power is no other than to say that it does so by itself; to deny this would be to deny that your carpenter had built the house himself because he worked with the aid of his hands."

"This advocate of riches certainly is stubborn," said Charles. "But consider for a moment what profit he gains from his obstinacy. He will not concede that men seek riches for the end of being able to live because, he says, they desire to have more of them than are necessary to this end. But how does it help him to prove that they seek them merely for the sake of having them? It is clear that they who desire riches beyond what is necessary to life do so in order to win honor. To what end (for you would never say, I hope, that they do it without proposing any end at all) do you think men accumulate so much money except to make themselves stand out from others who have less? The Greeks, in fact, gave a name to this penchant of the rich, using the verb *pleonektein*,[14] as if to say that enriching onself is nothing else, in effect, than possessing more than others. If only men, in the distribution of riches, would think of an arithmetical propor-

---

[13] *sed ut totum est causa suae partis:* "as the whole is the cause of its parts."
[14] *pleonektein:* "to get more wealth."

tion, they would be content when they possess more than is necessary for one man to support himself. But, since it seems to them that this distribution, as if by geometrical proportion, follows the dignity of persons rather than their number, they do not rest content with any reasonable accumulation, hoping by having more than others to appear more worthy. But let us leave them and return to my final reply to you, Laurence. Riches, you said, are not the instrumental cause of honor and power, for these two have the same nature as the former, whereas the instrument is always distinct from the thing that the instrument produces. Who would concede this? I certainly shall not, for I know very well that riches and their effects are things not only as distinct as the instrument and the thing it effects, but even more so. Because where *utrique possint simul esse,* riches and their effects cannot meet under any circumstances, for the making of the one is the breaking of the other.[15] If you look at all the effects or pleasures that riches bring, you see perfectly well that they do not cause any of these without destroying and consuming themselves before those effects can exist at all. And if Laurence wants me to demonstrate this, let him order a few hundred of his scudi brought here, and I shall conduct a beautiful experiment that will give him ocular proof how money always disappears before any pleasure appears."

They all laughed when they saw how Laurence flinched at this threat to his money. More, still laughing, said, "Proceed, Charles, for I think that, if you wait for these scudi, you will wait in vain."

"In good faith, that is true," said Laurence, "because I would much rather concede Charles a whole argument than half a scudo with which to conduct his experiments."

"As you please," said Charles. "But, since you are so discourteous with your scudi, I shall show the same lack of respect in my arguments. I shall force you, in two words, to agree with me that happiness cannot be found in riches, which, I am sure you will concede, are desired either with respect to some further good, or else for themselves. If men desire this good as a means to another good, then that good must be greater than riches, and, consequently, more worthy to be called happiness; the end is always more noble than that which has it for its end. If you say that money is desired for itself without seeking any other good, this is extreme avarice; to tell us that a miser is the happiest of men would be a fine paradox, for no one doubts that they are the unhappiest and most miserable of living men."

[15] *utrique possint simul esse:* "both can exist at the same time."

Then Laurence said, "Were I not afraid that Mr. More would suspect me of being one myself, I would say frankly that, as far as this life goes, misers are the happiest men in the world."

More said, laughing, "Speak freely, Laurence, and rest assured that you could never say anything that would make me suspect that you are a miser," at which everyone smiled and grew quiet.

"Gentlemen," said Charles, "you do not expect, I presume, that I shall argue any further with Laurence. I do not know how I could make a better case against him than I already have, for I have reduced him to the absurdity of affirming that misers are the happiest of men. Leaving aside their damned state in the next life, consider that, even in this life, they taste neither pleasure nor any sweetness. Placed in the midst of great abundance, they are like Tantalus, whom the poets describe: they endure an unendurable fast."

Laurence then turned toward Charles and said, "It is not as foolish as it seems to you to say that misers are the happiest of men. First of all, their damned state in the other world in no way checks their great happiness in this one; on the contrary, it is proof of it. As you know, nothing is more prejudicial to happiness in the other life than too much enjoyment in this one.[16] But I am amazed that you have denied every sweetness to their lives just because they do not eat so delicately as some others. Until now we have put happiness in the delight of the soul, not in the pleasures of the body. Since to displease me you do not want to abandon that definition of pleasure now, you will have to concede that misers are the happiest of men. Where others get brief pleasures that the bodily senses afford in spending money, misers, by keeping theirs, enjoy a continuous delight of the soul brought about by the happy thought of the infinite supply of money they see themselves provided with. If you want to see just how much more complete this pleasure is than that other, notice that misers do not envy the pleasures of those who are enjoying themselves, but the latter never think of the great riches of the miser without being consumed by the excess of desire that they feel."

Charles, laughing at this, said, "You are greatly mistaken about the state of misers, making a perturbation into a delight of the soul. But I do not care to reason at greater length about this, lest we do wrong to the judgments of these other gentlemen. Now, however, I very much want to make clear to you, not as a reply to you but, rather, as an explanation of the

[16] Laurence's last argument anticipates Paul's.

cause of avarice, that avarice proceeds not, as it seems, from a delight in knowing that one is excessively wealthy but, instead, from a more immediate fear of finding onself unprovided for in this life. This notion seems the more reasonable to me in that each of us has a natural feeling that he will live a very long life. Since none of us knows exactly when the prescribed end of his life will come, we go on in hope, always passing this point and that without stopping at anything just as if we were immortal. This belief, fixed obsessively in the minds of those who burden themselves with money, is the real reason why they cannot limit their desires for riches any more than they can fix an end to their lives. Fearing always that they will be miserable in the end, they conduct their whole lives in extreme misery. Not being able to see with their eyes that their lives and their hoard diminish, they never let themselves believe that they, too, are hastening toward their end. Once they see clearly that they have reached the end of their lives, however, they spend and waste money obscenely, like a neighbor of ours a while back who had never enjoyed himself one day in his whole life. He had himself covered in perfumes up to his neck as he lay on his deathbed, whereupon one of our friends said, 'Here is a fellow who never lived until he died.' "[17]

"On the other hand," said Peter, "I remember the old notary who itemized the expenditures for his funeral in his will. Remembering that, among the other things, he had specified six yards of cloth for his winding sheet (as the custom is in our country when we bury our dead), he said to his executors that five yards and three quarters would suffice him if they were bought at bargain measures."

They all laughed, whereupon Charles said, "I think that if we look closely we will see that Peter has falsified a testament. Now, if he is agreeable, I intend to pursue Laurence's happy fellow, and I do not intend to leave him until I have brought him to the gallows. I say then, that these foolish misers degrade themselves into beasts, driven by fear of a lack rather than by any delight in abundance. This, I think, is obvious enough in their very faces, which show fear and suspicion rather than happiness. What confirms me in this belief more than anything else is seeing the desperate deaths to which loss of money often goads them. It is clear that the mere loss of goods without the addition of some great evil would not lead them to such violent conclusions. But I think that when a fresh misfortune, as it were, confirms that one which they have always feared,

[17] A similar joke about a dying miser is in More's *Latin Epigrams*, ed. and trans. Leicester Bradner and Charles Arthur Lynch (Chicago: University of Chicago Press, 1953), p. 168.

which is to lack the necessities of life, they try to shorten a long and miserable life by the noose. Paul told me of one yesterday who wanted to kill himself but did not have a rope handy. When he went to a shop to buy one, he was told that they cost two pennies. Leaving in high dudgeon, he muttered, 'Two pennies for a rope, huh? Looks to me like nobody but a gentleman can afford to hang himself. Either I find a cheaper rope, or, by the blood of the Virgin, I won't hang myself at all!' "[18]

They all joked about this proud miser who refused to hang himself out of spite, and they laughed so hard that all their teeth could have easily been pulled. Someone pointed out the fine irony by which an excess of avarice drove a miser to hang himself and save himself at the same time. Someone else criticized the shopkeeper severely for being too rigid with the miser in not reducing the price by a penny, and added that the miser would have done well to have gotten the rope on credit and then hanged himself without paying anything.

After they had laughed over the miser, Laurence turned to Charles and said, "I cannot agree with you that avarice is born from any other feeling than a great delight in one's riches; for if (as you will have it), it proceeded from a fear of lacking something necessary to life, it would be a vice more appropriate to young men who find themselves at the threshold of life than to old men who find themselves at the end of it. But we see the contrary every day, and, when you know the cause, you will see how much it supports my argument. The reason is that young men, who have so many pleasures to choose from, do not bother themselves with this one, whereas old men, deprived of every other pleasure because their senses are failing, cling to this one remaining pleasure. It is obvious from their faces, as you say, that they are fearful rather than joyful, but who does not know that this fear comes from the failing of old age rather than from anything else? Finally, I do not see how the violent and fearful deaths that misers often choose help at all to prove your argument; nor do I not understand at all the point of your distinction between the mere privation of good and the positive attainment of evil. It seems to me that no evil is anything but a privation of the opposite good. For instance, blindness is an absence of sight, servitude is an absence of liberty, and sickness is an absence of health.

---

[18] "Yesterday, Glaucus, Dinarchus the miser being about to hang himself, did not die, poor fellow, all for the sake of sixpence; for the rope cost sixpence, but he tried to drive a hard bargain, seeking perhaps some other cheap death. This is the very height of wretched avarice, for a man to be dying, Glaucus, and not able to die, all for the sake of sixpence." (*Anthologia Graeca*, trans. W. R. Paxton [London: W. Heinemann, 1916–1918], IV, 153.)

In the other world the greatest evil is no other than privation of the greatest good. Thus, in our case, the miser who sees himself deprived of the greatest good in this life turns to the greatest evil, that is, death."

Then Sir Thomas More, who had listened to this discourse on the happiness of misers with some amusement, said, "How Laurence has tricked us, persuading us with his gilded promises that he intended to direct us to the greatest good and, instead, putting us in danger of running headlong into the greatest evil. I think we had better not let him go further since, up to now, he has kept going from bad to worse. At first, he made just a small error when he put happiness in riches; then a greater error when he tried to make us believe that money is the best kind of riches, while in truth it is worthless except in respect to the others; and, finally, the most outrageous error of all when he claimed that, of those who possess money, they are happiest who do not use it. In fact, his 'happiness' has achieved that end reached yesterday by Patenson (More's fool) who was standing by my table while we were eating and saw among the guests a gentleman with an unusually large nose. After staring in the man's face for a while, he said, 'By my blood—this gentleman has one whale of a nose!' We all pretended not to hear lest we embarrass the good gentleman. Realizing that he had erred, Patenson tried to put himself in the right again by saying, 'I lied in my throat when I said that this gentleman's nose was so large. On my word as a gentleman, it is quite a small nose.' When they heard this, everybody wanted to laugh out loud, and they ordered that the fool be chased away. But Patenson, who wanted to preserve his honor, would not let the affair end this way because, of all his virtues, the one he most often bragged of was that whatever he set out to do always came out right. To arrange the matter more to his own advantage, he went to the head of the table and said, 'Well, I just want to say one thing: this gentleman has no nose at all.' " Everybody laughed so hard at this tale that they almost dislocated their jaws.[19]

When they were almost exhausted, Alexander, still laughing, said, "The difference between the ugliness of that nose, and the beauty of these riches, is that the more Master Patenson set about diminishing the former, the greater it grew, whereas the more Laurence goes about increasing the latter, the smaller it gets. But this is your fault, Charles, for you have treated him

[19] This tale of More's fool was printed as No. 86 in the "First Hundred of Epigrams" of Ellis Heywood's father, John Heywood. See "Of the foole and the gentlemans nose," in *John Heywood's Works and Miscellaneous Short Poems*, ed. Burton Milligan (Urbana: University of Illinois Press, 1956), p. 135.

with such friendliness in this trial of riches that it occurs to me that perhaps you expect some recompense. I am unwilling even to concede that we should understand riches to be a means to happiness since, as we see every day, they cause great unhappiness. Since poverty is the intimate friend of happiness, it follows that money is its enemy."

"I will never agree with you about this," answered Charles, "nor would it be appropriate for me to do so since I have already equated happiness and honor and do not doubt that I can prove the equation when it is my turn to speak. Now, since liberality is the virtue above all others that leads to honor and since riches are the proper instrument of liberality, who would not prefer them to poverty, which is nothing else but a deprivation of riches and thus a very great impediment to liberality? You really cannot say to me that the poor man as well as the rich man can be liberal, for they cannot equally put it into practice. Since the greatest praise we spoke is that happiness is in the doing, clearly both cannot be equally happy."

"Although it may be less than reasonable," said Alexander, "that I defend poverty before this tribunal, especially when I have already defined happiness in an entirely different way, still I fear that this poor waif will not easily find an advocate because she is so poor, and I would rather that she be defended poorly than completely abandoned. Let me begin by saying, Charles, that if you think riches are the only means by which we can put liberality into practice, you certainly must have forgotten the example of Eutrapelus who gave his riches to his enemies because he considered them more fit for getting revenge than for practicing liberality.[20] Actually, poverty is no more defective in exercising liberality than it is defective in any other way. How much liberality was demonstrated by that poor student of philosophy who said to the master who had taught him precepts of philosophy, 'Since fortune has made me so poor that I have nothing in the world to give you, here, I give you myself.' 'And I,' said the other, 'Will give you back to yourself better.'[21] You see how those gentle hearts, in spite of fortune, found a way to give freely and to return a benefit with increase. I do not, however, plan to vanquish you by examples or authority, but by that method that has most force of all, that is, reason itself. You must

[20] "Whomsoever Eutrapelus had a mind to punish, he presented with costly garments. For now, [said he] happy in his fine clothes, he will assume new schemes and hopes; he will sleep till daylight; prefer a harlot to his honest calling; run into debt; and at last become a gladiator or drive a gardner's hack for hire." (Horace *Ep.* 1.18, quoted from *The Works of Horace*, trans. C. Smart, [London, 1870], p. 267.)
[21] This anecdote is told of Socrates and his poor pupil Aeschines in Seneca, *De beneficiis* 1.8.

grant that liberality is nothing else but a determination to enrich others with that which is our own. Therefore, the closer those things are to us with which we intend to show our liberality, the more lively and perfectly they achieve their desired effect. How much more intrinsic to a man, do you think, are virtue, knowledge, and other things of the mind (which he possesses inside himself) than riches and other accidental things that come from without? And if you think I have argued this according to some logic more subtle than true, look at ancient history. You will see that those who were liberal with their interior goods are the ones whose liberality is clearly remembered, while the reputation of those who were liberal with money has grown dim. The wise storyteller, desiring, in his discussions of liberality on the last day, that each story might surpass its predecessor in describing an act of liberality, begins first with a king who gave away a chest laden with riches and then proceeds to those who were liberal with their praises, then their virtues, and, finally, their very lives.[22] Internal things are more effective in putting liberality into operation than riches are, and, consequently, we must allow that the poor man is as effective in this as the rich man. But let us leave the means that lead to honor and pass directly to honor itself. What will you say if I prove to you that poverty is enough of itself to bring honor and that riches are not? To understand this, you must grant that every honor we give is given to someone as a recognition of some virtue, either of the soul or of the body. Now, since riches are something completely separate from both the human soul and the body, it is evident that, although they are able to make a man conspicuous, they do not have the power to make him honored for his merit. No one may, therefore, presume himself more virtuous simply because he has riches; one might, however, presume this from not having them, as is readily apparent in the case of that great Roman consul Valerius Publicola for whom it was considered a great honor to be so poor he could not pay for his own burial. This generous consul's inability to pay for an honored burial has made his burial honored throughout the world. Similarly, Crates, the philosopher, was never esteemed as a man of lofty soul while he was rich, but he was held to be very virtuous after he had thrown his riches into the sea.[23] Have

[22] The tales exemplifying liberality, the theme set for the tenth, and last, day in Boccaccio's *Decameron*, culminate in the story of Patient Griselda, a story treasured by another ascetic scholar, Chaucer's Clerk of Oxenford.

[23] Publius Valerius: "Publius Valerius, universally regarded as the foremost citizen, both in military and civil qualities . . . was a man of extraordinary reputation, but so poor that money was wanting for his burial, and it was furnished from the treasury of the state." (Livy 2.16. 7–8, quoted from *Livy*, trans. B. O. Foster [London, 1909–1959], I, 271.) Crates:

a care, then, Charles, since you have taken up the burden, how you defend riches in this connection. For it seems to me an easy matter to prove that the simple lack of riches generates some opinion of loftiness of soul; the mere possession of them can, then, create a certain suspicion of something mean and trivial. I have now defended poverty before your tribunal. Had I been defending it before mine, I would have set it above riches for other reasons: poverty is the cause of a man's knowing himself, while riches make him forget by their very nature; poverty brings repose to the soul, whereas riches bring a thousand troubles; and, finally, poverty represents a state full of hope for improvement, while riches lead to a state of fear that change will be for the worse. Laurence well knows that the rich are continually agitated while the poor are secure. Or, as Juvenal put it: *Cantabit vacuus coram latrone viator.*[24] These things I say, and there are other things I might say, but I shall hold my tongue lest I get off the subject."

As Charles was about to respond, Laurence interrupted, saying, "I am unused to finding a new advocate in an old adversary. So I think I had better make out my own case lest Charles do here what bad women do to their husbands: they drag them into their battles and then beat them, all the while crying out wildly against their enemies."

"Familiarity with such pitiful creatures," said More, "makes you suspicious where there is no need. You may rely on Charles, for he will act above me as a good and loyal agent. If at any time he does not, you may renounce his services."

"I am content," said Laurence, "since you bind yourself to be his surety."

"You do not need any security at all," said Charles, "especially when I am, in this case, an agent *in rem suam.*[25] Because I must disagree with Alexander, I will agree with you in everything. Well now, Alexander, though I concede to you that there are other goods aside from riches that are fit to show our liberality and that internal ones are more productive of this end than external ones, still it cannot be denied that rich men who have both external and internal goods are better off than poor men who possess

---

"[Crates] threw his wealth into the sea, saying, 'I'll drown you, lest you drown me.'" (*The Apophthegms of the Ancients* [London, 1663], II, 247.) Diogenes Laertius, *Lives of the Eminent Philosophers*, VI, 85–93, relates that the Cynic Diogenes persuaded Crates to throw his wealth into the sea.

[24] Juvenal *Sat.* 10.22 "the traveller without a penny in his pocket can sing before a thief." Professor Hans Baron points out the popularity of Juvenal's verse in medieval moral literature in "Franciscan Poverty and Civic Wealth as Factors in the Rise of Humanistic Thought," *Speculum*, XIII (January 1938), 4.

[25] *in rem suam:* "in his own case."

only the latter. Both are necessary to the desired end, the internal ones to show liberality more readily to those in need and the external ones to show it more often and to everyone. When your storyteller wanted to portray the greatest liberality in the story of Nathan as I interpret it, he showed him to be very liberal in both kinds of goods.[26] The possession of riches, Alexander, is an advantage in practicing liberality; the lack of them is a great impediment. Now we must look at your final statement that poverty is enough of itself without any other consideration or means to make us honored. For what you have set out to prove, the examples of that poor consul and of the philosopher who lacked money are extraneous for you have conjoined poverty to another quality, either the authority of a consul or the wisdom of a philosopher. In both examples poverty alone did not make these men honored; it merely furthered the conjoined quality. The consul was praised for being just and loyal, and the philosopher was praised for his wisdom. Neither was praised for being the poorest of men. If you were to put before us two men completely unknown in every respect except that one is poor and the other is rich, you would see exactly the opposite of what you said. Just having money generates a certain presumption of prudence and wisdom, whereas a lack of it causes suspicion of a certain carelessness and disorder. Though this is obvious enough in itself, it is made even clearer by the fact that everyone has a natural shame and repugnance about borrowing money that proceeds from these first impressions that the lack of money gives birth to in our souls. Where honor is concerned, riches are not only worth more than poverty, they are also beneficial, while poverty does more harm than good."

Charles paused, and Laurence, without waiting to see what he might say, said: "I did not expect this defense would go any further into the matter than Charles found necessary to defend his honor. But money means too much to me to leave the defense of it half furnished. As for what Alexander really said while pretending not to say it, I deny it all. What appeared most absurd to me was the claim that the rich man is troubled and the poor man is at ease. It would be enough to simply note the very word itself which calls 'rich' men 'well-off,' but I shall not use any subtleties. Instead, let us turn to the facts themselves. I put this to your honest judgments: can all the trouble he pretends to find in riches equal the misery a poor man feels from hours of constant harassment with naked children screaming at

[26] The rich, elderly Nathan offers his life as well as his hospitality to a young gentleman in Boccaccio, *Decameron* 10.3.

him on one side and bill collectors pressing him on the other? If that is the means by which, according to Alexander, these men come to sing, it must be, in faith, a fine piece of music! But even if that little verse (now that I remember it) lets poor men sing in the presence of thieves, I still would not want to be one of those who may well sing in the face of thieves and afterward cry before honest men. Well, now! let us just see if poverty is truly preferable to riches because the first is a state filled with hope of change for the better, while the second is filled with fear of change for the worse. I do not think, Alexander, that you have persuaded yourself any more than you have persuaded us. Can you expect us to believe that, if it is good to desire a thing that it is not better to have it when the desire is to have it? It is perfectly obvious that this argument is one of those you call 'andro stephonda.' "

"Perhaps," said Peter, "you mean to say *antistrephonta*. But you have made an antistrophe for us when you set out to *antistrephein*."[27]

"Enough of that!" said Laurence. "I mean that this is one of those arguments that uses a contradiction which proves both sides equally well. You say that poverty is better than riches because it is a state of hope of changing into a better, that is, riches; therefore, I say that riches are better than poverty because they are a state of fear of changing into a worse, that is, poverty. Therefore I say that poverty must be worse than riches. You see that I can use the contradiction in this argument just as well as you can. But I will argue in a different fashion so that my reply will work only to my advantage. The poor man hopes to improve his state, and the rich man fears falling into a worse, I admit. I must add, however, that the hope of acquiring riches is so slight for the man who has none and the fear of losing riches is so small for those who are well-off in an orderly nation that I think no one would choose the hope rather than the fear. I have never known any man who does not recognize that a little fear is better than a little hope since the diminution of one means the increase of the other."

At this point Laurence stopped and Alexander turned toward him and Charles as though to answer them both, but More interrupted, saying, "With your permission, let us act toward Laurence in this trial just as at one time the people of Rome acted toward a criminal who was accused of a capital crime and made no attempt to defend himself. He appealed, instead, to the consulate. When this was refused, he had to undertake his

[27] *antistrephein:* to make an antistrophe (antistrophe: [a] the repetition of words in inverse order; [b] the figure of retort, or turning an opponent's plea against him" [Oxford English Dictionary]).

own defense before the very court in which he had appealed to the consulate. When the people saw that he would be hard put to save himself, they became so sorry for him that they let him go without considering further the right or the wrong of his deed. In the same way now, let us show ourselves neither more nor less compassionate toward these poor little riches of Laurence's. After claiming the title of the greatest good, they have not only been denied that honor, but they are also in danger of being preceded by poverty itself. At first we condemned them; now let us say rather that, since riches and poverty are, of their own nature, neither good nor bad, there is no reason for one to be esteemed more than the other. The value of either in relation to a man will depend upon the man himself. And thus, having demolished the bulwark that Laurence raises in front of his riches, let us present the vacant place to Charles to explain his honor and turn back, in order to continue this inquiry into happiness, to the point where Laurence left it."

"If you remember," said Laurence, "I ended happiness with the hanging of the misers. If we take Charles and his honor as far back as the gibbet, it will not be very much to his honor. But I shall leave the affairs of others where they belong and turn back to my own. And let me say to you, Mr. More, that your speech has left me greatly satisfied, for I expected nothing but condemnation from you. Since I don't have to pay a penalty, however, I call myself content. As far as removing my riches from here is concerned, you need not force me to it by a fine. I am ready to take not only my own riches, but also yours as well, whenever you so command. I laugh at the fine present that you give to Charles, seeing how honorable it is to present him with a place from which I have already extracted what was of value."

"However it is," said Charles, "I accept that place with all my heart, and strive, to the limit of my ability, to shore up my honor more solidly than he did his riches lest I in turn must present it to someone else, as Laurence did to me. I had better, for I stand to lose more than he did. Though he did not know how to make his riches win the trial, he has lost nothing; I must conquer or else suffer a terrible loss.

"I shall, without further delay, first show what honor is and then prove that it is not, as Laurence maintained of riches, a means to an end, but rather the true and ultimate end itself for which all other things are desired and beyond which, speaking only of this life, we desire nothing. Let me be more specific: I say that honor is simply to be distinguished from others and to be raised above the multitude by the merit of some virtue, which is why the Romans, as you know, called honored persons *eximiae*, that is, 're-moved,' and *egregiae*, that is, 'separated from the mass.' Who would deny that this is the natural goal of everyone who, in order to experience his own individuality, desires to raise himself as much as possible above the mass of his species? Only thus can he enjoy to the fullest that existence as an individual which touches him more intrinsically than his existence as part of the species. Those who are without any talents whatsoever to distinguish themselves nevertheless attempt it in whatever way their small competence will allow. Many with neither genius nor learning write simply to get their names on the covers of books; others, unable to do even that much, gain publicity by writing their names on all the walls and public places in the city. Others who cannot distinguish themselves by good actions are determined at least to distinguish themselves by bad, like the Herostratus who burned the temple of Diana in order to win fame. As far as honor is concerned, such men get away from the mass in the same way prescribed by the simpleton for his friend in prison. When the friend grumbled about having to stay locked up, he said, 'I had a relative who was here for a long time but in the end he got out.' The prisoner asked how he got out, and the simpleton answered, 'He was taken out to be hung.' "

After they had laughed at this a while, Charles resumed. "Those who try to make themselves famous by wicked deeds leave the multitude in such a way that, as far as honor is concerned, they might better have stayed within. But let us leave them in their misery and turn directly to those who seek to distinguish themselves by means of some virtue. This is a desire so conformable to the excellent nature of man that, if you examine the exploits and pursuits of all the men in the world, you would find that none (of this I am certain) ever had an end other than this. If we look at history, what else can we say of that glorious example of the two Decii, who took up arms and sent their enemies packing in disarray? What of Mucius Scaevola, who liberated his besieged country so dexterously with his left hand? What of Curtius, who plunged into the burning crevice and had *rogum et sepulchrum* at the same time? You may be certain that such generous souls could expect no reward for merit won at the end of their lives except the only one that lasts after death—honor.[28] Let us leave aside the history and

[28] Decii: For the dramatic story of the Decii, the father who sought death on the battlefield in response to a prophetic dream, and of the son who imitated his death, see Livy 7.34; 8.6; 10.7, 27. Mucius Scaevola: Plutarch tells how the warrior Mucius entered the camp of the beseiging Tuscan army to kill Porsena, the Tuscan leader. Seized and interrogated, "Mucius held his right hand over the flames and, while the flesh was burning, stood looking at Porsena with a bold and steadfast countenance, until the king was overcome with admira-

turn our eyes to the present. What shall we say inspires the great deeds of all princes today? What inspires those who exercise their strength and wits in watching over their affairs? What, to reduce many words to one, inspires those who either perform great deeds themselves or else record those of others? What, if not honor, prompts them to undertake what they do? I will not insult your intelligence by listing those who all too obviously seek honor. Instead, let me speak of those who slyly pretend to seek exactly the opposite goal and pursue honor while no one is looking. I am talking about those greedy philosophers whose every action seems to scorn honor. But be not deceived by those rascals, for, in spite of their torn cassocks, they hankered more after honor than those who wore silk and velvet. And as they were wiser than the latter, so they were better able to fulfill their desires. Thus, while the memory of all the glittering courtiers of that time is so thoroughly extinguished that not a spark remains, the fame of their wallets and their shaggy gowns and other such miserly trash still burns brightly throughout the world. Those rascals saw very clearly that scorning all bodily ornament was much more effective than praising it would have been in distinguishing them from the customs of the vulgar multitude.

"This was most certainly the end that the philosophers had in that affected poverty of theirs. I do not know what other end could be postulated, for I do not understand to what end anyone who wants to give the appearance of disdaining honor could be working if not to be honored— a point that did not escape the divine understanding of Plato when Diogenes and certain other philosophers came together to pay him a visit. His house was finely furnished with tapestries and other lovely decorations on the walls and even on the floor. Diogenes walked on the tapestries and said with his customary rudeness, 'Look how I tread upon the pride of

---

tion and released him, and handed him back his sword, reaching it down to him from the tribunal. Mucius stretched out his left hand and took it (on which account, they say, he received the surname of Scaevola, which means *left-handed*)." Overcome by this act of generosity, Mucius revealed a plot to kill Porsena, and Porsena thereupon came to terms, "not so much, I suppose, through fear of the three hundred, as out of wondering admiration for the lofty spirit and bravery of the Romans." (Plutarch, "Life of Publicola," quoted from *Parallel Lives,* trans. Bernadotte Perrin [London: W. Heinemann, 1914], I, 547–549.) Curtius: In response to a call from the soothsayers for a sacrifice to ensure the endurance of the Roman Republic, Curtius jumped into a chasm that had appeared in the middle of the Forum. *Rogum et sepulchrum:* "funeral pyre and burial." The Decii and Curtius are joined together by Folly as examples of empty vainglory (Erasmus, *Praise of Folly* [Ann Arbor: University of Michigan Press, 1958], p. 40), but Heywood perhaps expects us to recall Augustine, *City of God* 5.18, where St. Augustine cites the Decii, Mucius, and Curtius as examples of the lengths the Romans went to achieve earthly glory even without the promise of the eternal reward that Christians have.

Plato,' whereupon Plato replied, 'You trample upon one pride with another.'[29] And what he said was true, for it is clear that disdain has in its nature a certain carelessness, so that where anyone takes any pains about something, then it can be said with certainty, that he is not disdainful, but rather extremely attracted. If you consider then the tribe of philosophers, I am certain that you will not find any content to scorn the things of this world in a simple manner unless he can concoct some unusual means to make others take notice of his actions. When Crates, for instance, wanted to get rid of his riches, he could have disposed of them very simply, as a person would do to whom they meant nothing. Instead, he had them carried solemnly down to a ship so that they could be thrown into the sea. Diogenes, who scorned the mansions of great princes, did not take the first miserable hut he happened to light on for his quarters; he chose, with subtle calculation, a tub, thus getting a house famous throughout the world at no expense, whereas others who spend many scudi can hardly find means to make their houses famous even in the towns where they live. You see, then, that to those who look carefully at the words and deeds of these philosophers, their affected disdain of honor appears to be none other in effect than a very ardent desire for it. This was shown clearly by the penetrating genius of Cicero with one of his acid comments against those books that they write in dispraise of honor: 'The philosophers,' he says, *'scribunt libros de contemnendo honore, scribunt quidem, sed nomina sua inscribunt,'* a clear enough argument that philosophers do not undertake their literary labors to insult honor but to get themselves more honor.[30] You may then, gentlemen, very easily deduce all our other actions whatever from this, since even that which in appearance is undertaken to flee honor is, in reality, done for no other reason than to acquire it. With this prejudgment I believe I may conclude most judiciously that honor is the true and final end

[29] This anecdote is recounted in Erasmus *Apophthegms,* III, s.v. "Diogenes Cynicus," No. 11. (Erasmus, *Opera omnia* [London, 1703–1706], IV, col. 173.

[30] *scribunt libros de contemnendo honore, scribunt quidem, sed nomina sua inscribunt:* "they write books in contempt of honor, but they put their names on the titlepages" (slightly altered from Cicero *Tusc. Disp.* 1.15.34 [Translation mine.]). Cp. Sydney, *Defense of Poesy:* ". . . the moral philosophers, whom, methinks, I see coming toward me with a sullain gravity, as though they could not abide vice by daylight, rudely clothed to witness outwardly their contempt of outward things, with books in their hands against glory, whereto they set their names, sophistically speaking against subtility, and angry with any man in whom they see the foul fault of anger." (Quoted from Hyder Rollins and Herschel Baker, *The Renaissance in England* [Boston: Heath, 1954], p. 609.) Sydney's emphasis is on the hypocrisy of the philosophers; Charles's, on their rudeness, egoism, and grubby appearance. Charles reflects the gentleman's contempt for the otherworldliness of the cleric and the academic ideal of the contemplative life.

of all the actions that we undertake, but I will add that if any of you has the courage to bring forward an action that can be referred to some other end, I will yield submissively."

"Yield, then," said Peter. "Give yourself up to no one else than that lord who makes everyone submit—I mean love. You surely cannot mean to say that anyone falls in love in order to gain honor; in fact, in this matter, love is superior to all other actions in the world, for all others have some further end; love has no goal but the enjoyment of love itself. Here, then, you have an action whereby honor is not only not the end; it has no part at all. Every day of our lives shows us that lovers who have fallen into the snares of passion let honor fly with the wind."

Charles smiled and said, "You need not expect me to concede anything out of love for you, Peter, that goes against my honor. Do not suppose you have persuaded me with this example of love that we ever undertake an action for any motive other than honor. As for this example of love, let me say, first, that there are many who deny that love is an action at all or that being loved is a passion, but just the opposite. What they say seems right to me, for loving is, in fact, a certain compulsion toward love and being loved is simply compelling someone else toward love. But, lest I appear to you too stingy toward love by measuring it out so subtly, I will concede that it is in some sense an action, though not a free action that proceeds from our will; rather, the performance of the action is motivated by some other cause. When I say that honor is the end of our actions, I mean those actions that proceed from our will and are actually and essentially our own. I know very well that, in others, that which motivates us to act is both cause and end; thus for love, there is no other end to be given than to love. But however much you may boast, this is not a privilege of love alone; the same must be conceded to all other perturbations of the soul which, because they are forced and not free, have no end beyond themselves. A man fears for no other reason than to experience fear; he cries for no other reason than to cry. I could say the same about anger, joy, and all the others, but it is perfectly clear that these examples are of no use in proving that honor is not the final end of all those actions that we freely will. These, I repeat, have no other end than honor. Thus you see, Peter, that I shall not surrender to your great lord Love, who, according to the proverb, would not be accepted as a lord even in the land of the blind."

"That is true," responded Peter, "for Love only reigns among men furnished with eyes. But let us leave aside love as of now, for I do not want to dwell on this part of my reply as though I had no other arguments to establish that countless actions are undertaken for ends other than honor. I could prove this to you by that very example in which you trusted so much to prove the contrary—the example of princes. For it is certain that, in all their broils and endeavors, they have power and not honor as their principal end. No one, I think, will ever doubt this who considers carefully how princes think only of being able to subjugate cities without caring in the slightest whether the methods used are honorable or vile, unless we are willing, perhaps, to say that the use of crafty deceits and treachery that would disgust the vilest rogue is honorable in princes."

"In these deceits, you deceive yourself," said Charles, "because you cannot judge the actions of princes and of private citizens by the same measuring stick. You know that, when an army is defeated, the praise of the victor is no less lavish if he has attacked the enemy from behind, but it would hardly be honorable for a private citizen to overcome an adversary in this manner. To undertake a fight with an advantage or by deceit in private quarrels shows a mistrust of one's own valor. In a battle between two armies, where Fortune generally rules the field, however, you might say that taking any measures that will ensure success proceeds from a mistrust, not of valor, but of Fortune. Do you not remember that the Romans, who were the most perfect models of honorable behavior in every thing they did, always put in their standards the insignia of a fox and a lion together? Their meaning was that a victory gained from an equal is honorable whether gained by strategy or by force. It is not discreditable for a prince to seek his honor in the way that he understands best, even if he has to resort to deceit or betrayal."[31]

"Perhaps," said Peter, "what you say regarding deceit can stand, since that shows us to have wits superior to those of our enemies, but I do not at all see how the same can be said of treachery, for that derives, not from our wits, but solely from the baseness of the traitor. If you look at the deeds of the Romans in their histories and not just the emblems on their banners,

[31] The image of the lion and the fox seems to point directly to Machiavelli, *The Prince*, Chap. xviii, where the image appears in a very similar context. The long passage in *Utopia*, in which the same topic at issue between Charles and Peter is discussed, is one of the most bitterly ironic in the book: "Wherefore it may well be thought, either that all justice is but a base and a low virtue and which avaleth itself far under the high dignity of kings, or, at the least wise, that there be two justices: the one meet for the inferior sort of the people, going afoot and creeping low by the ground, and bound down on every side with many bands because it shall not run at rovers; the other a princely virtue, which like as it is of much higher majesty that the other poor justice, so also it is of much more liberty, as to the which nothing is unlawful that it lusteth after." (*Utopia*, p. 106.) In the final sentence of this paragraph in *Il Moro*, I have written "seek his honor," where the Italian has "seek his *cinanza*," a word that, as far as I know, does not exist.

you will see how much they always scorned such a victory for they believed that it did no honor to their valor in war. This was made very evident in their war against the Falisci, when a schoolmaster offered to deliver up to them practically all of the most noble sons of the enemy. The Romans refused the offer and, seizing the schoolmaster, they handed him over to his own pupils for a beating. Then they wrote to their enemies, warning them to beware of treachery.[32] But let us leave these tricks and betrayals now. Since you have presented me with Fortune herself to conquer you with, I will seize the occasion by the forelock, since the nape of her neck is bald."[33]

"In that case," said Laurence, "occasion and I are at sixes and sevens," whereupon he bared his forehead, upon which there was not a sign of any fuzz. Everybody laughed, and More said, "This has probably come about because your wife seizes you every so often in the same way that a man would like to seize the occasion."

"Let her try that——," said Laurence, at which they laughed even louder. Then Peter said, "Laurence's baldness came close to making me miss the forelock of occasion, but I will not let such an opportunity get away. Now then, Charles, after equating happiness with the praise of our virtue, do you mean to tell us that Fortune is the governess of all? I, for one, thought you would surely come to the opposite conclusion. To give a wider scope to honor which, according to you, proceeds from our merit, you have to remove it completely from the hands of Fortune as an imaginary thing and ally yourself entirely with the opinion of those who say only that the wise man makes for himself the fortune that he desires."

"I wish," said Charles, "that it were this way, yet I cannot honestly affirm that it is. If we could assume that all events could be ordered by counsel alone, it would always follow that better counsel would produce a better result. Every day, however, we see that foolish schemes succeed very well and wise counsels end in misery. Perhaps this does not seem so remarkable if you consider that the conditions of our lives depend not only on our actions, but also on those of others, which may or may not coincide with our own. Although the wise man may be certain that all of his actions are directed toward the best end, who can be sure that others propose the same end for their actions? Whoever wants to exclude fortune from his affairs, hoping to lead them all along the road to success by wisdom alone, must not only be wise himself, but he must also find the way to instill the

[32] See Livy 5.27.
[33] bald: i.e., difficult to grab hold of.

same wisdom in everybody else. Whoever sets out to do this is, I think, as wise as Patenson."

By chance the fool passed by on these last words. Hearing himself put among the sages by Charles, he very solemnly doffed his hat and said it was in acknowledgement of the compliment.

When everybody had stopped laughing, Peter said, "Enough, Charles. You have set up Fortune for a lady and governess of the affairs of this world. It may be that she is, but, if she is, I do not see how that honor of yours can be very solid. For, if honor comes solely from the merit of our own virtue, as you have already affirmed, how can it hope to receive any benefits from those things that come from fortune? Everyone knows that whenever we want to take away from someone all merit for some good that he has said or done, we always say 'he must have done it by accident,' as if to point out that no one need expect to be praised for those things that proceed from fortune."

"True it is," said Charles, "that those things which we customarily direct by judgment alone, as, for instance, speeches and writings and all those actions that may be done completely by a man himself are praiseworthy only if performed by the judgment alone; but in other matters, where, along with virtue, Fortune plays a role so large that she is truly called the consort of virtue, we attribute the title of the one and of the other as a great honor to everyone who merits it. Therefore the title of 'Most Fortunate' must be added to the other titles of great princes in order to make out of Fortune as well as virtue a habit (which is necessary to honor since no one is justly honored for that which he does not have)."

"Certain it is," said Peter, "that no dialectician would ever concede this uncertain habit to you, seeing how easily it is lost. Nor can I agree that being fortunate deserves to be praised by anyone. If that were true, it would follow that the converse is dishonorable, and thus, when Fortune changes her style toward a man, no matter how virtuous, the less favor he finds with Fortune the less he would be honored. Thus, without having otherwise deserved it, he would suffer the most terrible affliction possible."

"How many are those," said Charles, "who suffer wrongly every day, although it ought not to seem such a great wrong if Fortune, withdrawing herself from someone, but not otherwise disturbing his honor, carries away with her that part which she herself gave to him as a loan, not as a gift."

"Well," said Leonard, "it would perhaps be bearable if she did not take away any more than just what belonged to her. But this fugitive goddess, when she departs from great lords, generally without even bidding them goodbye, strips them clean of every honor, taking with her not only the title of Most Fortunate, but also Most Serene, Most Prudent, Most Virtuous, and all the others too."

"And do you think, then," asked Charles, "that true honor depends upon titles alone?"

After this question, he grew silent, whether because he had no intention of saying anything further or because he mused upon that which remained for him to speak. Leonard then said: "It would be well, Charles, if, instead of speaking from a cloud of generalities, you would make clear what you mean by the term 'honor' so that we, informed in this matter like litigants *ab editione actionis*, might know whether it would be to our advantage to oppose or to subscribe to your contentions.[34] But until you instruct my judgment, giving me a token by which to know true honor from false, I know of no way to decide which of the many opinions about honor is the true one. Some say it is nothing but purity of blood. They firmly believe it enough to earn them the highest honor that they are descended from those who knew how to perform valorous deeds, however limited their own knowledge in these matters might be. Others, who are neither offspring of virtuous men nor endowed with virtue themselves, think that honor comes from riches or a position of prestige. And there are those who have nothing to swell up about except that, at great cost, they manage to dress like lords. Some equate it with fighting skillfully; still others, with intellectual feats and learning, and so on. Everybody holds true honor to be that at which he is most competent and rejects as counterfeit that with which he finds himself unprovided. Therefore, Charles, since you have equated happiness with honor, give some plain indication of which is the true one."

"This," said Charles, "is truly a burden for other shoulders than mine; however, since I find myself entered this far in this undertaking, I shall go on with my eyes closed, though I am afraid that this honor will be the instrument of my shame. It is certain that those things you enumerated—nobility of parentage, riches, offices, and the others that can come to the basest men as well as to the most virtuous—may certainly be called great ornaments of honor, but it is not possible that the very substance of honor can consist in something external that is not essential to the nature of man. Honor consists solely in what a man possesses inside himself by means of the soul or even of the body: that is, virtue. For example, having an office

[34] *ab editione actionis:* "at the beginning of the trial."

in the government does not in itself create honor, as infinite examples testify; if virtue is present, honor is created because virtue is honorable in itself, while the office is not. An office is, in fact, none other than a clear indicator, as ready to make evident our defects as our sufficiency, and, as a consequence, as apt to bring us contempt as honor. But honor, which resides solely in virtue, manifests itself by external signs which, meeting our senses, make the virtue of others known to us. That these external signs—riches, offices, and such—are universally reputed for honor itself proceeds from the ignorance of the masses which cannot distinguish between the symbols of things and the things themselves. Honor, then, is founded solely in the working of virtue, whether of soul or of body. First, in regard to the body: though it is true that man does not have one bodily power that cannot be surpassed by other animals, he can still be honored since honor comes from advancing beyond one's own species. The perfect honor, according to me, is the power to surpass humanity itself in that very thing in which humans surpass all the other animals, that is intellect."

Here Charles paused and Leonard said, "I still do not know where to put this perfect honor. I very much doubt that intellect can claim her since a short while ago you derived honor from virtue, and you know that intellect falls among those things that are indifferent, no closer to virtue than to vice. I could give you many examples of people with most acute intellects whose worldly success has been so great that, as far as honor is concerned, it would have been better for them to have been born feebleminded. I think, Charles, that you intend this word 'intellect' to refer only to that kind accompanied by virtue, and I also think that we are getting overly general, confounding under the term 'virtuous intellect' many diverse kinds. You know how different are wit and prudence, and yet both require intellect and virtue."

"We can easily find the knot in this difficulty," answered Charles, "by saying that intellect is superior or inferior according to whether it is or is not directed toward an honorable end, that is, whether it contributes more or less to the common life of the human community. Thus the prudent man, whose intellect is more judicious and has utility for its end, is superior to the wit, who is more creative but has pleasure for his end. The masses, on whose mouth depends honor, always admire more those things from which they feel they derive greater utility. Since government is needed above all else to maintain community among human beings and preserve them from the confusion that encumbered them in the state of nature when they led a savage life suitable only to brute animals, it is just that the prudence of great princes and other magistrates in the government should be honored above all else. And since, after government, the most useful thing is the knowledge of teaching men how to govern themselves, the second honor goes to those who have been or are proficient in that knowledge. Passing through all the occupational levels, we always find that the more generally useful the worker, the more universal the acclaim he receives."

"It cannot be denied," said Leonard, "that this rule is reasonable, but experience, I think, proves just the opposite, so much so that even the two examples you presented to confirm your position actually negate it. If it were not too far off the subject to discuss magistrates and writers, I would demolish your so-very-solid rule with these two examples. It is clear, as you say, that magistrates are more useful than writers, just as doing good is more useful than writing well; nevertheless, writers continue to enjoy shining reputations much longer than do magistrates. You know Livy told of many consuls and tribunes whose reputations have faded and practically been erased from memory while the reputation of Livy shines brightly even today. A deed continues to exist in an unchanged state only while it is being performed. Books, on the other hand, remain forever in that very form set by their authors. And since these divine geniuses continue to speak, they live on inside us far more vividly than do those about whom they speak."

"You make," answered Charles, "an unequal comparison between doing well and writing well, confronting mediocre examples of the one with a most excellent example of the other. Nonetheless, you have accomplished nothing. To prove that writers are more famous than rulers does not help to prove that they are more honorable than rulers. You cannot define honor as a clear or vivid memory in the mind of man, for, by such a definition, Nero would be the most honorable emperor of all. Honor means rather to be held in great esteem for virtue, and there is no one, I think, who, remembering any consul whatever who was competent in his office, would not judge that consul to be a man of greater virtue in his time than Livy was in his."

Then Paul said, "This discourse is too long to enter into now. To draw you back from these irrelevant trifles to which, it seems to me, you have been attracted for some time, I shall oppose directly your honor, which for many reasons it appears to me ought not to be accounted the happiness we seek. First, the very method of obtaining it is wrong. We acquire honor in the same way that the dog drank at the Nile River, that is, by fleeing it.[35]

[35] For the dogs who lap at the Nile running fearfully from the crocodiles, see Pliny *Naturalis Historia* 8.48.

You know that it is those who do good deeds for the sake of making good prevail that find themselves honored for disdaining honor; those who run to meet honor with open arms find those arms as empty as the arms of Tantalus before the unattainable apples. Honor truly resembles a shadow. Not only is it without substance, but it flees from him who follows and follows him who flees it. I do not see how it is possible to enjoy to the full a happiness that one must always flee from in order to possess. Besides, this makes me wonder if honor is not something evil, for it is never unpraiseworthy to pursue the good. Finally, we cannot consider honor to be the happiness we seek; it has no existence in the person honored and, by its very nature, it demands a kind of comparison whereby one person is preferred over another. Men distinguished among men of the lowest classes must give place when they are put in a class superior to their own and others take precedence. Thus it may be said that the happiness of an honored man is nothing at all in itself and its existence or nonexistence depends on all those with whom he is compared. Such instability does not suit the nature of happiness, which must be a thing certain in itself, and he who would be happy must have a certain disposition inside himself that can never be hoped for from honor since it is nothing in itself. And even if it were something, it is tied, as you will have it, to the doubtful gifts of Fortune, whereby a man, although he has won much, cannot count what he has gained as being his own. In a card game where there are several hands to be played, the player who is ahead cannot consider himself the winner until the set is finished. In the game of life, a man, as long as he has not reached the end, cannot consider himself as honorable. Fortune ever rules the game, dealing out the cards as it pleases her, now a King, now a Jack and then, all of a sudden, whenever it is her pleasure, she sends you a reversal as great as the advance you had made. It seems to me then that you reach this honor, which can never be perfect this side of death, a little late to make you happy in this life. And so, to what you have expounded at such great length—that men desire honor as the ultimate end—I will answer in few words: since honor is such as I have outlined, those who seek her are not guided by reasoned judgment, but misled by empty and loose desire."

At these words of Paul, More said, "From what I have understood, it seems to me, Charles, that you have accomplished little in the defense of your happiness by demonstrating that men have claimed honor for their goal. Showing that men do this is not enough; you must also show that, in doing it, they act as men, that is, using reason."

"I will be glad to," said Charles. "Nor will anyone deny that there is good reason to put honor above all things, seeing that even God Himself takes more account of His honor than of any other thing. Having given us this beautiful habitation of the world to fulfill our needs, He has asked nothing in return except honor alone, of which, as He Himself says, He is so jealous that it is easier for Him to forgive man any other fault than that of having denied Him honor in order to bestow it upon another, false God. Do you not think the example of so great an author worthy to be imitated by us? If you deny that it is, I will show expressly that God Himself has invited us to imitate Him with a most precious gift. Do you not remember, gentlemen, that the Lord God, among His many infinite benefits, gave us one more important than all, that is, our great excellence above all the other animals? And what else is honor but excellence and preference above others? Invited, then, by the example and by the gift of our Lord God, let us confess honor to be the greatest good of this life. It certainly seems to me most fitting to so confess, since honor preserves every facet of our political life which, without honor, would not last an instant. Tell me who, if you took away honor, would trouble himself to govern the mob? Who would labor at writing books? Who, to sum it up, would do anything to help anyone else? I think we will all agree that the answer is: no one. Admit, then, that honor is our happiness. If not conquered by her just arguments, at least honor her for the benefits she bestows. Should you still hold out stubbornly, I will add another argument against which you can oppose nothing unless you are determined to quarrel with Truth herself: since the soul finds contentment only in those things that are, like herself, infinite, she never finds complete satisfaction in those things of which she is able to discern the end; thus, nothing in this world can content her except honor alone. For who does not see that everything dies save honor alone, but that honor, like the Phoenix, arises from death more alive than ever? Before such clear-sighted judges, I think I may presume that what I have said will preserve the honor of honor itself. And now, lest my defense of honor become as infinite as its virtue, I will end my praises with the hope that the praise of honor will have no end."

"Honorably, indeed," said More, when the others remained silent, "have you defended your honor; still, I fear that your defense, like all things whose honor consists only in appearance, may be more honored than true. Let us therefore consider each of your points one by one. First, God Himself (you say) is so fond of His own honor that He seeks no payment other than this for the infinite blessings he has given us. Ah, Charles, if you believe that our Lord values honor so highly that He feels honored by the honor or by any other good that we can do Him, then you are certainly fooling yourself. Our Heavenly Father does not require honor for any personal pleasure, but rather to have a pledge of that sincere love toward Him in which, as He Himself has said, rests all the Law and all that He asks from us. For we sinners have nothing else to give Him except honor alone. When we give it to Him willingly, He accepts it graciously, not for the sake of the gift itself, but as a firm witness of our love for Him and as proof that, as we give Him that, so would we give Him a thing of greater value if we were able. If the Almighty got pleasure from the honor that our little rituals do Him, small indeed would be the pleasure He would get since the entire world is to be destroyed in a very short time and, while it lasts, we do not pay Him the third part of this tribute. Even that which we do pay is paid so badly and with such ill will that no great prince here on this earth is so lacking in courage that he would hold himself an honorable man if he did not vindicate himself. But then, even if I concede to you that our Lord, Who deserves every honor, does desire it simply for the sake of the honor, do you think that you can infer from this that we sinners ought to do the same? I would think the exact opposite is true, for if our Lord intends to receive every honor Himself, then we should not expect any at all.[36]

"But God (you say) invites us, by His great gift to have respect for our honor, giving us the special blessing of pre-eminence over all the other animals, and honor is nothing else but a pre-eminence over others. Charles deceives himself in this, equating excellence, which is the virtue itself, with honor, which is none other than an opinion of excellence and can as well exist without virtue as virtue can exist without her. It is, therefore, most beneficial to us that we surpass other animals; without this virtue, there would be no order by which we might ever lift ourselves from the earth and reach the heavens. But no one would maintain that the opinion of this virtue, that is, honor, is also essential to this end unless he would also say that Jesus Christ has been driven out of Heaven. You know how He was honored, not only not more than other animals, but, in fact, far less. Shall I then, now that you have brought up the example and gift of God to confirm your honor, show you in one word that honor which God has approved by His example and that honor which He has given us as a gift? Certainly it is none other than the Cross."

[36] Charles's argument, "By seeking glory man seeks to imitate God, Who seeks glory from men," is introduced and refuted by St. Thomas (*ST*, II, ii, Q.132, A.1); cf. Augustine, *City of God* 10.5. Charles's argument is used by Satan in John Milton's *Paradise Regained*, III, 108–145.

Here More paused, and the others waited attentively for his next words. Laurence, on the verge of laughter, said, "Did I not tell you at the beginning, gentlemen, that this honor of Charles's must finish at an end like the Cross that is now presented to you? Did I not prophecy the same?"[37]

"To be sure," said More, "exactly like Pilate, who, speaking of Jesus Christ, said that someone had to die for the people. Be quiet for a little while, Laurence, and let me go over these two last arguments of Charles's concerning the merit and infiniteness of honor. By the first of these he intends us to understand that every good in our lives derives from honor. Now who would concede that? Rather, it is apparent that quite the contrary is true. All the calamities and the devastations that fill the world, even more today than in the past, come from no other source than this wild and unruly appetite for honor. To show this, I shall not depart from examples already introduced. Who can recall without sorrow how Christian rulers, under the mask of empty honor, have constantly built up their territories and succeeded in tearing down Christendom? They have ripped open the central part with their claws and left the outlands prey to the Turks—too much preoccupied, if it please God, with their own honor to see to the honor of Christ. May God protect us from that judgment which the Highest Judge will make of that honor of theirs, whatever value it may have in their foolish judgments.[38] The second example concerned writers. Who, I ask you, can put into words the evils loosed on the world by the immoderate ambition of those men who put all of their efforts toward making truth conform to their opinions instead of making their opinions conform to truth? In regard to divine and human law, they have created such confusion in the express commandments of the authors of each—some exulting in their strange opinions, some in their singular turn of intellect—that, though both laws were established solely to teach us, first of the will of God and second of justice and goodness, now, thanks to the good offices of the expositors, we are more uncertain than ever. The cause of all this is the blessing of honor. I do not see how anything else could be the cause, for it is difficult to believe that so much discord could ever have reared its head

[37] Laurence means the gibbet he previously mentioned.
[38] The horror felt by More for war among Christian princes is discussed by Robert P. Adams, *The Better Part of Valor* (Seattle: University of Washington Press, 1962). Cf. "As for fame and glory . . . This maketh battles between these great princes, and with much trouble to much people, and great effusion of blood, one king to look to reign in five realms that cannot well rule one. For how many hath now this great Turk, and yet aspireth to more? And those that he hath he ordereth evil, and yet himself worst." (*A Dialogue of Comfort* 3.12, quoted from *More's Utopia and A Dialogue of Comfort*, ed. John Warrington [London: J. M. Dent, 1951], p. 341.)

among us, being rational creatures, in these most rational things if we had wanted to follow reason instead of subverting it. Look, Charles, how well those actions succeed which are aimed at your target honor. Not only in these examples but in others as well, if we examine all the most excellent works of human life, do we find all perverted from their true ends and directed toward this one. Humanity might well complain of this cursed honor for the same reason that Charinus of Terence complained of Davus, that is, *quod interturbet omnia.*[39] There remains only your final argument, that honor, as though privileged above all other mortal things, has the power to resurrect the dead. Whether this is true, we shall shortly see. First, what that life might be that the dead live here from the fame of their names, I have never been able to understand. A name is not a substantial part of the soul or body of anyone, and, since beyond these two there is nothing, I do not see what the difference is, as far as this life is concerned, between the existence of Orlando and that of Julius Caesar. The latter feels no more pleasure from his praise than does the former. But we foolish mortals, more unstable than reeds, in abandoning ourselves to the deceits of that flattering appetite for the delights that praises bring, think that even after death we will find some pleasure. We forget that when we die we put off, along with this flesh, all desires whatever, and without them we get as much pleasure out of honor as a blind man gets out of colors. To long in vain for impossible things is indeed nothing else but to build castles in the air. For reason, we may be certain, does not allow the soul, after having bid an eternal farewell to this world and wholly absorbed in waiting for that important decree of the High God, to take any account at all of that which the world babbles concerning its own affairs. For, once having discovered the corruptibility of the world, reason has that regard for it that one has of the basest things." And More grew silent.

Charles said nothing for a while, as though doubtful whether to answer or remain silent, saying, at last, "You think then, Mr. More, that honor is not worthy to be prized by anyone? Certainly you debase all those gifts that Heaven, more liberal to one than to another, gives to us; if you remove this reward of honor, I do not see any reason why they should be dear to us since we could derive no benefit from them."

"On the contrary," said More. "Do you not think, Charles, that a virtuous man, realizing Who has given him his virtue and directing it toward the sole end of pleasing Him, does not await with greater contentment the re-

[39] *quod interturbet omnia:* "because he brings everything to confusion." (Cf. Terence *Andria,* 663.)

ward of immortality from this honest paymaster than he who seeks to make himself immortal in this mortal world, from which, after that very short space that life lasts, he will be so completely cut off that he will hear nothing further of it?"

"All you say is certainly true," said Charles, "but you are speaking of supreme perfection."

"And we," replied More, "are speaking of perfect men. But let us give some place to our desires, as long as we have to live indissolubly joined to them. I concede that a man who knows himself to be endowed with intellect, learning, and other virtues may feel inside himself a great feast of contentment and joy at finding himself so much in favor with his Creator that He deigned to adorn him with so many jewels. But whoever glories in them and uses them to obtain honor for himself is in grave danger that the Donor will retract His gift because of his ingratitude—or else, will not retract it in order to damn him further."

The others stood attentive to hear how Charles would answer to this. But he submitted very courteously, saying, "Mr. More, all your reasoning about honor is so true that I consider it more honorable for honor itself to submit to reason than to contend further without reason." And he stopped.

Noticing the lateness of the hour, More said, "You see that these discussions have grown longer than we had expected and, if what has passed is a measure of what is still to come, I think we must recognize that, if we are to discuss the matter adequately, we will be here until nightfall. Before we proceed further in this matter, however, you must promise to remain with me this evening. And I will counter with another promise: before the time comes for supper, we will most certainly provide happiness, for at that time you yourselves will feel how misery begins."

They all thanked him for his invitation, saying that they would agree quite willingly to what he asked except that necessity required them to return home since they had departed that morning intending to return in the evening.

"And besides," added Peter, "I am certain that, though you might get Laurence to stay the night here, no one in the world would be able to get him to sleep here, for you know his habits well. He can go to sleep when he is next to his happiness, but not when he is three miles from it."

"As to that," answered Laurence, "I think that rich men who are sleeping let themselves be pulled from the side of their happiness more easily than you lovers from yours."

After they bantered together for a while, More, seeing that they were determined to leave, said: "Well, now, it seems to me that you do not care to do anything I have asked you this evening. I would press you if I did not believe that your excuses are quite justified. I leave the decision to go or stay this evening up to your judgment, lest I put my pleasure over your convenience; yet you must promise that at least you will all return together tomorrow to dine."

They all agreed without making More importune except for Charles, who was somewhat punctilious. When he began to spin out new excuses, More smiled pleasantly and said: "Dear Charles, leave ceremony to those who have more concern for courtesy than for friendship, though how they can be called courteous I do not know, for courtesy consists in treating everybody in the appropriate manner. To me it seems as great a discourtesy to show many scruples toward your friends as to treat strangers without respect."

This speech brought Charles out of his mood. "Mr. More," he said, "you know very well without my reminding you how little scrupulous I am with you about invitations as well as other matters. I really do have to get a certain document off tomorrow; it is, however, not the most important in the world and can be deferred without any harm."

Thus, in friendly fashion, he accepted More's invitation. And More, contented, said: "It is enough that we finally agree. But, although you have accepted these invitations so ceremoniously, thanks to your shyness, I shall, nevertheless, give you the simple fare that I am accustomed to give to my friends."

"If you are accustomed to treat your enemies better," said Laurence, "I shall come as one of those."

"And so I am," answered More. "Do you know, then, who my enemies are? Those who treat me as Eutrapelus was accustomed to treat his."

Peter laughed and said, "With this reply you have made peace with Laurence. You may be sure he will never come as your enemy," at which they all laughed.

Seeing that they were keeping More from his studies, they left and boarded a small boat that was waiting. Whether because of the freshness of the air or because of the stimulation of the arguments, the crossing was so pleasant that they were in London almost before they were aware of it.

BOOK II

The following day the gentlemen returned, as they had promised. After they were greeted and had dined, they wandered slowly out into the garden as they had done before. After a relaxed stroll, they returned to their little park where each sat down and waited to see who would be the first to resume the discussions. After they had remained silent for some time, Laurence began to smile to himself. He covered his face so the others would not see, but Peter noticed and smiled a little in turn.

"Now, Laurence," he said, "do tell us why you are laughing so that we can laugh too. We will think you much too envious if you do not enrich us with your happiness when you can do it without diminishing your own."

"The reason for my laughter, since you want to know," said Laurence, "is no other than the thought of your predicament. Frankly, I think it totally inappropriate for you to speak of a thing as trifling as love, especially before these sober judges and after those grave discourses of yesterday."

"True it is," answered Peter, "that the judges are so revered and that the discourses were so serious that, when I put this naked little son of Venus before you, I might well expect that he would faint from shame were I not sure that his blindness will protect him from your presence and that in the discussions nothing of weight was spoken against him."

"In connection with those discussions," said Laurence, "let me give you this other consoling thought: to judge from the useless solicitations of lovers, love is just as deaf as he is blind; I just wish to God he were also speechless."

"Had I not heard it myself," said Peter, "I would never have believed that there could live a man so inhuman as to hate love itself. But what he has said will not shake my intention to exalt the great power of love, knowing how many enemies he has overthrown, and those more powerful than Laurence. And I am certain that one day even he will forego these arid little heaps of silver, and I shall see his icy heart consumed by the beams from the beauteous eyes of some fair lady just as the snow is consumed by the rays from the sun."[1]

---

[1] "Whether it is possible for a miser to love" was one of the *dubbi* often discussed in fifteenth- and sixteenth-century Italian treatises on love. See John Charles Nelson, *Renaissance Theory of Love* (New York: Columbia University Press, 1955), p. 74.

"Let me tell you," said Laurence, "that, if I abandoned myself to such folly, I would deserve the punishment of those who are condemned to pay a large amount of money for some great crime. But you need not worry about that; you can be sure that I will guard myself from such a whimsy as I would from a headache."

When he saw that Peter was ready to begin, Laurence stood up as though to request a special favor of the others. He asked if they would mind letting him carry the burden of answering Peter in this conflict about love. They agreed unanimously. Laurence, taking the stance of a combattant, said "Begin!" to Peter, who answered that he would gladly do so.

"In the first place," he said, "I am encouraged to argue my case, knowing it to be free of every prejudicial flaw that has been alleged against the others: for example, that riches are desired for an end other than themselves and that honor lies in the opinion of someone other than the person honored. Everyone will admit that in love the situation is quite the opposite. I would certainly consider myself dense if I undertook to defend this case which is so free of all prejudicial factors without being able to support it well, and, like some unpracticed lawyer, left it in a worse way than I found it. This is especially true since I do not have to argue with anyone but Laurence. If I were to use the arguments by contraries against him, proving that love is the greatest good of all since hate is the greatest evil, I do not know what arguments he could use against me. But, lest it be unpleasing to God that love should conquer through the weakness of his enemies instead of his own proper virtue, I will put hate aside and use only love in arguing against Laurence."

Here he stopped to collect himself for a moment, like one who was about to begin some long discussion. Just as he was about to speak again, Laurence cried, "Stop! Do you suppose that I am content that you set hate aside, just because you have said the worst you can of it? Let us just go back a moment to that argument by contraries. I say that you are tricking me with love, but I will make sure that you do not confuse me from here on out with the ambiguity in this word 'love.' Before we go any further, I am going to make a clear distinction that will both clarify the terminology of our dispute and, at the same time, will refute the argument by contraries. Now, it is clear that there are two kinds of love: the first is for the goodness of the soul, which, to give it its proper name, is friendship; the other is for the beauty of the body, and this truly may be christened love. Hatred then, which is nothing else than a state of enmity toward someone, is the opposite of friendship, not of love. Since hate is truly a great evil, it follows, therefore, that friendship is a great good. But if we chose to argue about love on the basis of its contrary, we would soon see just how contrary everything would go. For, after all, what is love? To burn with too much desire for the person you love. What, then, is its contrary? To grow quiet and stop thinking about it? This is certainly good. It follows, then, as the night the day, that its contrary is bad."

"It is wrong," said Peter, "for you to make such a crude distinction between friendship and love, separating things born together of the same root. If you hold to your distinction, what would you say to all these discussions of the many prominent thinkers of today who write of love, identifying it in the end not only with friendship but even with the love of God?"

"Let me tell you," said Laurence, "if I had to answer such discussions, I would say that they are more clever than true, like those paradoxes by which verbal jugglers prove the contrary to what everyday experience tells us is true. Aside from the fact that reason denies that the same heart can love two contrary things at the same time, experience itself shows how often these two kinds of love are at sixes and sevens. Neither of them ever enters a man's heart without diminishing or extinguishing the other."

"But I," answered Peter, "by means of reason and experience will join together these two kinds of love, and you will see that they agree very well."

"Now, now," said Laurence, "for shame, Peter. Leave these subtleties to the logicians. Argue with us plainly, as the rest of us have done, and try not to get off the subject. Take that son of Venus for your love and show him naked as you have promised to do."

"You treat me," said Peter, "like those considerate thieves who steal the best part of their victim's belongings and leave him the refuse. Nevertheless, although you have taken away a great many of my belongings, you have not taken so many that I have nothing left to defeat you with. Now then, to make clear to all of you the high worth of love, even of beauty, consider this: God, who endowed the world with so much beauty that in the Greek and Latin languages it has taken its name from the word for beauty, left love as His vicar to preserve its glory.[2] If you want fully to

---

[2] "word for beauty": cosmos. ("This composite of all the Forms and Ideas we call in Latin *mundus,* and in Greek *cosmos,* that is, *orderliness.* The attractiveness of this orderliness is Beauty." [Marcel, *Marsile Ficin,* p. 140; translation mine].)

appreciate how well he performs the duties of his office, then observe how, among the creatures endowed with souls, even those who have only vegetative souls (for example, the plants), feel, insofar as their base condition permits, the force of love, and it leads them to draw near to things that have like natures and to produce, in the appropriate season, the fruits, leaves, and flowers that ornament this beautiful world. When you move up the ladder from these to those nobler animals who have sensitive souls, you discover (for love and the soul, as it were, grow together) how tenderly they observe the sacred laws of love in producing and nourishing their young. Finally, mounting higher still to that complete life of the rational soul, see the force and the effects of love in human kind so powerful that, in two lovers, each has the soul of the other instead of his own and, together, they have one single soul that animates both. Nor ought it to seem strange to you that those animals that are more reasonable feel more strongly the force of love, for, in truth, reason and love, though some fools have held that they are contraries, differ from each other only in the sense that the genus differs from a species. Each of them is none other than a mode of comprehending the true nature, the first, of everything, the second, of beauty. For what else does it mean to love a woman than to understand how beautiful she is? If you would object that love is not only a discovery of beauty but also a desire for it, I would answer that the discovery of and the desire for beauty are one and the same. I do not think that I need to prove that, for, since desirability is the only quality by which beauty makes itself known, to know that something is beautiful is none other than to know that it is desirable and to know that a thing is desirable is none other than to desire it. If we were to say that a man could know that something is desirable without desiring it, we would get into the great difficulty of trying to prove that the same thing can be both desirable and not desirable at the same time. In fact, to desire beauty is no different from knowing it; thus it is that the most awakened spirits, because they comprehend more fully the perfection of beauty, long for it so much more than less sensitive minds who pass it by as something quite ordinary. We often see this happen among spectators looking at beautiful pictures: the ignorant give them a superficial glance and quickly become wearied; those who understand art consider them more deeply, and, the more fixedly they gaze, the more stupefied they become till finally they become enraptured."

Seeing that Peter was going to ever greater length in his discussion, Laurence said: "It is better that I stop Peter from further effusions on this paradox, lest what happened to that spectator looking at the picture happen to me. What I mean is that he was stunned by the proportion and I will be so stunned by the disproportion of this answer that I shall not recover in time to answer him. Let me tell you, truly, Peter, it has been difficult for me to keep from laughing at the presumption with which you sublimated that love of yours to the office of God's vicar, commending it for managing so well the government of the universe when everybody can plainly see that it destroys all laws, divine, natural, and human. It is plain that the only way this blind lieutenant of God serves Him is by keeping Him out of every place where he manages to get a foot in the door. And tell me sincerely, on your faith, do you really believe, Peter, that a man who is head over heels in love with a woman thinks about religious matters? To me it seems, as I told you, an impossibility for the same heart to love two contrary things at the same time."

"I would like," said Charles, "to help Peter out of this difficulty with the example of a niece of mine who fell in love, over the opposition of the whole family, with a person whose social station did not equal hers. At one time she was being urged by her father confessor to forgo her love. He tried to persuade her to change her mind by several means, one of which was to ask her, 'How do you think you can love God when you love this man against the will of your father? He is your enemy, rather than your lover, since he is the cause of so much trouble.' 'That is why I love him,' answered the young lady, 'to please God, Who, you know, commanded us to love our enemies.'"

After all had laughed a while, Laurence, still laughing, said, "Truly, that was a saintly reply, though I fear she would have been more than willing to disobey another of the Commandments in order to keep this one strictly. But let us leave her aside and turn directly to the final part of this discussion, where, if we are to believe the words of Peter, love becomes a kind of reason. Blessed Lord, how many has this kind of reason driven insane? How many have hung themselves because of the overwhelming burden of this kind of reason? I suppose these lovers are so courteous that they want to be companions for my miser. Lest he be the only one to hang himself without a motive, they hang themselves as well —for love, as they call it, though to me it looks more like hate. Behold, gentlemen, the 'reason' of Peter. If I were to itemize here the impetuousness of love, its blindness, its fickleness, its desperation, and all of its other beautiful parts (including all that are the reverse of reason), I am certain that you would all be after Peter, shouting that he fabricates this 'reason' out of untruths. So that my answer does not get too far from the preceding arguments, let us consider for a while just whether or not love is a good judger of beauty because Peter has tried by means of this proposition to join it to reason. Do you really believe, gentlemen, that love, as he says, is comprehension of the true perfection of beauty? It certainly would be an ugly error to believe so, for you yourselves see every day lovers who delight not only in women of few attractions but even in the most grotesque and artificial ones you can find. Not long ago my servant Checco fell violently in love with a woman who, though she had only one eye, had as many eyes in her head as Checco had in his. A friend of his joked about his infatuation, saying, 'Now you see just how blind love is; Checco's lady has only one eye, and he, it seems, has none at all.' Men fall in love with ugly women as well as beautiful ones, and I think that I need search no further for a clear means of showing that love is not a discovery of the true perfection of beauty. Thus, there is no question of pairing it with reason, as Peter has labored to do. Now, shall I show you plainly what love is? Certainly it is nothing else but a sickness of the soul caused by surplus desire. Just as, when the physical body is surcharged with one humor, the body contracts some disease, so, when one of the desires of the soul steps over its limits, it disturbs the soul just as sickness upsets the body and drives it out of its natural state. This analysis of love—that it is born from some defect in our feeling rather than from the perfection of someone's beauty—is truer than yours for it explains why a man does not fall in love with a beautiful woman the first time he catches sight of her. Rather, this occurs only when he himself is ready to take fire. This explains why those who perhaps have seen a certain woman a thousand times without falling in love are then, suddenly, caught when they have become susceptible to the disease. It is obvious that this love proceeds not from the beauty of the thing loved, which has remained practically the same, but from the feelings of the lover, who is prone to take fire at one time but not at another according to the disposition of the body. Do not then, Peter, attribute to love that sharpness of insight that penetrates to the true nature of things. Admit that he is, as you said at first and as the whole world says, blind."

"Truly," said Paul, "it seems to me that Laurence has sharp eyes for uncovering the blindness of love. I do not see, Peter, how you can possibly offer a reasoned argument in further defense of your proposition that love is a perfect perception of beauty since we love the ugly as well as the beautiful and, further, since we love the same beauty more at one time than at another. It appears to me that Laurence's answer is firmly based."

"Wait a moment," said Peter, "and you will see that his firmly based answer will not triumph over me. Do you not see that whereas I joined together reason and love, taking both of them in their pure nature, Laurence has replied, in his example of those who love ugly women, with a love caught up in our weak and deceptive senses? But I, understand, have compared these two together on an equal basis, that is, either pure reason and pure love, or human reason and human love. And you know that reason, as it exists in a living man (which is where that love exists that Laurence spoke of), is not a comprehension of the truth of all things either, for it never achieves this effect. Human reason deceives itself so often that everyone deviates from the truth more often than he knows, or takes its exact opposite for the truth in the majority of cases. Considered in themselves, reason and love are both kinds of perfect comprehension, the first of truth, the second of true beauty. As they actually exist in men, however, they either fail in their effect or mislead us into their direct opposite according to the honest or degenerate nature of him who uses them. What do you think, then, gentlemen? Do you not agree that this single distinction suffices to remove completely all the opposition of my adversary? Rather more than suffices, I think both you and Laurence will agree. But, just to show you that love, which sharpens everybody's wits to find the means in his greatest needs, is not so poorly provided that he has no means but one out of this difficulty, I will help him by a different and strange means that, like the greater number of his stratagems, will seem at first impossible. I will maintain, gentlemen, that the love for an ugly woman proceeds from no other cause than the very perfect perception of her beauty. This will be clearer to you when you remember that no man or woman is so perfect that he does not have some imperfection nor so imperfect that he does not have some perfection somewhere. Thus, anyone intending to draw a true portrait of supreme ugliness must, like that excellent artist who painted perfect beauty, use many models: here a forehead, there a nose, elsewhere a mouth, and so on for the other parts. Although every woman has some beauty as well as some ugliness, the beauty is of such force that, in whatever tiny part of the face the sympathetic viewer describes it, it is never overshadowed by the ugliness to which it is joined. She so engrosses all the thoughts of the viewer that he cannot turn his eyes again to the disproportionate parts or, if by chance he looks at them, he endows them with the beauty of those parts that are proportionate, excusing them to himself and reforming them as much as possible in his imagination. The same is also true when someone notices the slightest similarity of eye or mouth in a portrait that barely resembles its original; the resemblance takes hold of his mind and, in order to find the person there, his imagination turns the dissimilarities into features he is familiar with. Thus, it seems to him that this portrait resembles the original, while someone who had never noticed that particular resemblance would never see it no matter how long he gazed. This is why we often see that the same portrait appears a just likeness to one person and not to another. The same is true of a woman. She may appear beautiful to one man and not to another. Resemblances and beauty are alike in that each is a proportion that relates one thing to another, but they also differ in that resemblance is the correspondence of one individual to another while beauty is the correspondence of the individual to the *idea* of his species. Men and women have reciprocally impressed in their souls a perfect form of their species, and, when they find that form in the features of another person, they are informed with certitude that the person is beautiful. When they run into that which they were seeking, they eliminate from their minds every other *idea*, content to exchange an *idea* for a deity."[3]

Laurence derided this, saying, "A fine idea, that lovers carry deities around in their heads like Jove carrying Athena, though one could say that they feel similar labor pains and often the goddesses do not come from their heads except by a ministration similar to that which Vulcan gave to Jove with his axe."

"You see," said Peter, "how Laurence would break my head with Vulcan's axe. But please, have patience and see if I am able to give birth by myself to that which I want to say to you. To return then to the point: I say that your last argument was completely pointless. You argued that love cannot proceed from beauty since we often see a beautiful woman without falling in love with her and, also, since we fall in love with the same beauty more readily at one time than at another. Laurence, you have fallen into the great error of equating a beautiful woman, that is, a material body, with the discovery of her beauty, which is a subtle proportion that only strikes our eyes by rare good fortune. So I will answer your argument by saying that it is exactly like that stroke of genius of Madame, your wife, Mr. More, which I have several times intended to tell you. It was one time when we were instructing your

[3] In this sentence, Heywood puns on *dea*, "goddess," a technical term in the exaggerated rhetoric of the Petrarchan love tradition, and *idea*, a technical term in Platonic philosophy.

daughters in the properties of the line and were having difficulty making clear to them that it is mere length without breadth or depth. After the lesson was over, she had the children called to her room, saying, 'What is the matter with my girls? Does their father have to beat his brains for a whole hour to show them what a line is? Look here, you silly things,' and she pointed to a great beam that crossed the roof of the room, 'this is what a line is!' "

At this they all laughed for a long while, and would have laughed longer had Laurence not been so eager to reply that he turned to Peter and said, "Your arguments are so subtle that, to tell the truth, I have not been able to understand them too well. As far as your words made sense to me, however, I gather you intended to tell us that, since men and women have the perfect impression of their species stamped reciprocally in their minds by a natural instinct, love is nothing else but a certain recognition of that proportion in some individual. This notion might find some defense if lovers remained constant to one form of beauty, but they continually change their opinions, now admiring long faces, now round, one time the most plump, another time the most slender and angular. They generally reverse their opinions so often that I cannot imagine what that *idea* to which they refer so often in their infatuations could be unless perhaps it is the Chimera. It is time to rid yourself of these subtleties and to show without any more nonsense the effects of love so that we can decide how conducive they are to happiness. It seems an easy thing to me to discover in the very faces of lovers how unhappy they are; I have never been able to get through my head how continual weeping, sighing, sleeplessness, and solitude can be conducive to happiness. If they are—you see what a simple man I am, without any sinful thoughts—I have never, when in my downy bed at night or with my jolly companions in the daytime, felt any envy of the happiness of a lover off in the forest talking to the birds or languishing all night at the door of his goddess, doubly chilled by the night air and by his cold mistress."[4]

Here Laurence stretched as though to survey the spacious field of the misfortunes of lovers, but Peter halted him in midcourse. "Laurence," he said, "the sorrows that lovers endure, such as solitude, anxieties, and sleeplessness, will not serve your turn. How can they? Do you not know how much more pleasing is the sweet that is mixed with some bitter? Every pastime in this life is, in fact, none other than a continual change

[4] Ovid *Amores* 1.6,9, and 3.11; Propertius 1.16; Horace *Od.* 1.25 and 3.10.

from one thing to its opposite. Eating, drinking, and sleeping only give pleasure after we have felt the need for them, and the greater the hungers, the greater the pleasure when they are satisfied. Excessive thirst makes drink more satisfying just as excessive fasting enhances the flavor of food. No one gets pleasure from just one of these contraries, even sweetness itself, unless the other be added. Pharmacists do not mix their finest concoctions out of sugar or honey alone, but, along with these, they mix in things that have an equal amount of the opposite quality, such as orange peels, walnuts, unripe fruits, and other things which, the more sour they are in themselves, the more delicate they are to the taste when they are sweetened. Just imagine, then, what an expert our pharmacist love is! He can blend tears, sighs, and torments (things in themselves very bitter) that, if we credit those who have experienced them, become sweet sighs, sweet torments, and sweet tears."

"Oh, fine, fine!" cried Laurence with a snicker. "Look how this lawyer for lovers, as the lovers themselves, tries to cover his words with honey so that I shall not notice the deceit underneath. He does not fool me. What good does it do you, Peter, in answering my enumeration of the discomforts of love, and love brings a world of them, to tell me that every pleasure is born of its contrary? Who, except a lover, would be so stupid as to concede to you that the opposite of sadness or sleeplessness is falling in love? No matter who says it, I will never believe it. I know well (and necessarily so, since I have experienced them so often) that no contraries can relieve sleeplessness and sadness except sleep and merriment. It seems to me, therefore, that your pharmacist, who compounded his pills out of contraries, went contrary to the right way. He was a pharmacist as skillful as that servant of Mr. George, the apothecary who, having prepared an enema for a simpleton, ordered him to eat it. When the good man returned to complain about the taste the following morning, the servant brought him certain pills, just as before. Since these too were for the relief of the body, the servant prescribed that he take them in the way that one is supposed to take an enema. This business benefited the poor man just as much as love benefits these miserable lovers in their discomforts; it never relieves them as a contrary, but, like a greater ache among minor ones, it makes us oblivious to the others. Let us leave aside this argument by contraries and turn directly to the subject. First, I have never understood, if the human intellect is as divine as you are always predicating, why it is not great folly to pull it down from its very noble subject, that is, contemplation of the highest things, and set it to mooning perpetually in the face of some miserable female with the most vile and bestial intentions imaginable."

"Softly, Laurence," said Peter. "You are now so far from the right way that it would be a sin to give you free rein any further. What man but you would ever say that love pulls the mind down from lofty enterprises? The truth is that it incites the mind to them. Many authors there are (and not authors of licentiousness or foolishness, but of profound, learned and acutely argued treatises) who attribute to love whatever worth they have. Furthermore, the intention of love, to answer you in this point, is not that end which you imagine. It is as repugnant to that as is the delight of the soul to the pleasure of the body."

"Oh, to be sure," said Laurence, "though I could cite the example of every lover in the world about what the intention of love is. But, as I do not intend to go into that, I shall put it aside and ask you to please clear up one doubtful point that just now came into my mind: where do you find any place suitable for making this wretched lover happy when happiness is a contentment of the soul? For until he satisfies his love, he longs for it, and in this state, which is the contrary of contentment, he is, you must admit, miserable. Once he gets satisfaction in love, you cannot say that he is happy because of something for which he no longer cares. It seems to me that our poor lover always comes too early or too late to catch happiness, just as the creditor always happens to come early for an insolvent debtor, either before he has gotten up or after he has left the house."

"Just see," said Peter, "how officious Laurence is in my affairs. Fearing, I suppose, that I shall lack time to guide our lover to happiness, he has assigned every moment of the lover's time to either desire or satiety, both of which extremes are contrary to contentment. But Laurence is too hard on poor lovers. Do you not suppose that the contentment they find in attaining love is as great as the pain they took to win it? It is my very firm belief that such contentment far surpasses every other in this life, and you will say the same when you recall that love never wears out its welcome though all other pastimes soon pall. Have you ever heard anyone confess himself glutted, as do merrymakers and gamblers, with too much love? Love enters our souls with greater force and efficacy than other delights; thus, it is most worthily held to be the greatest of them, just as those annoyances that weigh most heavily or afflict us longest are held to be the gravest."

"Just look," said Laurence then, "how green he would have to be who put any faith in the simple words of these lovers! Now Peter denies that love is perpetual desire, after having just conceded a moment ago that love was, in effect, nothing other than a certain comprehension of beauty, and comprehension is nothing other than a desire for it. The very words he uses are the clearest evidence that love is a perpetual desire. And even if, as lovers are accustomed to do, he intends now to go against his very words, the thing itself is only too obvious. What is love, after all, if not a yearning, a longing, a desire? Clear it is, then, that, while a man loves, he yearns and desires; beyond the point where he stops desiring, it is impossible to continue to love. Because love is a desire, it does not satisfy as do the other pleasures. They satisfy because they are, so to speak, fruitions, whereas love, because it is nothing else but desire, never satisfies since desire is directly contrary to satisfaction." At this Laurence whooped, as though he had won the trial.

"I am not yet in those dire straits," said Peter, "where you think you have conducted me. You will see, Laurence, that I do not intend to deny my own words; nor do I intend to concede yours. While it is true that love is a continual desire, it does not follow that it cannot be a perfect contentment. But here I have to explain that there is not just one kind of desire, but, rather, two. The first is when we desire that which we lack, and this is truly desire. Among the Romans, 'to desire' signified also to be lacking, since that which is desired is always lacking. Because this kind of desire is a lack of the thing desired, it is undeniably contrary to contentment. But there is also another so-called desire, through which we find ourselves longing for that which we already possess. Not only is this desire not contrary to contentment, it is essential to it. For how can a man find contentment in that which he does not prize or desire? And you know how, in that perfect contentment of the life eternal, souls in bliss find perfect contentment in contemplating the divine majesty and yet yearn to contemplate it. You must admit, Laurence, that this desire is not at all contrary to contentment. If I were to explain here part by part the inestimable grace of that woman whose soft glances, pleasant words, sweet laughter, and gracefulness in all her actions show a smooth interworking and harmony between her body and soul, I do not doubt that Laurence himself would concede that to find himself clasped to the heart of a woman like this would so satisfy any man that he would have no other desire."

"In faith, Peter," said Laurence then, "you do wrong to try to blind the eyes of our judges with your rhetoric. But since you have tried with all these colors to paint the beauty of women when whoever has looked into their faces would say that you need not have taken the pains, I myself intend to set my own rhetoric to work to discolor their applied beauty and their forced and pompous behavior. I, too, have read my part of Tully's *De inventione*, though you perhaps do not think so."

"We take for granted," said More, "that, if you have studied the rhetorical works of Cicero, you read the book *De inventione* with greater readiness than *De partitione*."[5]

"Enough," said Laurence, and struck an attitude as though he were about to launch a solemn invective against women. Peter, stopping him with the words on the tip of his tongue, said, "Laurence, I understand quite well at the very beginning what the end of your argument will be, but I shall concede to you, without your taking the trouble to prove it, that affectation takes away the grace from anything, and most especially when those things that use it should be produced by nature, not by art. And such a thing is the beauty of women. There is nothing attractive in the beauty of those whose open affectation shows more pains than wit, or those whose red cheeks show more care than shame. But this does nothing to disgrace those whose winsome, refined, and pleasing ways exhibit, in everything they do, a graceful decorum showing that the same Nature that gave them such beauty taught them the secret of using it. This, Laurence, is enough for a brief answer to that which you intended to say, and, even if you argue further, I shall not change my answer. I only regret that you other gentlemen have assigned to me an *antagonista aneraston* in this dispute of love.[6] I feel like a fencing master facing some ignorant student whose hands flail about artlessly. Such a student makes the master forget the rules of the game and gives far more trouble than would a serious student who could parry and thrust with judgment. In the same way I have, in this discourse with Laurence, lost track of what I had intended to say; I have gone so superficially into the matter that, if you do not let me begin again this argument of love, I have little hope of showing well in this trial."

"The hour is late," said More, "and there are many who still wait to be heard in this matter. There is no way at this time for you to reweave

---

[5] *De inventione*, etc.: that is, Laurence is more apt at finding matter to talk about ("invention") than at breaking it up for coherent discussion ("partition").

[6] *antagonista aneraston:* "an opponent who lacks love."

BOOK II

your finished cloth. But how does this please you? We will do you the courtesy of setting a limit within which you may bring in these new proofs."

"What good would this do me," said Peter, "since you intend to give a sentence in this controversy tonight?"

"The sentence," answered More, "will not be definitive, nor will it be prejudicial to anyone, not even to you in that very just allegation of new-found instruments. However, Peter, since there is no harm done to you, and great benefit to others, show yourself amiable. Put aside love and do not delay Alexander any further, for it appears to me that he is prepared and has delayed beginning his reasoning only until we have finished ours."

"Assuredly," said Alexander, "what I intended to say can be said quickly, yet is important enough that I am eager to hear what you will have to respond. My assertion was that the greatest happiness in this life is knowledge, and to prove it I shall use no other method than this one. You know, gentlemen, that, of the three kinds of souls, the rational is the most noble and most perfect, and that human life surpasses that of plants and animals only in the sense that it enjoys the most perfect soul. Who, then, does not perceive that those men are happiest who enjoy to the fullest that faculty by which men are made more happy than the other animals? I do not think I have to prove that the only means of enjoying perfectly the rational soul, and its only substance, is knowledge since this is obvious enough in itself. We see that just as the plants, those with vegetative souls, naturally desire the sustenance of earth and as the animals, those with sensitive souls, seek food for their bodies, so men, those with rational souls, seek knowledge of everything down to the most minute. Since, then, knowledge is the true nutriment of the rational soul, it is clear that, just as the other two souls languish when they lack their nutriment, so also the rational soul languishes and dies when it lacks knowledge. Thus it seems to me well said that ignorant men not only are not happy, but that, speaking of human life, they are not even alive. Although they do not lack a soul in the general sense, they certainly lack that excellent soul that distinguishes men from plants and animals. Thus, while they are alive in respect to animals, they are dead in respect to human beings. In conclusion, my sentence concerning happiness is that, as the happiness of our soul in its pure state will be to contemplate God in His presence, so now, while the body impedes it from arriving at such a height of contemplation, the closest happiness is to consider His works, that is, the construction of this universe, the wondrous work of a great artisan."

Having said this, Alexander suddenly stopped, whereupon More, who saw that no one was ready to argue, said to him, "You have stated your opinion in few words, but with great effect; with your permission, I shall defer my judgment of it until the conclusion of this dispute. In this way you will be able to alleviate your eagerness to hear a reply with the delight you will get from the argument that must arise between Leonard and Paul, whose opinions are completely repugnant to each other: the first putting happiness in everything; the second, in nothing."

"True it is," said Leonard, "that I was of the opinion at the beginning (and I am of the same still) that happiness cannot be limited to this or that type. It must be put equally in everything, according to what is most pleasing to us. It seems to me, gentlemen, to speak frankly, that you are all wrong in trying to limit happiness to one single species, for instance, love or honor, for 'happiness' is a general concept, that contains every good within itself. Such affirmations appear to me similar to these: *Animal est homo. Ubi species praedicatur de suo genere.*"[7]

"Now, now, dear Leonard," said Laurence, "if you have any consideration for me, discuss this happiness so that I can have my part in it, too. You know that I am little skilled in the terms of Aristotle, and you, as far as I can tell, intend to argue about happiness with predicaments and syllogisms. If you intend to continue thus, at least tell me so, and I shall leave without wasting any time, for I am quite certain that such arguments will drive me mad before they make me happy."

"You need have no fear on that score," said Leonard, "for you will soon see that I shall prove my happiness, without any logic whatsoever, and in a simpler fashion than anyone has used up to now. Now let that one among you who considers himself the greatest master tell me this: how could it ever be possible that happiness, which is a contentment of the soul, could lie in one thing alone, when our souls find contentment in the most diverse ways? Were you to deny me that our souls find such diverse contentments, I would not have to go outside this very company to find proof, for, up to this point, everybody has disagreed with everybody else about contentment. But why do I speak of others? No one

---

[7] *animal est homo, ubi species praedicatur de suo genere:* "man is an animal—where the species is predicated according to its genus." In the following line, I have altered "caro Signor Allesandro" to "dear Leonard," since Laurence's remark is clearly addressed to Leonard.

disagrees with himself about what contentment is; we are bored by what pleased us a little while before, and pleased by what we found unpleasant an hour ago. Our life is nothing but a continual going around in a circle, ever finding pleasure in the same things in succession, just as the sun retraces the year through the same signs of the Zodiac. Therefore, the happiness of this life, in my opinion, is not a thing determined in itself, but determined according to the structure of our souls, and consequently to be found equally in everything in whatever measure that our souls find contentment."

When the others remained silent, Alexander said, "Leonard has tried to prove by two arguments—the generality of happiness and the variety of our souls—that happiness lies not in one thing only, but in many. Unless I deceive myself, both of his assumptions are false. First, who would concede to you that 'happiness' is a general noun? It is, in fact, a very specialized noun, for happiness, as you know, is no other than the greatest good, and to be the greatest, among the species of the same genus, can only be said of one; therefore, this first assumption not only does not support your assertion, it utterly destroys it. The other assumption was of the variety of ways in which our souls find contentment. This one, too, is far from the truth. Since our souls are rational and the determination of reasons is certain and conclusive in itself, I do not think that, if we follow the judgment of the soul, we can propose more than one kind of happiness when there is but one alone. What then shall we say to Leonard's argument wherein everyone disagrees about contentment, not only with others but with himself as well? Just this: in his discourse Leonard has exchanged satisfaction of appetite for contentment of the soul and thus pleasure for happiness."

"Here," said More, "you have hit the nail on the head and with such plain truth that no one, I think, not even Leonard, could ever deny you."

"In truth," answered Leonard, "the reply of Alexander was most true in itself, and now that you, Mr. More, have given it the authoritative stamp of your approval, it becomes clearer than ever. Since there is no point in wearing myself out in an impossible enterprise, I will say no more." And he stopped.

When Paul, who was sitting close by, saw that it was his turn, he spoke up without waiting for any further invitation. "It is up to me," he said, "to prove that this life is deprived of all happiness. On that score, everyone can see how little remains that I need to say since each of you has confirmed my opinion in part. I do not see how I could find any quicker way to prove that there is no happiness to be found in this life than by showing that our principal delights do not lead to happiness. But you yourselves—for which I thank you—have conceded completely without any effort on my part. But, lest winning my cause in such a way, I remain without the victory and with the shame of having led it into the field without giving it any aid, I shall arm it with some arguments for this happy undertaking against happiness.

"Well then, gentlemen, I tell you I am truly amazed that, after putting happiness in the contentment of the soul, you did not foresee at the beginning that it would be impossible to find it in this life, in which no one ever finds any peace or contentment. If you inquired of every man in the world, you would find none so comfortable that he does not have his own thorn that perpetually torments him. The poor man, beaten down by a thousand pressing necessities, wears himself out to get money; the rich man, his brains confused by continual losses, enmities, and lawsuits, dies from anxieties; the retired life is without honor, and the honored life without repose. Thus you see that, in every class of men, for every good portion, there is another portion of evil. Imagine, then, what contentment we may expect from this carefully weighed balance of pleasure and pain, when it is the cursed nature of our soul ever to long for the very thing that it lacks. Do I need to give examples for this? The man who owns a field itches to join another to it, just as he who owns one kingdom seeks a second. Alexander the Great, as we read, cried because he had no more worlds to conquer. Our desires are, in themselves, infinite, and to own much effects nothing except to redouble our desire. This very indisposition of our souls toward contentment is enough of itself to assure us of little happiness. But I will put aside all other arguments and bring one forward so striking that you yourselves will say it admits of no reply. You know, gentlemen, that this life is none other than a harsh exile and a grim struggle to return home. Do you not see, then, that to try to find any happiness here is a deadly blasphemy? It is none other than to forget both our condition and our debt to that very God Who, because we broke away from Him, gave an express commandment which exiled us from all happiness and set us in a valley of misery to wear us down in discomforts and trials. To try to find happiness in this life can be but an express contradiction to the will of God that scorns His just punishment, like those desperate servants who, when their masters beat their shoulders black and blue, act as if they took no notice just for spite. Here you have the great happiness of this blessed life! If we knew how to keep our account of pleasure and pain as accurately as we can that of debits and credits, we would soon see that the account can never be balanced. Do I really need to clarify item by item this account, explaining our imperfect infancy, our troubled youth, our weak and sick old age, or, dividing man up into his parts, to show that the soul is subject to the infinite chances of fortune and the body is at the mercy of sickness and deformity? But if you wish a plain demonstration, just remember that there is no good so capable of giving pleasure that it does not turn to gall if some injury be added to it. There are, however, plenty of evils so injurious that no stroke of good luck can sweeten them. Thus it seems plain to me that this life is more unpleasant than pleasant. But our harsh condition proceeds from nothing else than the abundant tenderness of our Heavenly Father Who, fearing that if He did not take away the sweetness of this life we would forget the life to come, tempered that sweetness with a very bitter aloe so that we would not savor it too long, just as we ourselves do with those fruits that we do not want our children to eat too much of. But why should I go to such lengths to show the evils of this life when I have at hand something to convince you?"

And, extending his hand, he showed them a ring on his finger, which bore the inscription MEMENTO MORI.[8] "The thought of this, gentlemen," he said, "is enough to destroy all our pleasures, no matter how perfect they might otherwise be, and all the sweetness of this life."

He paused for a moment, and Laurence, mocking as usual, said, "Paul, if what you have in your hand seems to you as evil and unsupportable as you say, free yourself of it immediately and burden me with it, for gold weighs more with me than do these words, for they can be understood in another sense, that is, that I should remember, not death, but you, Mr. More."

"I really believe," said Paul, "that, if Death himself came in person to Laurence with a bag of gold, he would be warmly welcomed. Well, his exposition of MEMENTO MORI may have forgotten death, but anyone who expounds it in its proper sense would soon see the cheating happiness of this present life go up in smoke. Let me give you an exposition more to the point than Laurence's, using the vivid metaphor that you, Mr. More, used in one of your books, which I hope it may please God to see translated into a more universal language as it is well written in the native language of this island. You compare our condition with that of those who, all guilty of the same crime, are condemned to death by the same judgment, loaded

[8] *memento mori:* "remember death."

together into one cart, and sent off to execution. They are sent to various regions instead of all to the same place, so that their exemplary punishment will be more vividly known, one to the closest city, another to a more remote place, and another to the very borders of the country. We humans, equally guilty of that first sin of Adam are all condemned to death by the Supreme Judge, sent off together in the same chariot, that most rapid chariot of time that rushes us over a street hard and rough toward death, and, as it pleases Fate or Fortune (who execute the sentence every day) we all die—this one in his early years, this one in middle age, and some, but not many at the extremity of life.[9] Let us turn now, gentlemen, to that happiness already spoken of and compare it, point by point, with this image of our present state. How great is the folly of rich men who make such a great provision for such a short trip? Or of those honored and powerful rulers who delight in being able to dispose at will of the lives of others, forgetting altogether that we are all on the same voyage and that maybe they will be among the first dispatched? Or of those who drown their happiness in love or some other pastime when they are most certain to arrive soon at that end that cuts short all our pleasures or turns them into bitter torment? I am certain, gentlemen, that you have already admitted within yourselves what I have argued, knowing it to be most true. I believe then I may conclude that our condition in this life is not only unhappy, but indeed, most miserable."

Alexander, seeing that the others were silent, said, "Gentlemen, we would be worth very little if we five allow one single man to bind up our happiness without offering any resistance or using anything to aid us, especially since we do not need to use anything but words. Since you have made no motion toward a defense, I shall answer very briefly to all that which you, Paul, have argued at length. Your discourse of the unhappiness of this life, if I have understood correctly, was based upon three assumptions: the discontent inherent in our souls, the punishment of God for our original sin, and, finally, the unpleasant fact of death, the certain end of all living things. Your first assertion, that neither contentment nor satisfaction of the soul are to be found in this life, has left me so dissatisfied that I cannot accept it. You tried to prove your point with the example of those whose insatiable desires pursue the empty smoke of worldliness. But it is clear that such gluttons seek not to satisfy the soul, but, rather, the ap-

[9] More uses the metaphor of the condemned prisoners in "The Four Last Things" (in *The English Works of Sir Thomas More*, ed. W. E. Campbell [London: Eyre and Spottiswoode, 1927-31], I, 460-461).

petites, which have no fixed limits. What wonder is it, then, if they never succeed in finding contentment? But, although such men wear themselves out searching in vain for contentment down the dark alleys of desire, we need not suppose that those who search for it reasonably will not find it readily. Here I could cite the example of many wise men who, recognizing the perfection of their state, are fully content with it, as with a thing true and certain. Such men laugh at those who let their contentment depend not on their own judgment, but on the judgment and favor of someone else, that someone being one who follows appetite instead of stable judgment. You see, then, Paul, that there are men who find contentment in this life and, if you reply that the number who do is very small, I shall answer that the number of those who can call themselves happy in this life is not great; it is indeed very small. And now, watch me overtake you as you fly for aid to the wrath and disdain of God. You affirm that the Lord has thrown us into this valley of misery to punish us for our evil deeds and to wear us down with troubles, rather than to let us enjoy any happiness. I do not see how I can agree with what you say. It does not seem reasonable to me to say that God has given us this beautiful dwelling place, a world filled with delights, in order to bring about a contrary effect, since He never did anything in vain. I agree that original sin has greatly diminished the happiness created for us in this life and made it harder to obtain, but let no one say that it has taken happiness away completely. Do you not remember, Paul, since you have laid your hands on things of Holy Scripture, how many who follow the commandments of God are assured by Him of worldly blessings for themselves and for all their posterity? Do you not remember how many times the Highest God has promised with His own mouth to bless those who observed His sacred precepts and make them fruitful in children, grain, wine, oil, and other worldly goods? If these things formed no part of happiness, then such promises would be vain and pointless. We must confess, for this reason alone, that there is happiness in this life; we cannot say that our Heavenly Father's testament has endowed us with a legacy of no importance. Besides, you see, Paul, that, even if I admitted that all the happiness in this life were taken from us by our first excess, what difference would it make in our present condition? After that scornful emancipation we have already been received again as sons in a solemn adoption consecrated by the very blood of the Highest God. To consider ourselves made happy in this life by the many gifts of our Father is not, as it seems to you, blasphemy or forgetfulness of our condition and the service that we owe to Him. On the contrary, it is a real recognition of both, for we love and revere God for the benefits we have received, like His sons, instead of fearing His punishment, like slaves. And this is enough of an answer to the arguments you have put together out of theology. But what shall I say against your terrifying sermon on death? The very memory of it, you say, causes so much anxiety and despair, that, if our life were in every other respect most sweet, this alone would turn it to gall. I think you are very wrong in trying to deprive us of our happiness by reminding us of that of which we are all very forgetful. You know, Paul, how little account we take of death; we almost never think of it, or, if we happen to, we do not view it with anxiety but, rather, with that attention we give to those things that do not concern us much. Even if it were not thus and if we thought of death almost every hour, there is nothing in it, as long as we think rationally, that should disturb us at all. Do you really think, Paul, that death is as fearful as your words have represented it? You deceive yourself if you think so, for there is no evil in death except our empty fear of it. I do not think I need to prove this in the house of Mr. More, where the only books read are those of excellent authors whose very clear arguments and examples have made us realize that there is no evil in death except its horrible appearance. Death is like a terrifying mask whose outward appearance is truly fearful; seen inside, however, it is immediately discovered to be empty and far from that which it appears to be. Do not suppose, Paul, that you can frighten us speechless with this mask as you can children. And what does that metaphor of the condemned man prove against the sweetness of this life? What is there in death, then, to cry out against? Let us but think of it rationally, and we may be certain that, when death comes, it will bring us more good than harm. I would defy death itself to prove that our condition in this present life is not happy."

"You would gain nothing in a battle with death," said Paul, "where the most you could hope for is the power to flee." And with this he struck an attitude as though he were about to rebuke Alexander with the ferocity of death itself.

But Laurence, who took little delight in listening to discussions of this sort, said, "Paul, are you not content to have paralyzed us already with this bitter comparison? Do you have to give us up to death once more? For Heaven's sake, be content to have broken the law of Mr. More only once and do not continue your crime with another reply. If you are in love with death, then keep it, embrace it without fear of horns whenever you please, and let us enjoy our happiness."

When he saw that the smiles on the faces of the others confirmed this speech by Laurence, Paul said: "Since it so pleases you to find happiness in this empty happiness, like children who become rich with imitation jewelry, I will leave you to your own devices. But of this I am certain: when Mr. More reviews the arguments, he will add up the bill in another way."

"If you are trying to learn my judgment," said More, "it is that I cannot agree with you or with any of the others about happiness, for, although there is no happiness to be found in the things already mentioned, it does not follow that there is none to be found. To demonstrate this, I intend to reintroduce a happiness so perfect in itself that you yourselves will agree that all your arguments cannot hold out against it."

After deliberating for a while, he began thus: "It is strange indeed that men, the only animals endowed with reason, are, nevertheless, more irrational in pursuing their desires than the beasts, which distinguish clearly their pleasures and thus enjoy to perfection the humble sweetness of their lives. But man constantly deceives himself about them, putting the lesser pleasure ahead of the greater or mistaking for a pleasure its direct opposite. There is no need for me to give examples of what you see every day: how men put more happiness in the acquisition of riches than in the use of them, more in the life of labor than in the life of rest, more in the appearance of well-being than in the thing itself. How much these motives are repugnant to reason, we ourselves confess with our mouths, solemnly denouncing riches as base and honors as a puff of smoke whenever the occasion presents itself. But our eyes are so filled with that smoke that we cannot see the bright fire that burns within. How laughable it is that none of us ever loses the occasion either to dispraise these things or to seek them. The cause of all this is our cursed appetite that so overwhelms our thoughts that we can barely descry the rays of reason. Just as the sun often appears behind a mist with a light so ambiguous that you feel you are seeing it and not seeing it at the same time, so reason appears behind the dense fog of our appetite with a light so weak that we grant it recognition in our words and deny it in our deeds. Since we are all rational beings, however, we would grant it recognition in all things if we could see it clearly. Therefore, if we intend to reach happiness, we will, in my opinion, have to find out how to draw a distinction between reason and appetite that will satisfy our judgments. This is not easy; indeed, it is most difficult. For, although reason and appetite fight each other like all contraries, they do not fight in the same style as others where, when one diminishes, the increase of the other is clearly apparent, especially as the disproportion between them increases. With appetite and reason, everything goes in reverse. The greater the lack of reason, the less it is missed, for the absence of foolishness is the only means by which foolishness can be discovered. Thus it often happens that the further our desires are from reason the more obstinately we maintain that they are reasonable. But, let us leave this for now and return to the search for happiness. That happiness builds its home in the soul alone is a truth so evident that you will all concede it. Every good and evil that we experience in this life relates only to the soul. The very pleasures and pains of the body are incapable of working their effect if the soul refuses to accept them for pleasures or pains. For instance, an idiot does not feel any injury when he is beaten because his soul has no power to distinguish between pleasure and pain, though all his senses may be in perfect working order. If our happiness were placed anywhere else but in the soul alone, we would have a fine time of it, for all things except the soul, even the heavens themselves, are subject to continual change. But Nature, our common mother, has shown us favor in this matter. She who made man so excellent in his nature that he deserves that great title of *microcosmos* has not failed him in the main thing of all, his happiness.[10] To keep such a great treasure safe, she has put inside him an impregnable fortress, so constructed that nothing in the world can penetrate it except its own ministers, that is, the affections. If we guard ourselves carefully from betrayal by these, then nothing can disturb our sleep. But it is certainly true that these servants are the most disloyal and untrustworthy traitors in the world, always standing at our ear, on the alert for an opportunity to betray us, carrying back lying reports on every occasion for the instruction of our judgment. It is almost impossible not to be trapped sometime by their devices. Very few indeed are those who have been able to protect themselves completely, although some have held such strict watch over these traitors with the guidance of reason that, after assault by the most grievous torments of the affections, their happiness has mounted higher at their victory than it sank low from seeing themselves besieged by evil. A fitting place for happiness is the soul of man.

"Now that we have looked at the model, let us turn directly to the consideration of this happiness, leaving aside the hairsplitting intricacies of those who, never having understood the ultimate good, spin out subtle discourses that have given us a happiness easier to demonstrate with arguments than to enjoy effectively. Let me say plainly that, according to me,

---

[10] *microcosmos:* "microcosm." The honorific use of this term among such Renaissance writers as More's favorite Pico della Mirandola, is discussed briefly by George Perrigo Conger, *Theories of Macrocosm and Microcosm in the History of Philosophy* (New York: Columbia University Press, 1922), p. 11.

happiness is none other than, as you have all admitted already, contentment of the soul. But we must realize that to content oneself within a certain limit consists not only in not desiring more, for this would be better called not being miserable than being happy, but also in understanding why there is nothing further to be desired beyond that limit. When animals stop at a certain limit by a natural instinct, we do not say that they content themselves with that since they are incapable of going to excess. Man alone finds contentment in the limit at which he stops: his will controlled by reason, as if it were the ultimate end. Perfect happiness, then, comes when a man fully contents himself with a certain good, understanding perfectly why it is the final and highest that he can desire. There is no need, I think, gentlemen, for me to go on speaking, as they say, in 'letters writ large,' to clarify further what I mean. For what is there in this whole universe of such quality that it may be set up for the highest and ultimate good except that alone from which proceeds and to which is directed every other good, that is, the most high and single God, Who is everything in Himself and in Whom is to be found perfect contentment and outside of Whom is neither contentment nor satisfaction? I greatly wonder, gentlemen, at the way you have handled this matter. Since we have in the past so many times and with such clear arguments concluded among ourselves that there is no other happiness for man except to find contentment in God, how has such a clear and express truth in this argument slipped through your hands?"

The others remained silent, as if half confessing themselves in error, but Alexander, still obstinately clinging to his belief, said: "Mr. More, if our dispute were about happiness in general, we would have to be careless indeed to maintain anything other than what you have pointed out to us. But, since we have argued in this dispute only about the happiness of this life, I do not see how it is possible to equate it with anything except knowledge. To say to me that this is an imperfect happiness, while yours is perfect, is irrelevant, for the only happiness that befits this present life is that which conforms to its conditions. Furthermore, happiness is an enjoyment, and there is no enjoyment except of things that are present. So where will your happiness, which is a hope in future things, find a place here? Finally, contentment in this life is a controlling of the will by reason, but, for this happiness that you describe, we must abandon reason altogether and use faith alone. We will find our happiness in divine things, as far as I can tell, when we cease believing in them and begin to know them. But in the meantime, before our souls arrive at such an altitude, we must put our happiness in those lower things that we can understand by means of reason. True it is, that this happiness is infirm and weak in comparison with that other and unworthy to be pursued by us except where it aids, or at least does not hinder, that other."

More smiled. "See," he said, "how Alexander has given you a happiness that, as he himself says, he is not certain of enjoying very much. Certainly he is in a great error when he assigns to the soul, which is always one single thing in its nature, two different objects for happiness. How far this is from reason is obvious to everyone. For how is it possible that the soul can propose two objects for its ultimate good without deceiving itself about one of them? Or how can it have such a weak judgment that it could take the works of God for the ultimate good without recognizing that these works had to have a creator, who in all likelihood must be a thing more noble than the works of his hand? The soul, then, when it judges aright, will never have more than one happiness, nor any good other than the highest, which is God Himself. What shall we say then to that reply of Alexander about the two different conditions of the soul? Just this, that we recognize according to their different conditions, not, as he would have it, two different kinds of happiness, but one only, with two different ways of enjoying it. In its perfect state, the happiness of the soul will be to enjoy the immediate presence of God, and in this imperfect life it is to enjoy Him by understanding His works and His words. Of these two means, the more important is His words, for they have teaching as their proper end. Thus, Alexander, we have set your happiness in such order that it is no longer a true happiness, but just a means to it. I do not think that I need to answer that objection that my contentment is found through faith and not through reason, for who does not see how much more perfect it becomes if that is true, since faith is more noble and more perfect than reason? And yet I could show you that finding happiness through faith is truly a finding through reason.

"But leaving aside for now everything else, I turn to your affirmation, Alexander, that the happiness I described cannot be enjoyed since it concerns not present things but future hopes. What then? Do you think that contentment in God is not the most perfect enjoyment of a good that this life has to offer? It would not be pleasing to God that such a thought should creep into our hearts, for certain it is that, when we consider our condition soberly, it is more than obvious that this is the only good that we can enjoy in this life. If a man puts his happiness in some other good, he does it with extreme carelessness. He does not understand his true worth, nor how much more noble he is than the other creatures, for Almighty

God created him for the glorious end of finding contentment in Him. If each of us were to examine most carefully his state, considering that he possesses within himself an eternal soul, a thing of such inestimable worth that the very government of it is of far greater importance than the acquisition of the rest of the world, certainly then every happiness would seem vain in comparison with the happiness of knowing that his most precious jewel was in the hands of Him who cared for it so much that His own blood seemed to Him a small price to give for its redemption. For as He is a just and true God," and here he raised his eyes toward Heaven, "when man offers Him this soul, He will embrace it tenderly, as He has promised to do, filling it with such a joy and consolation by His divine power that he will feel inside himself a happiness so complete that no mortal tongue can express it."

And here More stopped, leaving a great admiration in the souls of those who listened to him when they saw how exactly his life corresponded to the words he spoke. Not long after, that admiration was greatly increased by his truly Christian death, when he lowered his head to the very blow of the axe with a happy and open face, reassured by his pure conscience, like one whose great courage faced that final end with more hope of life than fear of death.

ITALIAN TEXT

IL MORO
D'HELISEO
HEIVODO
INGLESE.

*All'illustriſſimo Cardinal
Reginaldo Polo.*

Con Priuilegio.

IN FIORENZA

Appreſſo Lorenzo Torrentino.
MDLVI.

ALL'ILLVSTRISS.
MONS.IL CARDINAL
REGINALDO
POLO

*Primate della Chieſa nell'
Inghilterra.*

E IO a guiſa gli altri(Re
uerendiſsimo Signore) i
quali a gran perſonaggi
indrizzano l'opere loro,
m'ingegnaſsi hora a vo-
lere inalzar l'infinite virtu voſtre, certo è, che ad vn'inſtaute m'intopparei in
duoi errori grandiſsimi, l'vn d'hauer
quegli lodato, che foſſe più toſto da ri
uerire, l'altro d'hauer voluto moſtrare
re al mondo coſa, che già da ſe ſteſſa era
manifeſtiſsima. Non è però non mi vo

4

lendo io ſcoprire per vn troppo inauue
duto, che mi metta a dire delle voſtre
lodi, nè altro m'impediſce ad honorar
ui, ſenon che voi troppo ſiete d'hono-
rare. Che ſe la fama del valor voſtro,co
me quella delli altri virtuoſi foſſe di qua
lità tale, che poteſſe o da malitia riceue
re macchia niuna,o qualche ſminuimen
to da inuidia, forſe nõ ſtarebbe male l'a
moreuole ufficio di chi a queſto s'inge-
gnaſſe d'opporre. Ma poi che ella ſi
truoua per modo priuilegiata, ſopra di
tutte le altre, che non s'è fin qui viſta nè
lingua tanto velenoſa, che non l'habbia
incontra hauuta riſguardo, ne perſona
tanto inuidioſa, che non la predichi al-
l'vltimo ſuo potere, io per me non mi
auueggio, come ſia poſsibile,che a quel
la ſublimità d'honore ſuo, ſi poſſa dalla
mia picciolezza aggiungere coſa, che
non foſſe, o da manco, in quanto al ſuo
merito, o di ſouerchio, in quanto al

5

biſogno. Et a chi poi ſcriuerei io del
voſtro valore, che non lo conoſceſſe
meglio di me? Chi è fra gl'Italiani,che
non ſappia, come per Roma la vita v'è
ſtata fra tutti per vnico paragone di ſantità,& di virtù? Chi tra Franceſi o tra
gli Alamani, che non conoſca, quanto
s'affaticò, il voſtro Chriſtianiſsimo ani
mo a comporre la nimicitia, che già tan
ti anni roina la Chriſtianità. De gli In-
gleſi? poi chi è, che non s'auueda,qual
mente dal voſtro ripatriare,hauete non
manco ripatriata la iſteſſa patria. Euui
niuno tanto nuouo nelli affari della
Chriſtianità, che non habbia ſentito, come à queſti pochi giorni paſſati,
la ſantità del N. S. P. per il biſogno,
che del voſtro aiuto lo premeua al gouerno della chieſa, con grandiſsima in
ſtanza v'importunò a Roma? la patria
dall'altra banda, mouendoui à pietà
con le ſue freſche piaghe, vi sforzò a re-

73

ſtare pur in dietro, trouando il voſtro
aiuto apunto come il ſuo biſogno.

Quando adunque ſiate addomandato
coſi caldamēte ad vn tempo et dalla pri
ma.et dall'eſtrema parte della Chriſtianità, non ſi potria egli meritamente dire, *quod huic orbi Chriſtiano* (non altramente, che a quello vniuerſo fingono gl'Aſtrologi)ſi richiedeſſe per ſoſten
tarlo, vn altro Polo? Ma queſte ſono
coſe troppo alte, & non ſtarebbe bene
alla baſſezza del mio ſtilo il volerſi ſali-
re ſino al Polo. Quello forſe mi ſaria
ſtato piu conueneuole ſoggetto, cioè
che confeſſata la pochezza di queſta o-
pera humilmēte confugendo alla pron
tezza del voſtro animo, la ſupplicaſſi di
accettarla. Et queſto harei anco fatto
alla diſteſa, ſe non mi accorgeſſi, come
a queſto modo, col tanto ſminuire il li
bro,l'hauerei accreſciuto,& col mio accreſcere .a voſtra prontezza l'haria ſmi-

nuita. Et però intorno al mio preſen-
tarui vn coſi fatto libro, non dirò già
altro, ſe non d'hauer ciò fatto all'eſem
pio di quelli della villa, i quali, benche
ſiano poueriſſimi, pure vedemo che la
vſanza lor habbia cōceduto queſto priuilegio,che non gli diſdica punto il pre
ſentare i grandiſſimi Signori, chi con
Noci,chi con Perſiche, chi con Pere &
altre ſimili coſette di neſſuna importan-
za, le quali quanto in ſe ſteſſe ſono di
manco pregio, tanto ſtanno meglio,
& a quelli, che le offeriſcono ,& à colo
ro,che le riceuono. A queſto modo mi
parſe che foſſe di dare qualche conue-
nienza fra l'altezza voſtra, e la baſſezza
di queſta opera. La qual, riguardando alla condition ſua,benche temo non
v'offendeſſe,il vederne quell'acutiſſimo
ingegno del S. T. Moro introdutto con
vno parlar coſi freddo, che ne ancho al
Moro morto corriſponderebbe, pure

A iiii

riſpetto alla mia pura affezzione uerſo
quel venerando nome,ſpero certamen
te che la preſente opera per queſto ver-
ſo non vi ſia diſcara.

Di V. S. Reuerendiſſ.

Affettionatiſſ. S.
Heliſeo Heiuodo.

IL MORO'
D'HELISEO
HEIVODO
INGLESE.

All' Illuſtriſſ. C. Reginaldo
P O L O.

 RA molte diletteuoli *v*ille et
*ca*ſtelli, i quali lungo il bel *r*a
migi , ne luoghi ameniſſimi ſi-
tuati , ſi uedono , una n'è aſſai
uicina alla città di *l*ondra , do-
ue il *S. r*omaſo *m*oro (huomo per la ſua uirtù
aſſai conoſciuto) tenne una ſua bella & com-
moda ſtanza , nella quale , quaſi ogni uolta,
che lo ſtare nella *c*ittà gli tornaua in faſtidio,
ſoleua ritirarſi. *A* queſta caſa , ſi dalla uici-
nanza del luogo , ſi anchora dall'eccellentia del
padrone inuitati, ſpeſſo uſauano de i piu rari &

eccellenti ingegni, che nella Città si trouauano.
I quali trouandosi assai uolte insieme senza ha
uer altro da fare, molto si dilettauano d'entrar
in qualche bel ragionamento, o discorso delle cose piu appartenenti all'humana Vita, & ualen
do ogniun di loro d'ingegno & di dottrina assai, recauano con queste lor dispute l'un all'altro
marauiglioso frutto & piacere. Et quantunque, ricordandomi io di una cosi rara compagnia, come era questa, mi sento tirare à douer-
ne scriuere, per far un uero ritratto di una uera & assoluta Academia; pure à coloro lasciando l'impresa i quali per essere in quella uiui-
ti, piu a pieno n'hanno conoscenza, io per hora
solamente un suo ragionamento mi son posto à
scriuere, il quale (s'il mio auuiso non m'inganna) non passera senza utile, & diletto di chi
si mettera a leggerlo. Che se in questo discorso
o ragionamento, che uogliam' dire, per sorte
si uedra qualche cosa men che perfetta, come io
son certo, che se ne uedranno assai, forza è, che
io tutto quello riconosca dal mio poco sapere, o
uero da quel di coloro, i quali a bocca me lo rac
contarono, (perche presente non sono stato.) &

quanto per adesso io m'apparecchio a scriuere.
Nè punto mi uarrebbe qui altra scusa, perche,
come io di questi difetti uolessi dar la colpa a chi
in quella disputa è stato il giudice, fra coloro
che l'hanno conosciuto, non trouerei, chi mi
credesse, sapendo ogn'uno che il suo limato giu
ditio altra cosa che perfetta non passò mai. Que
sto adunque S. Tomaso Moro sbrigatosi per certi
rispetti d'un suo ufficio, perche era ad ufficio
del gran Cancelliere d'Inghilterra, il quale
appresso gli inglesi, daquel del Re in fuora,
è di grandissima dignita hauendo dico procac
ciato d'abandonar questo ufficio cosi malage uol
mente, come altri suole acquistarlo, a considerar il uero bene tutto si riuolse Et benche duran
te il magistrato, egli non hauesse punto trala-
sciato gli studii, scriuendo ogni di, & insegnan
do egli stesso alle sue figliuole le lettere Greche,
& Latine, nè mancando però all'ufficio, anzi
più sodisfacendo ad esso (come ne fa testimonianza il numero delle piu importanti contro-
uersie per lui decise,) che niuna per lo passato
hauea fatto, nondimeno libero di tanto carico
più che mai, alla uera sapienza haueua il pen-

siero. Pure quantunque egli hauesse, quanto
per se stesso, abandonati quei desideri da quali
noi altri diuentiamo ciechi, non si mostrò però uerso gli altri, cosi rigidamente conteg no-
so, o μισανθρωπος, come ueggiamo fare a mol
ti, i quali con troppa spiaceuolezza, due mali
ne fanno seguire, l'un', che di se stessi mostrano un non so che di costretta uolontà, l'altro,
che i piu imperfetti spauentano, dando loro a
uedere, che la uirtù, non come si ragiona, di
fuora solamente, ma etiandio di dentro tenga dello spiaceuole. Ma il S. T. Moro si come quegli, che con allegrezza & prontezza
ubbidiua alla uirtù, oltre ad ogni altro era faceto, & piaceuole molto, & trouandosi in com
pagnia, ilche ne l'hore del mangiare et altre non
buone dallo studio, facea molto uolentieri, assai si dilettaua con alcuna dubbiosa propositione
di metterla in dispute di qualche cosa gioueuole,
in tutte le quali cosi facilmente sapeua scalzar
il dritto, che ben sarebbe stato ritroso colui, a
cui a pieno egli non hauesse sodisfatto. Fra gli
altri, che piu dimesticamente a casa il S. T.
Moro si riparauano, sei n'erano, de quali (per

hauere essi i sopranomi piu all'Inglese accom-
modati, che non si confà a questa lingua) io so
lamente citarò i nomi proprii. Furono adunque questi, il S. Lionardo, il S. Paolo, il Sig.
Alessandro, i quali per apprender lettere, &
costumi lungamente per tutte le piu famose cit
tà fuor della lor patria stati s'erano insieme,
& oltre a questi duo'altri gentil'huomini frate
gli chiamati, l'un il S. Piero, l'altro il S. Car
lo, con un M. Lorenzo Cittadino di Londra, huo
mo in quanto alle lettere assai materiale, & ro
zo, ma per altro d'ingegno perspicace & mol
to piaceuole, con cui, perciocche era un grandissi
mo ammassatore di danari, spesso scherzando
il S. T. Moro, imputandogli questo a sciocchiz
za, con si chiari ragionamenti, che non si sape
ua come acconciamente negare, ne prendeua
(come in cosi fatte cose soleua) grandissimo pia
cere. Questi gentilhuomini, tali come io ui l'ho
conti, essendo un giorno stati a desinare col S.
T. Moro, doppo pasto in un giardino, che quasi
duo tratti di pietra, discosto era da casa, tutti
di brigata andarono, et in un pratello posto in
mezzo il giardino sopra un uerde monticello,

ſtauano à riguardare. Era il luogo à maraui
glia bello , ſi per la conmodità del ſito (perche
da una parte quaſi tutta la nobiliſſima città
di Londra , et dall'altra il bel Tamigi con uer
di prati & boſcherecci monti d'ogni intorno ſco
priua) ſi per la bellezza propria . Perche eſſendo
coperta quaſi d'una continua verdura , haueua
delli appariſcenti fiori , & de ramicelli de frut
tiferi alberi , che ſtauano appreſſo , in coſi bello or
dine inteſſuti , che à riguardanti non pareua al
tro , che una animata tappezzeria fatta dalla
Natura iſteſſa , tanto piu nobile di tutte le al
tre , quanto queſta piu à pieno ſodisfaceua , doue
quelle con la ſomiglianza delle coſe diletteuoli
laſciano gli animi piu deſideroſi , che contenti .
Stranamente à tutti era piaciuto il luogo , ma
ſopra gli altri à S. Piero , il quale tanto ſene in
uaghi (come le piu delle uolte ſogliuno i piu pia
ceuoli ingegni d'ogni bellezza facilmente inua
ghirſi) che à pena in ſe capiua , & all'ultimo
largando la uoce à caldi affetti dopo molte ecceſ
ſiue lodi , affermò il luogo eſſere tanto dilette
uole , ch'il trouarſi in quello , baſterebbe à qualun
que huomo foſſe , per farlo felice . A cui ſorri

dendo il fratello , et ditemi di gratia diſſe , quan
tà ui parrebbe la felicità di coſtui , che ſi trouaſ
ſe qui tutto il giorno col mal del capo ? Io , ſe
m'hauete inteſo , riſpoſe , il S. Piero , affermai
la piaceuolezza di queſto luogo , baſtar ad un
huomo , & parlando d'un huomo intendo di
quello , che in tale ſtato ſi ritroua , quale natu
ralmente ad huomo ſi richiede , hor ſu replicò
il S. Carlo , togliendo uia la prima parte della
mia demanda , pigliamo il reſto . Quale dun
que credete uoi , che prouerebbe la felicità colui ,
che tutto il dì haueſſe à ſtare qui , dalla mattina
fin alla ſera ? Non poſſo negarui (riſpoſe il S.
Piero) che il troppo in ogni coſa non generi faſti
dio , nè però ui ho preſcritto io à queſta felicità
termine alcuno , auuedendomi bene , che niun di
qual ſi uoglia coſa continuamente puo dilettar
ſi , eſſendo le coſe tutte (o per difetto loro , o noſtro)
coſi fatte , che dopo hauere alquanto piaciuto ,
uengono altrui à noia . Non uoglio in queſto con
ſentirui , diſſe M. Lorenzo , perche io ſo bene
d'inſegnaruene una , della quale quantunque
l'huomo ne pruoui , mai però non gl'increſce . Et
non uolendo uoi in queſto di me fidarui , ditemi

di gratia , qual'huomo hauete uoi mai conoſciu
to , à cui le ricchezze per hauerne troppo ſiano
uenute in faſtidio ? anzi gl'huomini , quanto
n'hanno piu , tanto piu ne deſiderano . Donde
fra le felicità di queſta uita , che che ne paia al
S. T. Moro , ſempre l'ho tenute io per ſomme .
Di pari (riſpoſe il S. Piero) nimiche ſono di
felicità le coſe , che non ſodisfanno , & quelle
che ſatiano . A queſto modo (diſſe M. Loren
zo) non ci ſarà felice niuno , ſe e quello che ſatia ,
& quello che non ſatia hà ad eſſer contrario alla
felicità . Io non ui ho detto coſi , riſpoſe il S. Pie
ro , & non è (come ui pare) una coſa medeſima
il ſodisfare , & il ſatiare ; eſſendo il ſodisfare
un far ceſſare il deſiderio , & il ſatiare un gene
rar faſtidio , ma fra queſti duoi eſtremi , cioè il
deſiderare , & il faſtidire , c'è ben da dare un
mezzo , come il contentarſi . Di queſti mezzi ò
eſtremi non ſo io , diſſe M. Lorenzo : ma queſto
conoſco bene , che ogniuno in farſi ricco , con ſen
za ogni mezzo s'appiglia all'eſtremo , che non
ſi contenta d'altro , nè ſi ſatia di queſto , donde
io per me non uedo coſa per metterui la felicità
della preſente uita , altra che queſta . Taceua-

no gia tutti , quando il S. T. Moro , ſorridendo ,
diſſe à gli altri . Et che Signori , laſcieremo noi
M. Lorenzo con tante ricchezze andar felice ,
coſi chetamente , ſenza pur fargli motto , o uero
à guiſa gli ſbirri , inanti che con queſte ci paſ
ſi , cercaremole tutte , eſſaminando ſottilmente ,
quali ſono , donde l'hà tolte , & doue le porti .
E parmi ben fatto , diſſe il S. Paolo , poi che ſia
mo certi , che M. Lorenzo non ci darà mai qual
che coſa per gentilezza , di cercarne minuta
mente tutto il drappello , non tanto per ſaperne
la qualità (eſſendolo coſi mal compatto per non
hauer M. Lorenzo ſaputo troppo bene ουλλογιζε
ϭϑαι che di fuori , ſenza guardarlo dentro , tutto
ſi manifeſta) quanto per dargli impaccio . Ma
quantunque ſi uoglia , far coſi , non per tanto ,
eſſendoci preſente uoi (nella cui preſenza ceſſa
l'autorità de minori giudici) à niun di noi da il
cuore di farlo . Ma fatelo ſicuramente , diſſe
il S. T. Moro , perche qual ſi ſia qui l'autorità
mia , io ui uoglio delegarla tutta , & per ciò
ciaſcun di uoi dica intorno à queſto , liberamen
te , quel che gli pare . ſe ui ſete riſoluto , diſ
ſe il S. Aleſſandro , di uoler delegar queſta

causa, mettendola nelle nostre mani, prescri-
ueretcci almeno qualche ordine, secondo il qua-
le habbiamo a procedere in questa essamina del-
la felicità. L'ordine, disse il S. T. M. (benche
questo sia vn gran disordine, che io vel prescri-
ua) sia questo, che voi inanzi che vi mettiate
a disturbar la felicità di M. Lorenzo, v'accordia-
te prima fra voi stessi d'un'altra. Perche a que-
sto modo, & piu facilmente sbiancherete que-
sta contrafatta felicità, affrontandola con la ve-
ra, & a voi stessi, & a me anchora proude-
rete meglio, non togliendoci vna felicità sen-
za darcene vn'altra, doue altramente facen-
do per sorte ci lasciareste infelici. Ma essendo
d'accordo infra voi della vera felicità, ilche fa-
cilmente credo vi verrà fatto, fatcui intorno a
M. Lorenzo tutti quanti, & questo gran ca-
rico di denari (se'l sentirete contrario alla feli-
cità) ingegnatcui di leuar lielo da dosso, per
farlo felice. A questo ridendo, M. Lorenzo
a che hora mi venisse fantasia, disse, di voler di-
uentar felice a questo modo, non mi pigliarei al-
tro partito, che di darm'in preda a ladri, concio-
sia ch'ad una cosi fatta felicità piu forz'hanno i

loro argomenti, pur io piu uolentieri ascolterò i
nostri. Però cominciate, et liberatemi di vna
tanta paura, quanta è quella, ch'io ho del fat-
to vostro, voi forse per felicità ci partoria-
te qualche gran mostro di tante teste, quante
ne hauete voi cinque. Allhora il Sign. Carlo
guardando verso gli altri. Signori, disse,
per cacciar in vn tratto a M. Lorenzo la paura
& la speranza insieme, facciamo publicar que-
sta nostra felicita. Non vi par dunque, essen-
do ella vn sommo diletto dell'animo, che stia
bene di volerla mettere nell'honore, cosa piu ag-
gradeuole a gli animi nostri, come tutto il di si
vede all'effetto, di tutte altre. In questo dis-
se il S. Piero, io non vi posso mai consentire, che
l'honore, il quale non si puo dire, che habbia es-
sentialmente la sua essistentia, nella persona ho-
norata, si debba a quella accettarsi per la sua fe-
licità, ma per far questo effetto bisogna troua-
re vna cosi fatta cosa, che realmente consista
nell'animo di colui, che vuole esser felice, &
questo, secondo me, sarà quel piu nobile affetto
di tutti, dico l'Amore, il quale non solamen-
te dimora egli stesso nel cuore dell'amante, ma

B ii

anchora non vi lascia entrar'altro. In tale opi-
nione, non sono io, disse allhora il S. Alessan-
dro, che l'attuffarsi nel disiderio o d'honore o ve-
ro d'Amore, essendo elle amendue perturbatio-
ni dell'animo, siano a quello cagione di felicità
alcuna, non piu che la febre al corpo, per far pa-
rergli piu grato il bere. Ma essendo l'animo,
cosa in se perfettissima, quello che nello stato na-
turale il mantiene & conserua, sarà senza fal-
lo la nostra felicità, & questo chi non sà, che
è il sapere, il vero nutrimento dell'animo, non
altramente che il cibo del corpo. Allhora il
S. Lionardo, hauendoli vn poco guatato, io mi
marauiglio, disse, di voi tutti quanti, che non
essendo altro la felicità, che vn dilettarsi dell'a-
nimo, l'hauete messa in alcuna specialità, con
voler dire, che sia o di questo buono, o di quel-
lo. Conciosia che gli animi nostri si vedono cosi
diuersi, che a pena due se ne trouano, i quali da
vna medesima cosa a vn modo si dilettino. Et
però, al mio giudicio, la felicità non sara di
mettere in vna cosa, piu che in vna altra, ma
vgualmente in ogni cosa secondo che all'animo
di ciascuno piu va a grado. Restaua solo il S.

Paolo a douer dire, il quale stando vn poco so-
pra di se, all'vltimo disse. La legge dataci dal
S. T. M. se io non erro, è questa, che ciascuno
intorno alla felicità dica quel che gli pare, sì ve-
ramente, che in ogni modo ne habbia da consti-
tuire poi esso vna. Essendo adunque il mio pa-
rere, che in questa vita, non se ne possa dare al-
cuna, eccoui, che per osseruar questa legge, a
me bisogna, che io non l'osserui. Ma perche io
non ho per legge, quello, che qualche impossibi-
lità in se contiene, si dirò pure. Parmi dunque,
che la felicità (parlando di questa vita) non
sia da mettere in cosa alcuna, & che tutta la
nostra vita, considerandola bene, non sia altro
che vna continuata miseria, coperta (come a
gli infermi porgono i medici le lor piu amare ri-
cette) d'vna specie di dolcezza. Qui, hauen-
do cosi detto il Sig. Paolo, M. Lorenzo con vn
grandissimo riso, guardate, disse, s'io sono stato
buono indouino a predirui la natiuità di que-
sta felicità. Eccoui che ella è tanto mostruosa,
ch'i suoi parenti proprii stanno confusi come che
battezarla, mettendola l'vn nell'honore, l'al-
tro nell'Amore, il terzo nel sapere, il quarto

B iii

in ogni cosa, l'vltimo in nessuna . Per certo dis
se il S. T. Moro, mal'hauete procacciato , per
che doue io aspettaua da uoi certissimamente
vna vera felicità, uoi (mercè della uostra di-
scordanza) a si mal termine l'hauete condotta
ch'io per me non sò come che acconciarla ; donde
credo io , sarebbe ben fatto di lasciarla in tutto,
non forse impacciandoci noi troppo in questa in
tricata felicità ne diuentiamo infelici . Et il
dir così , & il forsi fuor del pratello , fu tutto
vno . Ma gl'altri gentil'huomini riscaldati
vn poco in sul ragionare, credendosi ogni vn dì
loro d'hauer nel suo dire piu ragione degli altri,
non voleuano per niente , che la cosa fosse lascia
ta in questi termini, & facendosi attorno al S.
Moro tutti quanti, con ardentissimi prieghi il
pregarono , che in questa lor controuersia gli des
se vn poco vdienza per dar all' vltimo la sententia in fauore , di chi gli paresse, che hauesse
a quella piu ragione . Et tanto seppero fare, che
il S. T. Moro tornato in dietro , eccomi (disse)
apparecchiato ad ogni vostro piacere, ragiona-
te pure quanto vi piace , che per certo io v'ascol
terò piu volentieri, che voi non me ne richiede-

te . Ma della sententia poi vi voglio ben dire,
ch'io son per darla in fauore, non di chi fra voi
piu n'haurà ragione , ma di chi n'haurà a bastanza a meritarla . Et però accadendo , che
vn tale fra voi non si troui, io vi lascierò questa controuersia indecisa , scriuendo pure quelle
due lettere de gl'antichi N. L. Fieramente mi
dispiacerebbe , disse il S . Alessandro, che noi
tanto tempo andassimo dietro a questa cerca, et
alla fine restassimo stracchi, senz' hauer poi fat
to niente . E se voi S. Moro ci mettereste per la
sententia quelle lettere, N. L. ogn'un di noi l'in
terpretarebbe , che le venissero a dire piu tosto,
Non Libet, che Non Liquet . Et però promet-
teteci almen questo , oue voi non vogliate dare
a niun di noi la vittoria, di dirci il perche, mostrandoci , doue siamo suiati della ragione , &
come facendo hauremmo potuto far meglio .
Questo , disse il S. T. Moro , non sarà altro , che
il dirui anchora io la mia opinione intorno a
quello , che voi andate cercando , & ben son
contento di farlo , ma non gia come giudice, ma
come litigatore , si , per non sententiare io stesso
nella mia causa propria , si anchora , acciocho

B   iiii

voi , oue io vi paressi troppo stretto giudice ne
vostri ragionamenti , ve ne possiate vendica-
re, facendo il somigliante ne miei . In questo,
disse M. Lorenzo , parlate benissimo , et mi pia
ce , che sia così, perche io (per quello, che l'altre
volte hò compreso dal vostro buono animo ver
so la mia parte) posso in questo giudicio sperar
piu contento della mia uendetta, che della vostra giustitia . Voi sete, rispose il S. Moro , via
piu sollecito , che non vi bisognerebbe , perche
voi in questo partito per quel che mi pare , non
hauete da far nulla , hauendo noi di gia mezo condennate le uostre ricchezze per troppo leg
gieri a voleruile mettere in bilancia con la felicità . Questo è ben bello, disse M. Loren. che noi
l'hauete condennate per leggieri senza hauerle
pesate altramente , o pur trouato il contrapeso ,
con che pesarle . Di gratia, disse il S. Alessan.
non rifutiamo di vsar con M. Lorenzo vna co
sì picciola cortesia , come sarebbe questa , di pe-
sargli vn poco questi suoi scudi, & chi sa , se
gli il fa per fargli cambiare ? Cotesto nò, dis
se subito M. Lorenzo , perche quantunque questi scudi non fossero di buon peso , non è però, che

io gli cambiassi con alcuna delle uostre felicità,
le quali al mio giudicio non pesano niente . Ve
dete Signori , disse il S. T. Moro , come sete ben
cambiati della cortesia vsata con M. Lorenzo,
ma poi che pure v'è a grado , che egli habbia an
ch'esso la sua parte di queste dispute , sia col nome di Dio , & per cominciare lo metteremo al
primo luogo , facendo , non come sogliono i Re-
thorici ne loro argomenti , ma all'vsanza de
mercatanti ne lor drappi, i quali al primo mo
strano sempre la lor piu cattiua robba . Però
cominciate M. Lorenzo , & gouernate di gratia le uostre parole intorno alle ricchezze, non al
tramente , che sogliate le ricchezze istesse, del
le quali mai non spendete piu che , non vi bisogna . A questo modo , disse ridendo M. Lorenzo , non ci farei motto io , conciosia cosa che
mai non spendo vn quattrino, se non in cosa, che
piu mi importa , che non mi fa hora il far que
ste dispute . Ma pur poi che a voi piace così, che
per me si dia principio al nostro ragionare , &
io il farò molto volentieri . Del luogo poi, quan
tunque il S. T. Moro m'ha messo inanzi a gl'al
tri , per cacciarmi dietro a tutti , io mi conten-

to pur'aſſai, ſtimando, che ben ſia conueneuole, che le noſtre diſpute delle ricchezze s'habbino ad incominciare, ſenza le quali, per quello che mi auuedo io, non s'incomincia coſa veruna. Et da queſta volendo io incominciar il mio ragionamento. ne cauerei vn'argomento ineſpugnabile, ma mi piace piu del drittamente contrario, cioè dal fine delle noſtre attioni, pigliare il principio di dire. Perche eſſendo la felicità vna ſomma contentezza d'animo, a trouar quella, non v'è piu dritta ſtrada da tenere, che di uoler cercare il uero fine delle noſtre attioni, dall'acquiſto del quale procede ſenza dubbio lo a pieno contentarſi. Qual dunque ſarà colui, il qual (conſiderandoli bene) non dica, che tutti i noſtri trauagli, tutti i ſudori, & fatiche non ſiano per altro da noi durati, che per poter con guadagno arricchirci? certo, che io credo neſſuno. In tanto che, ſe al S. Moro iſteſſo domandaſſi queſto, credo che il concederebbe anchora egli, o ſe pure il negaſſe, io lo sforzerei a confeſſarlo, inducendo gli a una a una, quante ſorti d'huomini al mondo ſi trouano, che ſo ben, che niuna ve n'è, che ſi habbia propoſto altro fine, che queſto. E là

ſciamo ſtar qui coloro, i quali facendo profeſſione di qualche eſercitio del corpo, troppo al diſcoperto tendono a queſto fine, ma vedete che anchora quelli, i quali andando dietro alle coſe d'ingegno fanno viſta d'hauer penſiero all'honor ſolo, piu fanno queſto lor meſtiero per denari, che per altro. Et mi piace vn poco ragionarui di queſti raccontandogli in quattro parole ordinariamente tutti. Eccoui prima, che di queſte ſette ſcientie, le quali ſi chiamano liberali, non ho mai viſto alcun profeſſore ſi liberale, che ſenza denari l'inſegnaſſe ad alcuno. I medici ſimilmente non per altro ſtudiano al rimediar gli altrui difetti, ſe non per guarir loro ſteſſi dal piu triſto che ſia, dico il difetto de denari. et però vedete, che mai non danno ad alcun vna ricetta di ſilloppo, ſenza farſi dare vna altra d'argento, come poco fa vn mio medico, il qual porgendomi egli una beuanda, et domandandol io ſe foſſe dolce, riſpoſe, che nel ber ſi; ma che dapoi facea guſto vn poco ſpiaceuole: e toſto che beuut'al'hebbi, ne domandommi un mezo ſcudo, a tal ch'infermandomi io, mai, non mi vien tanto faſtidio, del morbo, come del medico. De legiſti poi non ae

cade qui dir niente: i quali chi non ſa come con quel loro ius ſuum cuique tribuat, nummos ſuos cuique auferant? Ma volete forſe in queſto paſſo oppormi quei noſtri filoſofi, de quali voi tanto ſpeſſo ci allegate quegli arguti motti et ſententie in diſpregio delle ricchezze. Ma eccoui che coſtoro quelli loro belli diſpregiamenti di denari mai ſenza denari non proferiuano, anzi grandemente ſalariati fecero queſto lor meſtiere. Donde ſpeſſo mi vien da ridere fra me ſteſſo dicendo, e che diauol di modo non trouarebbono queſti ghiotti de i filoſofi per cauare i denari, poi che con dirne male guadagnano coſi bene? Vedemo dunque fra queſti, che molti ne erano diuentati ricchiſſimi, et mi ricordo d'hauer udito dir al S. T. Moro, che quel Seneca iſteſſo, il qual piu che neſſun altro per tutti i ſuoi ſcritti ſi fa beffe de ricchi, laſciò una ſoſtanza di piu d'ottanta mila ſcudi d'oro. Si che io del fatto de filoſofi non ſò che altro giudicare, ſe non, che queſt'huomini ueramente ſaui, diſpregiaſſero le ricchezze appreſſo a gl'altri, per poter piu facilmente recarle a ſe ſteſſi. Ma laſciamo hor queſto, che le ricchezze ſono il fine delle noſtre at-

tioni, accio non forſe il S. T. Moro mi dica del fine ſenza fine hauer parlato, e torniamo a dirui dell'effetto loro. Tornate pure (diſſe il S. T. Moro, che ſe voi non recate queſto effetto a miglior fine, che quel fine ad effetto recato non hauete, rendeteui ſicuro, che io in fine dirò, che voi in effetto non habbiate fatto niente. Vedete di gratia, diſſe M. Lorenzo, ſe io mai in queſto giuditio poſſo ſperare d'hauer buona giuſtitia per la mia cauſa, della quale il noſtro giudice comincia a parlare in pregiuditio, non hauendola io anchor mezo fornita. Et però ben lo potrei ricuſare, come ſoſpetto, & farei anchora, oue non credeſſi, che alle ricchezze doueſſe non poco accreſcere l'autorità l'hauerla eſſe mantenuta inanzi ad vn giudice poco fauoreuole. Ma per andar piu ſaldamente in queſta cauſa, come a colui fa dibiſogno, il quale non è troppo ben voluto dal giudice, innanzi che io mi torni a dir dell'effetto delle ricchezze, voglio, in acconcio del mio ragionamento, moſtrar agli miei auuerſarii un lor fallo pur troppo manifeſto. Et che Signori? non ui accorgete voi, come tre ſono le coſe, le quali ordinariamente ſi deſiderano da ogn'un in questa vita? cioè l'esser honorato, l'esser potente, l'esser ricco, senza i quali tre beni congiunti insieme nessun per conto di questa vita si chiama mai contento. Come volete adunque che desiderando gli animi nostri tutti tre di questi, la felicità, la quale, dite voi, è il contento dell'animo, sia da mettere in qualche un di questi senza gli altri duoi? Vedete (disse il S. Carlo) come voi M. Lorenzo, a guisa di vn desperato, per vendicarui degli auuersarii, ruinate anchora voi stesso. Perche concedutoui pure, che la felicità sia quella contentezza, che risulta da questi tre beni, l'honore, il potere, & le ricchezze, non vi par così ragioneuole di metterla nell'honore, o nel potere solo, come nelle ricchezze sole. Cotesto nò (disse M. Lorenzo) & vedete, se fra questi tre le ricchezze non hanno piu ragione delli altri a torsi il nome della felicità. Perche doue gli altri nella loro operatione si stringono ad vna certa specialità di bene, fuor della quale non giouano niente (come l'honore solamente in farti honorato, ma in farti ricco nò) le ricchezze vedemo, che fanno non solamente il loro vfficio, ma anchora

quello delli altri due, come mettendoci quà qual si voglia ricco, ne seguita ben cotale esser conosciuto, & honorato, fornito d'amici & potente, & se voi mi neghiate seguire immediate questi effetti dalle ricchezze, eccoui che io vi voglio mostrar ben sessanta persone, honorate hora da tutti, alle quali leuando le ricchezze, non resta gia altro, perche alcun gli cauasse ia beretta, piu che ad vn asino. Le ricchezze adunque contengono in se in effetto l'honore & il potere, & sono, non come gli altri, vn bene particulare, che faccia della felicità la sua parte sola senza piu, ma generale, cioè quello, che in se contiene tutti gli altri. Et quando a prouar questo mi mancasse ogni altro mezo, il nome istesso assai il dourebbe mostrare, perche doue tutti gli altri beni godono vn solo nome speciale senza piu, come l'honore, il potere, vedete che le ricchezze oltra quello speciale nome di ricchezze, per una voce vniuersale si domandano i beni, quasi quel generale bene, che in sua natura realmente contenga gli altri. Et per questo credo io che gli antichi volendo dire, che quella prima età era abondante d'ogni bene,

per significarlo in vna voce sola, l'hanno chiamato l'età dell'oro. Dunque per finir il mio ragionamento, dico che contentandosi il nostro desiderio di tre cose, l'vna di sentirsi preferire a gli altri, cioè l'honore, l'altro di fornirsi d'amici donde nasce il potere, la terza di trouarsi accommodato delle cose del mondo, la prima vien dalle ricchezze come da cose, che piu s'apprezzano, la seconda da quelle medesime, come da cose, che piu s'amano, la terza non è altra, che le ricchezze istesse. Et però conchiudendo in una parola, dico, che il dire, che vn sia ricco, non è altro, che il dire, che sia felice. Taceua gia M. Lorenzo, quando il S. Carlo, hauendo alquanto aspettato, ne veggendo, che nessun s'apparecchiasse ad opporsi, assai poueramente, disse, difese ci ha le sue ricchezze M. Lorenzo; che se non fosse, che egli per la lor sicurtà, piu forti hauesse le serrature, che i ragionamenti hauuti non hà, tosto prouerebbe, credo, quanto maggior sia la noia, che si risente, in hauerle perdute, che non sia la allegrezza da hauerle salue. Ma in questo non temo niente per lui, perche voi altri sapete, come è bene for

tificata

tificata quella parte della casa, doue M. Lorenzo tiene questa sua indorata felicità. Percerto che ella è tanto spessa di lame, di chiodi, & di serragli, & altri così fatti argomenti, che par quasi tutta di ferro. A questo ridendo M. Lorenzo, Et che volete, ch'io faccia, disse, poi che siamo a questa piu trista di tutte, l'età di ferro, bisogna accommodarsi al tempo. Ma questo, disse, il S. Piero, pessimamente osseruate voi, quando per mezo di tanto ferro cercate di conseruarui non solamente l'età dell'argento, ma quella dell'oro anchora. In questo, disse il S. Carlo, facilmente si potrebbe difendere M. Lorenzo, che per certo l'oro & l'argento son metalli piu conformi all'età del ferro, che non è il ferro istesso, della quali, come vogliono i poeti, sono stati la cagione. A tal che l'età dell'oro spari a punto, come l'oro cominciò a spuntare, et mi par, che ne prese il nome (per risponder in questo a M. Lorenzo, per ἀρρεφαν, come i Latini hanno chiamato il monte, cioè da quello, che non si muoue. Non sò, come ringratiarui S. Carlo, disse M. Lorenzo, della vostra fatica, con la quale pigliate la mia difesa

C

contra me steſſo , veramente voi ſete vn auo
cato apunto coſi galante, come era quel medico,
il qual per conſeruar a vn ſuo infermo vn den-
te , gli guaſtò vn'occhio . Ma non voglio già
che voi mi riputiate tanto ſenʒa occhi , che io
non mi auueda , quanto ſia coſa piu comporte-
uole vno ſcoperto , che vn ſegreto nimico . Di
te però contra alla mia difeſa delle ricchezʒe ,
poi che ne hauete detto vna tanta villania , come è quella d'eſſer pouerà , il peggio , che voi po
tete , ch'io non dubito punto di poterlaui mantenere per buona . Voi fate a modo di tutti i
ricchi , diſſe il S. Carlo , i quali facilmente , er
per ogni minima cagione pigliano nimicitia
con gli huomini di piu baſſa conditione , mà a
voſtra poſta , er poi che pure v'è agrado , che
io mi v'opponga in queſto voſtro ragionamento per non voler con voi contraſtare , voglio con
traſtarui . Vedete dunque M. Lorenʒo , che vo
lendoui voi moſtrarci al fine delle noſtre attioni
la felicità , cioè il contento dell'animo , vi biſogna produrre vn tal fine , che fuſſe l'vltimo ,
perche quel ſolo a pieno ci contenta , doue quelli
fini meʒani . i quali s'hanno poi a riferir a vn'

altro fine , ſi puo dir , che tanto habbiano della
diſcontenteʒʒa , quanto del contento , della
qual ſorte di fini ſono le ricchezʒe , le quali non
ſi deſiderano per ſe ſteſſe , ma per poterne piu a-
giatamente viuere , er oue queſto fine non ſeguita , poco gioua quell'altro , cioè l'hauerle ac-
quiſtate . Sono dunque lé ricchezʒe un fine non
vltimo , ma mezzano . er ſe ui dee baſtar un
coſi fatto fine a moſtrar la felicità , eccoui , che
io ui moſtrarò , che il trauaglio ſia diſſa . Per
che vedemo , che ogn'un , il qual ſi mette ad ac
quiſtar qualche faculta , o dell'animo o del corpo , il fa per poter eſſercitarla , cioè per traua-
gliare in quella faculta , trauaglia poi per gua
dagnare , guadagna per poterne viuere , Ve
dete , che in quanto all'eſſer fine , a vn medeſimo modo s'hanno il guadagno , er il trauaglio
cioè , che nel riſpetto de loro efficienti ſono fini ,
er in conſideratione de lor fini , ſono efficienti ,
er parlandone propriamente ſi puo dire , che ſo
no piu toſto mezi , che fini . Ma veggiamo ho
ra l'eſſ tto delle ricchezʒe , le quali, vuol Meſ-
ſer Lorenzo eſſer cagione di farci honorati , e for
niti d'amici ; ma in quanto all'amicitia , non

che d'amicitia neſſuna : ma anchora di continue nimicitie grandiſſima cagione , dandoci
non ſolamente d'inimici aſſai , ma che peggio è ,
di quelli , chi ſotto la ſembianʒa di voler ben ,
a ſpada tratta nimici ſono . De veri amici poi
non ſolamente non dandoci neſſuno : ma facendo anchora , che ſe qualchun ſe ne ſia , a niun
partito il ſappiamo conoſcere da quello , che fin-
ge . Ma per non moſtrarmi io vn di quei poco
amoreuoli amici , vi concederò queſto , er per
dir il vero . non ſo come acconciamente negarlo,
che le ricchezze ſiano ben cagione di qualche felicità : ma che ne volete inferire ? che ſiano poi
poi d'eſſa felicità ? eccoui che l'eſſerne eſſe cag-
ne , non che vi gioua niente a prouar queſto , ma
anchora v'impediſce aſſai . Et per certo io per
me a dimoſtrare , che le ricchezze non foſſero
la felicita iſteſſa , non ne cercarei altro piu chia
ro argomento che l'eſſer elle vn inſtrumento di
quella , concioſia che non ſia mai poſſibile , che
l'inſtrumento ſia vna coſa medeſima , con la co
ſa operata , et coſi le ricchezʒe , per eſſer cagione
della felicità non ſon coſe vnite con la felicità ,
non piu che il legnaiuolo con la caſa . Vedete

dunque M. Lo. che non v'è riuſcito punto, quan
to intorno al fine er l'effetto delle ricchezʒe ci
hauete ragionato , er però , recandoui le molte
parole in vna , vi dico , che in quel voſtro coſi
proliſſo diſcorſo , non hauete (a mio giuditio)
fatto niente . Per certo (diſſe il S. Piero) o che
egli non habbia fatta coſa veruna , o ſe n'la fat
ta neſſuna , voi l'hauete coſi disfatta , che non
ne reſta pur, vn minimo ſegno , diſorte ch'io mi
ſto con gran paura , non forſe M. Lorenzo , laſciando (pro derelicto) queſte ſue ricchezʒe , ci
venga adoſſo per torre a qualchun di noi la ſua
felicità in iſcambio di quelle . Di queſto , diſſe
M. Lorenzo , neſſun di voi non habbia paura ,
er voi S. Piero , manco di tutti gli altri , che
per certo io non ſono per tramutarmi alla voſtra
felicità , fin che non habbia deliberato di laſcia
re (pro derelicto) co i denari il ceruello inſieme . Ma perche vi vedo io pur troppo apparee
chiati ad hauer queſte ricchezʒe , come per a-
bandonate dal patrone , io per faruene fede che
non mi ſia anchora , per abandonarle, riſponderò
a quanto l'è ſtato incontra oppoſto , mantenen-
dole et del fine , et dell'effetto (ſi come hò fatto ſin

qui) per la uoſtra felicità . Sappiate, perciò S.
Carlo, che doue voi contra il fine, riſpondete,
che ſiano vn fine non da ſe iſteſſe però . ma con ri
ſpetto d'altro, & contra all'effetto, che queſto
le conuiene piu toſlo, per vno ſtrumento, della
felicità ch'ella felicità iſteſſa, io vi niego et l'un
& l'altro . Et chi ſarà colui tanto groſſo come a concederui che le ricchezze ſi deſiderino per
il fine del viuere ? atteſo, quanto piu volentie
ri le conſeruino g l'huomini, che non le ſpendono
nelle coſe biſognoſe alla vita, & che (doue il fi
ne è quello, il qual acquiſtato fa ceſſare le noſtre
attioni) trouandoſi vn huomo coſi accommoda
to delle ricchezze che, per queſto voſtro fine, ba
ſterebbe a ben mille perſone, non rimanga però
d'acquiſtarle, anzi il faccia piu che mai . Ma
oltre a queſto, quando il fine delle ricchezze foſ
ſe il poterne viuere, mi pare (come ogni agente
deſidera ſempre il piu che ſi puo d'appreſſarſi al fi
ne) che tra le ſpecie delle ricchezze, quelle ſopra
le altre ci doueſſero eſſer care, le quali immedia
te, & (in actu) conſtituiſcono il noſtro viuere, come ſono il frumento, il vino, i buoi, &
coſe ſimili, ma da queſte vedete che diſcoſtia-

moci ſempre, riducendole in contanti d'oro, i
quali delle coſe neceſſarie al viuere, non conſtituiſcono (in actu) neſſuna, come che in potenza (ſecondo ſolete voi, tra noi filoſofare della
materia prima) tutte ne contengono . A que
ſla groſſa filoſofia di M. Lorenzo, ridendo il S.
Aleſſandro, ch'haurebbe mai creduto diſſe, che
M. Lorenzo, ſentiſſe tanto auanti nelle coſe di
filoſofia, eccoui, come egli in queſte poche paro
le intorno alla materia, s'ha ſcoperto vn filoſo
fo aſſai materiale . Et come volete (riſpoſe M.
Lorenzo) ch'io pratticando con voi. gia ſono tan
ti anni non ne rieſca almeno mezo filoſofo ? perche no replicò, il S. Aleſſandro, poi che noi,
vſando vn altretanto con uoi, non ne ſiamo per
tanto diuenuti mezo ricchi, le ricchezze, diſſe,
M. Lorenzo, ſono coſe piu difficili ad impren-
der, che non è la filoſofia, ma laſciate di gratia
andar queſto, ne mi ſiate cagione, con queſti
mezo filoſofi, et mezo ricchi, di laſciare la mia
riſpoſta mezo fornita, per tornar dunque alla
prima parte del mio ragionamento, ui dico S.
Carlo, che doue io diceſſi, che la felicità a buona ragione foſſe da metter nelle ricchezze, co-

C iiii

---

me quel bene, il quale nella ſua natura generale contenga realmente gli altri, voi mi ſalite
adoſſo, con vna voſtra loica inferendo che ſe ſie
no l'inſtrumento di felicità non ſaranno mai la
felicità iſteſſa . Ma vedete, che non v'ho detto coſi io, che le ricchezze, come vno inſtrumen
to, producono l'honore, ouer il potere, ma come
vn bene piu aſſoluto, nella lor propria natura
contengono queſti duoi altri . Et però, doue l'in
ſtrumento & la coſa operata, come dite voi,
ſon coſe ſeparate, le ricchezze, & queſte due
qualità, come v'ho moſtrato io, ſon coſi vnite
che cominciano, durano, & ceſſano inſieme.
Manifeſto è dunque, che le ricchezze ſon
cagione elle d'honore, & di potere, non a quel
modo, ch'el inſtrumento è cagione della coſa o-
perata, Sed ut totum eſt cauſa ſuæ partis .
Et però il dire, che le ricchezze ci rendono felici per mezo d'honore ò di potere, non è altro, che
vn dire, che il fanno per loro iſteſſe, & il negar queſto ſarebbe, come ſe negaſſe qualchun,
a quel voſtro legnaiuolo hauerne edificata la ca
ſa da ſe ſteſſo, perche l'haueſſe fabricata coll'aiu
to delle mani . E pur oſtinato, diſſe il S. Car-

lo, queſto auocato delle ricchezze . Ma ſtate-
ui vn poco a uedere, che bel guadagno ne farà.
Non mi vuole concedere, che le ricchezze s'ac-
cattano pel fine di poterne viuere, perche (dice
egli) gli huomini le appetiſcono oltre, che a que
ſto fine non gli biſognerebbe . Ma queſto che gli
gioua, a prouar, che per ſe ſteſſe s'acquiſtano,
Niente certo . Perche tutte quelle ricchezze,
che fuor della neceſſità di viuere ſono bramate,
chiaro è, che non per ſe ſteſſe elle, ma per honore ſono deſiderate . Et per che altro fine (poi
che non direte gia mai credo, che il facciano
ſenza proporſene un fine) credete uoi, che gli huo
mini ragunino cotante ricchezze, ſe non per pre
ferirſi a quelli, che non ne hanno tante, il quale
affetto di ricchi fattamente hanno eſpreſſi i gre
chi, mettendo loro per quella parola (arricchir-
ſi) quel ſuo πλεονεκτειν) Quaſi voleſſero dire,
che l'aricchirſi non ſia altro in effetto, che vn
poſſeder piu de gli altri . Che ſe in queſta parti
tione delle ricchezze penſaſſero gli huomini ad
vna proportione Arithmetica, facilmente
ſe ne contentarebbono, trouandoſi hauerne,
piu che ad un huemo ſolo in parte ſua non toc-

cherebbe. Ma perche gli pare, che in questa di
stributione, quasi con una proportione Geome-
trica, s'attende all'egualita, non del numero,
ma della degnita delle persone, sperando con ha
uerne piu de gli altri, apparer piu degni di quelli a niun conuenuole termine si lasciano star con
tenti. Ma lasciamogli, star noi, per ritornar
ci a quello, che ultimamente vi replico M. Lorenzo, cioè, che le ricchezze non come un instrumento son cagione dell'honore, & del potere, per esser si queste due qualita nella istessa na
tura di quelle, doue l'instrumento, & la cosa
operata sempre siano cose separate. Ma questo chi gli concederebbe. Non io certo. Perche vedo bene, che le ricchezze & i suoi effetti,
siano cose, non solamente tanto distinte, come
l'instrumento, & la cosa operata, ma piu anchora. Perche doue di quelli, utrique possint
simul esse, le ricchezze & i loro effetti a nessun patto incontrarsi possono, anzi il far dell'un
è drittamente il disfar dell'altro. Guardate
pero a tutti gli effetti o piacere, che ci arrecano
le ricchezze, scorgeretcui bene che mai non ne
fanno nulla senza struggere, & consumare se

stesse, inanzi che quelli pur cominciano ad essere. Et volendo M. Lorenzo, che io gli dimo-
stri questo faccia un poco portar qui un cente-
naio de suoi scudi, & io con un bel esperimento
gli disegnarò all'occhio, del come i danari spa-
riscono sempre, inanti che qualche piacere ne co
mincia a spuntare. Risero a questo tutti, per
veder, in che modo M. Lorenzo, a questa posta delli scudi si ristrinse nelle spalle. Et doppò
alquanto il S. T. Moro ridendo anchora egli, S.
Carlo, disse, andate pur su, perche il volerci in
dug iar per questi scudi mi par che sarebbe uno
aspettar indarno. In buona fe che si, disse M.
Lorenza, perche io son piu tosto per conceder al
S. Carlo, un argomento intiero, che pur un
mezo scudo per farne di questi suoi esperimenti.
A Vostra posta, disse il S. Carlo. Ma gia che
Voi sete tanto discortese dei Vostri scudi io per
far il somigliante ne miei argomenti senza ha
uerui piu rispetto veruno sforzaroui in due paro
le a consentirmi, che la felicita non sia da met-
terenelle ricchezze, lequali, so ben che mi concederete, che si desiderano, o per rispetto di qual
che altro bene, o uero per se stesse. Se per altro

bene s'appetiscono cotal bene, sarà cosa piu prin
cipale, che non sono le ricchezze istesse, & per
consequentia piu degna di metterne la feli-
lita, si come sempre il fine è piu nobile di quel
lo, a cui le per fine. Se direte, che si desidera
no per se stesse, senza ricercarne altra com-
modita, eccoui che questo (come sapete) non è
altro, che una estrema auaritia & se volete
ci dare un auaro per il piu felice fra gli huomi
ni saria a se un bel paradosso. Perche di costui nessun dubita, che non sia il piu infelice,
et disgratiato, che viua. Allhora M. Lor. s'io
(disse) non hauessi paura del S. M. non forse egli
ne prendesse sospetto di me, di essermi un di quel
li io stesso, direi pure, che gli auari per conto di
questa vita fossino i piu felici huomini del mon
do, A questo ridendo il S. T. Moro, M. Lorenzo disse parlate pure, & state sicuro, che uoi
non possiate mai dir cosa: che mi facesse sospi-
care di uoi che foste auaro. A questo sorriden
dosi un poco gli altri, & tacendone ogn'un, S.
Carlo, Signori, disse, non aspettiate, credo, che
io mi metta piu oltra a contrastare con M Lo
renzo, contra a cui io non sò quello, che io mi

posso fare di piu, che non gl'ho, di gia fatto re
candolo ad una tanta inconuenienza, come è
questa di volere dire, che gli auari sono i piu fe
lici. I quali, lasciamo stare, la lor dannabi
le conditione nell'altra vita, ma eccoui, che an
chor in questa mai non gustano, o di piacere, o
di dolcezza alcuna, ma possisi in una grandis
sima douitia, come di Tantalo scriuono i Poeti,
supportano un digiuno insopportenole, qui M. Lo
renzo riuolto al S. Carlo, non è, disse, cosa tan
to assorda, come ui pare, il daruigli auari per
i piu felici. Et prima il lor dannabile stato nel
l'altro mondo non faegli niente ad improuerar
la sua grande felicita in questo, anzi la proua as
sas. Perche, come uoi sapete, non c'è cosa piu
nimica alla felicita dell'altra uita, ch'il goder-
ne troppo in questa. Ma che voi gl'hauete tolto ogni dolcezza di questa uita anchora per non
mangiar loro, si dilicatamente, come sonno
gli altri, in questo mi marauiglio assai del fat
to Vostro, hauendoci noi sin qui posta la felicità
non nei piaceri del corpo, ma nel diletto dell'ani
mo. Della quale determinatione di piacere, non
Volendoui noi dipartirui adesso per farmi dispia

cere, forza è mi concediate, gl'auari essere i piu
felici de altri. Perche doue gli altri spenden-
do i danari, ne fruiscono quei brieui piaceri, li
quali ci arrecano i sensi del corpo, gli auari con
seruandogli, sene pascono d'vn continuo diletto d'animo, il quale gli arreca quel giocondo
pensar ad vna tanta infinita di danari, di
quanta si vedono forniti. Et volendo vedere, quanto questo piacere sia piu compiuto di
quell'altro, guardate, che gli auari, a piaceri
di quelli, che si danno buon tempo, non hanno
inuidia alcuna, doue all'incontro coloro delle
grandi ricchezze de gli auari, mai non si ri-
cordano senza struggersi per il troppo desiderio,
che n'hanno. A questo ridendo il S. Carlo,
voi vi ingannate di gran lunga, disse, nel fatto de gli auari, pigliando vna perturbatione
per vn diletto dell'animo. Ma in questo caso
non voglio ragionar piu a lungo, per non far
torto a gli giudicii di questi altri Signori.
Questo vi voglio bene chiarire, non tanto per
risponderui, quanto per ragionar vn poco della
cagione della istessa auaritia, che l'auaritia non
procede, come a voi pare, da qualche diletto

di sentirsi abondare, ma d'vna certa piu presto
paura di trouarsi mancare al uiuere. La quale opinione prima mi fa parer probabile la pre-
sumptione, che naturalmente ogn'un sente in
se stesso di vna vita lunghissima. Perche non
sapendo a punto nissun di noi il termine pre-
scritto alla sua vita, sempre se ne va passando
con la speranza et questo, et quello, senza a fermarsi ad alcuno, non piu, che se fosse immorta-
le. La qual opinione, con maggior efficatia
infissa nella mente loro, li quali con le ricchezze
piu s'impacciano, ueramente è la cagione di non
poter loro ne suoi pensieri, piu constituire termino alle ricchezze, che alla uita non constituisco-
no, donde temendo sempre, non forse mancando
gli all'ultimo, in quell'estremo della uita haues-
sero a restar miseri, tutta la sua uita reggono
miserissimi. Et non potendo comprendere al-
l'occhio così lo sminuimento della uita, come del
l'acceruo, mai non si lasciano credere, che di pari contendono al fine, ma chioriti poi di questo,
et giunti al fine della uita, veggiamo, che
spendono, et spandono sconciamente, come
poco fa un nostro uicino, il qual per tutta la vi

ta mai non s'haueua dato buon tempo del mondo vegnendo a morte si fece riempir tutto d'a-
romati fin alla gola, di che leggiadramente vn
nostro compagno, eccoui disse, che questo buono
huomo mai non uisse inanti, che morisse. In
questo passo, disse il S. Piero, son pur contrarii
i essempii, come n'è uno di quel uecchio notaio,
il qual hauendo nel suo testamento contato partitamente la spesa della sua sepoltura, ricordandosi fra le altre cose, di hauerui messo sei
braccia di tela per inuolgersi dentro, come è la
vsanza nostra nel sotterrare i morti, disse a
gli essecutori, che cinque braccia con tre quarte
gli basterebbono, comparandone a buona misu-
ra. Risero a questo tutti, e non dopo guari, il
S. Carlo credo disse, che, esaminandolo bene,
ci rauuedremo, che S. Piero c'hauesse qui falsi-
ficato vn testamento, ma a sua posta, io voglio
andar pur dietro a questo felice di M. Lorenzo,
ne lo voglio lasciare, sin che non l'habbia condotto sino alla forza. Dico dunque che questi pazzi degli auari, si conducono a tanta bestialità,
tirati piu tosto d'una certa paura di qualche
mancamento, che d'alcun diletto d'abondanza.

ilche

ilche mi par assai manifestamente esser da comprendere anchora alla lor chiera istessa, la qual
ogn'un vede quanto piu rassembra vn pauroso
sospetto, che qualche altro allegro pensiero. Ma
oltre ad ogn'altro mi conferma questa opinione,
il veder quella lor desperata morte, alla quale
spesso si conducono sospinti da qualche perdita di
danari, perche non è da credere, che il solo priuarsi del bene, senza aggiungerui anchora qualche gran male, fosse bastante a condurgli ad
vno così fiero proponimento. Ma credo (quasi
confermandogli gia la fresca disgratia quello,
di che sempre slati erano paurosi) cioè di man-
carli al viuere, per non voler vna lunga, et
misera vita con laccio cercano di scurtarsela.
Come d'uno mi conto hieri il S. Paolo, ilquale
volendo appiccarsi, et non hauendo alle mani
nè laccio, nè altro instrumento, atto a far vn
simile effetto, s'ando ad vna bottega per com-
prarsene vno, et non potendone hauer per manco di duoi soldi, disse, partendosi in gran cruc-
cio, duoi soldi per vn laccio eh?; Dunque l'appiccarsi non fa, senon per gentil'huomini mi pare. Pur trouarò ben vn laccio a miglior mer-

D

cato, ò al sangue della Virgine, che non m'ap
piccarò altramente io. A questo orgoglioso
auaro, che per dispetto non si volse appiccare, tut
ti se ne rideuan tanto che tutti i denti si sarebbon
lor potuti ben trarre, & motteggiando poi
insieme sopra questo fatto, diceuano, chi, che
questo fosse vn bel caso, doue la troppa auaritia
hauesse condutto l'auaro ad appiccarsi, & a
scamparsene ad vn tratto. Et chi forte incel
pando quello, che teneua la bottega, disse, che
si mostrò troppo discortese verso questo auaro,
& che douesse calar almanco vn soldo dell'ordi
nario per fargli piacere, & che egli saria ben
fatto, che l'auaro tolto in credenza quel laccio,
s'hauesse appiccato, senza pagargliene altra
mente. Ma poi che sopra questo caso hebbero ri
so, & cianciato a bastanza, M. Lorenzo, ri
uolto al S. Carlo, non posso consentirui, disse,
che l'auaritia si nasca d'altro, che d'un gran
de diletto di sentirsi abondare, che se (come noi
volete (procedesse da paura di mācare i qualche
cosa valeuole alla vita, saria questo piu proprio
vitio alli giouani, che si trouano nel primo passo
della vita, che alli vecchi, che se ne vedono ar

riuati all'ultimo. Ma tutto il dì, vi si vede il
contrario, & volendone cercare la cagione,
vederete, quanto per me la faccia. Et questa
sia che i giouani in tanta scielta de piaceri,
poco conto ne tengono di questo, doue i vecchi,
per lor indispositione de i sensi, priui d'ogni altro
piacere, a questo, che solo glie rimaso, s'appi
gliano, Anzi alla lor chiera (dite voi) si
vede ben, che stanno in paura, & non in gioia,
& questo chi nol sa, come proceda dal vi
tio dell'età piu tosto, che da altro. Vltimamen
te la violenta & spaurosa morte, che spesso san
no, non vedo gia io, che vi vaglia a stabiliru il
vostro assunto, nè manco m'intendo quel, che
vi volete dire in quella vostra distintione, fra
il solamente priuarsi del bene, & aggiungerui
appresso del male. Perciò che a me pare, che
nessun male non sia gia altro, che vn priuarsi
del ben contrario, come la cecità è vn priuarsi
della vista, la seruitù, della libertà, la ma
lattia della sanità. Et vedete mò, che nell'al
tro mondo il sommo male non è altro, che vn
priuarsi del sommo bene. Et così in caso no
stro l'auaro per sentirsi priuare del sommo bene

D	ii

di questa vita si conduce al sommo male, cioè
la morte. Alhora il S.T. Moro (hauendo
non senza riso sentito questo discorso sopra la se
licita de gli auari,) quanto ci ha vccellato,
disse, Messer Lorenzo, il quale con sue indo
rate promesse persuadendo di volerci inuia
re fin al sommo bene, c'ha messi a rischio di dar
di testa nel sommo male. La onde parmi
manco male, che non lo lasciamo andare piu
inanzi, essendolo fin qui andaro sempre di mal
in peggio. Perche hauendo prima egli, qua
si con picciolo fallo, posta la felicità nelle ricchez
ze, dapoi con via piu maggiore, fra lespecie di
quelle, i danari ci ha dato per le prime, i quali
non vogliono nulla, se non per rispetto delle al
tre, & finalmente col piu straboccheuole erro
re di tutti gli altri, fra i possessori di quei dana
ri, quelli c'ha messo per i piu felici, che non gli
adoprano, talmente che questa felicità a punto
n'è riuscita a quel termine, che hieri non l'al
tro riusci il fatto di M. Patensono, (era costui
il pazzo del S. Moro) il quale stando alla mia
tauola desinandoui noi, visto vn gentil'huo
mo fra gli altri col naso oltra il douer grosso, poi

ch'hebbe vn poco guatato nel viso al sangue di
me, disse, che que gentil'huomo ha vn terri
bile pezzo di naso, et qui facendoci vista ogni
vn dì non hauerlo inteso, per non suergognar il
buon gentil'huomo, M. Pattensono accorgendo
si a questo di hauer fatto errore, per indrizzar
lo a buon segno, mentiua per la gola mi, disse,
a dire, che il naso di quel gentil'huomo fosse co
tanto grosso a fede di gentil'huomo ch'egli è pur
picciolo. A questo ogn'un con la maggior vo
glia del mondo di ridere, accennaua, che il paz
zo fosse cacciato fuora. Ma M Pattensono non
volendo per l'honor suo, che il fatto stesse a que
sto termine (perche oltre ad ogn'altra sua vir
tù, di questa piu si soleua vantare, che quan
to si togliesse a fare, sempre gli veniua fatto in
destro) per acconciar dunque la cosa in guisa,
che stesse bene, fattosi al capo della tauola, in se
de mia vi voglio ben dire vna cosa, disse, quel
gentil'huomo non ha niente di naso egli. A que
sto fatto di M. Pattensono, tanto fu riso, che
ogni un n'era quasi per smascellarsi, ma poi che
tanto hebbero riso, che ne eran diuenuti stracchi,
il S. Alessandro ridendo anchora egli, la

D	iii

85

diuerfità, diffe, fra la bruttezza di quel nafo
& la bellezza di quefte ricchezze è, ch'in quel
la M. P. quanto piu l'andaua fminuendo, piu
l'accrefceua, & in quefta quanto piu M. Loren
zo la va crefcendo, piu la fcema. Ma quefto è
ben ftato vostra colpa S. Carlo, perche in veri
tà voi vi fete portato troppo amicheuolmente
verfo di lui, in quefta effamina delle ricchezze,
di forte che mi mette nel capo qualche foffet-
to, non voi vene afpettiate niente per guiderdo
ne. Io non gli volfi mai conceder io, ne ancho
quefto, che le ricchezze s'habbiano d'accettar-
fi per vn inftrumento di felicità, effendo (come tutto il dì fi vede) adoperatrici d'infelicità grandiffima, & effendo la pouertà, come
fapete che l'è, amica & intrinfeca della felicità, ne feguita, che le ricchezze nimici ne fono. In quefto (rifpofe il S. Carlo) non fon per
confentirui mai io, nè mi ftarebbe ben di farlo,
hauendomi gia meffa la felicità nell'honore, il
che non dubito ancho di prouarui, quando a me
toccherà di dire. Effendo dunque la liberalità
quella virtù, che oltre ad ogni altra ne conduce
all'honore, & le ricchezze il proprio ftrumen-

to della liberalità, chi non le preferirebbe alla
pouertà, la quale non è altro, che vn priuarfi
delle ricchezze, & cofi di liberalità vn impedi
mento grandiffimo. Ne mi vogliate dir qui,
che cofi il pouero, come il ricco poffa effere libe
rale, perche non potendo anchora di pari adope
rarla (effendo la fomma lode, la quale dicem
mo noi, che fia la felicità, nell'operare) chiaro
è, che non poffa di pari effer felice. Quantunque (diffe il S. Aleffandro) fia men che ragio
neuole, che io habbia a difender la pouertà al tri
bunale della vostra felicità, et maffimamente
hauendone io gia conftituita vn'altra, niente
dimanco temendo, che quefta cattiuella per ef
fer pouera di leggieri non trouera auocato ve
runo, voglio piu tofto che ella fia in parte mal
diffefa, che del tutto abandonata. Se voi credete dunque Signor Carlo, che le ricchezze
fiano il folo mezo, per lo quale fi poffa vfar la
liberalità, per certo mal vi ricordate dello effempio di quel Eutrapele, il quale le donaua
alli nimici, feminandole materia piu atta a
far vendetta, che ad vfare liberalità. Et per
certo la pouertà come in neffun altro conto, cofi

ne ancho in quefto, di moftrarci liberali non ha
diffetto neffuno. Ilche con una grandiffima
liberalità ben moftrò quel pouero Filofofo, ilqua
le al fuo maeftro che gl'infegno i precetti di fi-
lofofia poi che la fortuna, diffe, mi ha fatto co
fi pouero, che non ho cofa al mondo che darti, ec
coti, ecco che io ti dono me fteffo. et io, diffe l'al
tro, a ti tene renderò migliore. Vedete, come
i cuori gentili al difpetto di fortuna, trouaron
modo & al donar liberalmente & al rendere
il beneficio con vantaggio. Ma non voglio qui
uincerui con gl'effempii ò con autorità, ma con
quel mezo, che ha piu forza, di tutti, dico,
la ragione ifteffa. Sappiate però, che la libera
lità non è altro, che un certo propofito di volere
gratificar gli altri, con quel che è noftro. Le
cofe dunque, con le quali ci vogliamo moftrare
liberali, quanto fono piu noftre, tanto piu uiua
mente & compiutamente fanno quefto effetto.
Et quanto, credete uoi, che le virtù, la fcien-
za, et altre cofe interne fon piu proprie dell'huo
mo, le quali dentro a fe fteffo poffiede, che non
fono le ricchezze & altre cofe accidentali, che li
vengono di fuori. Et non uoi forfe mi credia-

fe d'hauerui detto quefto, per qualche loica piu
fottile, che vera, cercate l'antiche hiftorie, &
vedrete, che tutti quegli, rimangono con piu
chiara memoria di fua liberalità, li quali di
qualche lor bene interiore fono ftati liberali, la
doue fcura è la fama di coloro, che con danari
l'hãno fatto. Et però vedete, che quel giudiciofo
nouellatore trattando nell'vltima giornata del
la liberalità, volendo che le nouelle andaffero
fempre auanzando l'una l'altra con maggior
paragone di magnificenza, comincia prima
d'un Re, che donò vn fuo forzier carico d'ogni
forte di ricchezza, fcendendo dipoi a quelli,
che della loro propria lode, della lor virtù, &
della vita ifteffa fono ftati liberali. Le cofe in
terne adunque fono piu efficaci in adoperar la li
beralità, che non fono le ricchezze, & con-
fequentemente il pouero verrà ad effer cofi facen
te a far quefto effetto, come il ricco. Ma lafciamo andare il mezo, che ne conduce all'honore, et paffiamo drittamente all'honore ifteffo. Et che direte uoi, fe ui fia manifefto, che la
pouertà da fe fteffa fia baftante a farci honora
ti, & le ricchezze nò? Ilche per farui inten-

dere , sappiate , prima , che ogni honore si ne
da ad ogn'uno per merito di qualche virtù , o
dell'animo , oueramente del corpo . Essendo a-
dunque le ricchezze cose del tutto separate , et
dell'animo humano , et del corpo , chiaro è ,
che quantunque come per segno lo pot sino far
segnalato , non haurebbono però forza di farlo
honorato , come per merito . Et pero nessun si
può presumer punto piu uirtuoso dal solo hauer
le ricchezze , ma di non hauerle , si bene , come
si uede espressamente in quel nobilissimo consolo
di Valerio Publicola , al quale uoi sapete , come
è stato riputato per grandissimo honore l'esser
trouato tanto pouero , che tutto l'hauer suo ne
ancho alla sepoltura gli bastasse , di sorte , che
quel generoso consolo dal non hauer , donde si fa
cesse honoreuolmente sepellire , ha fatto la sua se
poltura per tutto l'uniuerso , honoreuole Et si
milmente Crate filosofo , il quale possedendo
le ricchezze non s'era mai conosciuto per huomo
di si alto spirito , poi pure , che l'hebbe gittate
nel mare , fu tenuto per uirtuosissimo . Vedete
adunque S. Carlo , poi che uoi ui haute tolto
il carico , in che modo uolete difender le ricchez

ze in questo articolo . Perche a me pare cosa fa
cilissima a prouare , che come il solo mancare le
ricchezze genera da se stesso qualche opinione di
altezza d'animo , cosi il tenerle da per se consi-
derato faccia certo sospetto d'una non sò che vil
tà , et d'esser da poco . Et questo mi basta alla
difesa della pouertà nel tribunale nostro Perche
s'io hauessi a difenderla nel mio , l'haurei prepo-
sta all'istesse ricchezze , per altri piu saldi rispet
ti , come per esser la cagione ad vn huomo di conoscer se stesso , doue le ricchezze ne hanno vna
naturale dimenticanza , per dar questa il riposo all'animo , doue quelle portano seco ben mille
disagii . Vltimamente per esser quella vno sta
to pien di speranza di andar in meglio , et que
ste di paura di non andar in peggio , stando si (co
me sa ben M. Lorenzo) di continuo solleciti i
ricchi , et i poueri sicuri , come ben disse Iuue-
nale , Cantabit vacuus coram latrone Viator .
Queste dico et altre simili cose vi voleua ben
dire , le quali per adesso lascio tutte , per non par
lar fuor di proposito . Alhora essendo il S. Car
lo quasi in atto di rispondere , M. Loren in quel
punto interrompendolo , io non sono vso , disse ,

d'un mio auuersario vecchio farmi un nuouo a-
uocato . Et però credo . che sarebbe manco male , che fossi a far il fatto mio io stesso , non for
se il S. Carlo , si porti in questa lite a quel modo ,
che sogliono le cattiue femine nelle mischie i loro mariti , a quali esse danno delle buone , gri-
dando tuttauia fieramente contra i nimici loro . L'esserui (disse il S. T. Moro) troppo auez
zo a queste triste , ui fa sospettoso anchora , la
doue non ne ne saria punto bisogno . Ma fida-
teui in questo bisogno del S. Carlo , perche egli
sopra di me fara da buono et leale procuratore .
Altramente uoi potrete ad ogni hora ben sal-
uarui da lui . Son contento , disse M. Lor. poi
che voi me ne fate sicuro , dandomi noi stesso
qui per fideiussore . Non ui fa mestiere , disse
il S. Carlo , sicurtà niuna , massimamente sopra
di vn (come in questa lite mi tengo io) procuratore in rem suam . Ma pure io , per poter di-
scordar dal S. Alessandro , son disposto d'accordarmi con uoi d'ogni cosa , vedete adunque S.
Alessandro , che come ch'io vi conceda , che ol
tre alle ricchezze siano dell'altre cose atte a mo-
strarcene liberali , e che quelle cose interne fusse

ro per efficaci a questo fine che l'esterne non sono ,
non è però , che per questo conto il ricco per hauer commodità et di queste et di quelle non stia
meglio , che il pouero , il quale di queste sole si
troua capace , essendo tutte et due necessarie
a questo effetto , l'interne , a farlo piu viuamen
te a chi ne bisogna l'esterne per farlo piu spesso ,
et ad ogni uno , et però vedete , che quel uostro nouellatore volendo in quella nouella di Na
than , secondo che io ne giudico , farci un ritrat
to di somma liberalita , l'introduce nell'un et
l'altro di questi duoi beni liberalissimo . Vedete
adunque S. Alessandro , che l'hauer le ricchez
ze gioua assai ad usar la liberalità , doue il man
car ne è vn impedimento grandissimo . Ma
vogliamo hora vedere , come sia uero quello , che
vltimamente ci haute detto , cioè che la pouer
tà per se stessa senza altro rispetto o mezo , ci pos
sa fare honorati . Nel quale vostro assunto poco ui giouano i duoi essempii di quel pouero Consolo et di quel filosofo senza danari . Perche ha
uendoci uoi a produrre la pouertà senza ogni al
tro rispetto , eccoui , che l'hauete sempre congiun
ta con una altra qualità , come con l'authorità

d'un Consolo, o con la sapienza d'un Filosofo. Et
vedete, come in questi duoi essempii la pouertà
non con la sua propria lode, ma con auanzar la
congiunta qualità, gli ha fatto tanto honoreuoli. Perche niun di questi duoi è stato lodato,
come il piu pouero huomo di tutti gli altri, ma
l'un come il piu dritto & leale Consolo, l'altro
come il piu sapiente filosofo di tutti. Ma se ci
mettete inanzi duoi, sconosciuti per ogni altro rispetto, senon per questo, d'esser l'un pouero, l'altro ricco, vedrete a rouescio di quel, che
ne dite voi, che il solo hauer danari genera una
certa presontione di prudenza, & di consiglio,
doue il mancarne fa sospetto, di vna non so che
trascuraggine, & di mal gouerno, ilche benche da se stesso sia assai manifesto, da questo an
chor egli si riesce piu chiaro, che ogniun a domandar danari in prestanza, ne sente vna naturale turbatione di uergogna, et di schifezza,
la quale senza dubbio non procede d'altro, che
da queste prime impressioni, le quali nelli animi uostri partorisce il solo non hauer danari.
Vedete adunque, che in quanto all honore le ricchezze non solamente vagliono piu che la po-

uertà non uale, ma che quelle giouano, & questa nuoce piu, che non gioua. Et qui facendo il
S. Carlo vn poco di pausa, M. Lorenzo non aspet
tando troppo, a che douesse riuscire, non aspetta
ua mai altro, disse, di questa procura. se non,
che non hauesse d'andar piu auanti, che al S.
Carlo per la sostentatione del suo honore facesse
di bisogno. Ma a me piu pesano i danari, che di
lasciarne la difesa mezo fornita. A proposito adunque di ciò, che il S. Alessandro facendo uista di non uoler dire, il dicea pure, gli nego il tutto, & in prima, (ilche sopra il resto
mi parcua assordo) che il ricco stia al disagio,
& il pouero al riposo. Et benche in questo assai mi potessi valere della uoce istessa, chiamandosi i ricchi huomini agiati, pure lasciado ogni
sottilità, e uegnendo simplicemente in sul fatto, questo solo domando a i uostri giudicii, se tutti i disagii, li quali si fingono nelle ricchezze
siansi d'agguagliare con quella sciagura, che
ogn'hora prouano i cattiuelli di questi poueri nel
poter così malageuolmente regger la uita loro, gridandogli adosso da un canto i figliuoli
ignudi, dall'altro gl'impertuni creditori Et se

quelli in questo mezzo (come dice il S. Alessandro) si mettano a cantare, saria ella, a fe,
vna braua musica. Ma quel versetto (adesso che me lo ricordo) licentia i poueri di cantare in presenza di ladri, pure io non uorrei gia
esser di quelli. i quali ben possono cantare inanzi a i ladri, & pianger poi inanzi a gli huomini da bene. Hor sù, veggiamo per adesso,
come stia ben detto quello, che la pouertà sia da
esser preferita alle ricchezze; per esser quella
vno stato pieno di speranza d'andar in meglio,
& queste di paura di non andar in peggio. In
che dire, non credo, che uoi S. Alessandro hab
biate persuaso a uoi stesso, non ch'a nessun di noi.
Et come volete, che vi crediamo, che di qualche cosa sia buono lo sperarla, della quale non vi
sia meglio lo hauer la essa, non essendo poi lo spe
rare d'altro, che di hauere. Ma vedete, che
questo uostro argomento è di quelli, che uoi chia
mate Andro stephonda, volete forse (disse il
S. Piero) dire ἀντιςρέφοντα. Ma uoi nell'istesso
ἀντιςρέφιν si hauete fatto vn'antristrophe. Basta
disse, M. Lor. uoglio dire, che sia vn di quei ar
gomenti. i quali di una contrarietà prouano
vgualmente

vgualmente & l'una & l'altra parte, come
vedrete in questo. La pouertà dite uoi è migliore delle ricchezze, per essere ella vn stato di speranza d'andar in meglio, cioè, d'arricchirsi,
dunque le ricchezze dico io sono migliori, che
non è la pouertà? di rincontra dite uoi le ricchezze sono peggiori della pouertà, per esserle un sta
to pauroso di non andar in peggio, cioè d'impouerirsi. Adunque dirò io la pouertà dee esser el
la peggio, che non sono le ricchezze. Eccoui
come in questo argomento io ne posso così seruirmi come esso voi, ma per far, che la mia risposta torni al mio commodo solo, risponderoui
ad vn'altro stilo. Il pouero spera d'andar in
meglio, il ricco teme di non andar in peggio, vi
concedo, ma vi aggiungo poi questo, che la speranza d'acquistar le ricchezze, a chi non n'ha
nulla è così pouera, & la paura, di quelli che
forniti sene trouano così picciola di perderle in
qualche ben regolata republica, che nessun credo io sarà chi non s'eleggesse piu tosto quel timore, che questa speranza, non hauendo io per me
fin qui conosciuto quell'huomo, a cui non sapesse
meglio il poco temere, che lo sperar poco, essen-

E

done fra questi duoi lo sminuimento del vno, è l'accrescimento dell'altro. Tacendo qui M. Lorenzo, & riuoltosi il S. Alessandro a lui, & al S. Carlo, come se all'vno & all'altro volesse adattar la risposta, il S. T. Moro interrompendolo, vogliamo disse, se a voi anco non dispiacerà portarci con M. Lorenzo in questa causa in tale guisa qualmente vna volta il Popolo Romano portossi con vn suo reo, il quale essendo stato accusato d'un capital delitto senza punto pur garsene, fece richiesta del consolato, al quale essendogli drittamente detto di nò, peruenendolo dapoi alla difesa del delitto, il popolo vistone che in quel medesimo giudicio nel qual haueua ricerco il Consolato, a pena poteua saluarsi la testa, tanto ne diuenne pietoso, che (senza guardar piu altramente al dritto o al torto che lo fosse) li berollo, medesimamente anchora noi, mostrandoci ne piu ne manco compassioneuoli in verso di queste pouerelle ricchezze di M. Lorenzo, a vederle dopo la domanda del titolo di sommo bene, non solamente di tanto honore ributtarsi, ma ancho poste a rischio d'esser cacciate di sotto all'istessa pouertà, hauendocile in prima condene

nate hora diremo tanto, che essendone le ricchezze, & la pouerta cose da sua natura, non mi ca ne buone, ne cattiue, non esser per che da esse l'vna si teng a o piu buona, o piu cattiua dell'altra, ma che, quali s'habbiano elle da essere rispetto all'huomo, questo non fondarsi su altro che nell'huomo istesso. Et così imponendo a M. Lorenzo, che pena la confiscatione, di fatto ci leui dauanti le sue ricchezze, facciamo del luogo vacante vn presente al S. Carlo per ispiegare il suo honore, tornandolo in dietro, a continouare la richiesta della felicità, fin doue M. Lorenzo la lasciò. Io, se tenete a memoria disse M. Lorenzo, finiua la felicità, con quell'appicarsi delli auari, & se noi ritornassimo S. Carlo col suo honore sino alla forca saria egli cosa poco honoreuole, ma per lasciar nei suoi termini il fatto d'altri, & tornarmi al mio, vi dico, da douero S. T. Moro, che nella vostra sentenza mi hauete benissimo sodisfatto, che nò speraua mai altra; che la condennatoria. Hora poi che non ci và qualche pagamēto di danari, io mene chiamo appagatissimo. In quanto al leuar di quà le mie ricchezze, non vi bisogno d'astringermi

E ii

sotto pena nessuna, perche eccomi apparrecchiato di leuar di quà, non che le mie ricchezze, ma (quando voi me'l commandate) anchora le vostre, del bel presente poi ch'voi ne farete al S. Carlo, io me ne rido assai, auuisandomi come egli habbia da esser honoreuol'il presentargli un luogo, poi ch'io n'ho cauato quello, che v'era di buono. Che che si sia, disse il S. Carlo, l'accetto con tutto il cuore, & accioche io non habbia anchora a farne vn presente ad vn'altro, sì come M. Lorenzo n'ha fatto a me vno, ingegnaromi, al mio poter, di comprobarui piu saldamente il mio honore, che non v'ha fatto egli le sue ricchezze, & ben mi fa mestieri, ch'io lo faccia, perche non mi trouo io, per far questo partito così al sicuro, come facea egli, il qual, ben che non ne seppe sì fare, che le sue ricchezze vincessero la proua, non però n'ha perduto nulla, la doue io, alla vittoria del honore non potessi mancare, senza che io ne facessi gran perdita. Ma per non perder anchora il tempo, voglio senza piu oltre differirui, mostrare prima, che cosa sia l'honore, prouandoui poi, che quella cotal cosa, sia d'ogni nostra operatione, non (secondo

che fece M. Lorenzo nelle ricchezze) a qualche modo un fine, ma il vero, & vltimo fine, per il qual ogni altra cosa da noi si desidera, & oltre a che (parlandoci di questa vita) non si desidera niente. Facendomi dunque al fatto, dico, che l'honore, secondo me, non è altro, che vn preferirsi agli altri, & vn solleuarsi sopra la moltitudine per merito di qualche virtù, donde i Latini come voi sapete hanno chiamati l'honorate persone, eximiæ quasi essempte, & egregie quasi scernite, della gregge del popolazzo. Et per certo, questa c'è cosa naturalissima ad ogni un, che, per essersi vn indiuiduo in se stesso, desideri il piu che si può di trarsi fuor della moltitudine della sua specie, con qualche singolarità, per godersi piu a pieno quel suo essere indiuiduo, il che piu intrinsicamente gli tocca che non gia, l'essere di quella specie. Vedemo però, che quelli anchora, i quali sforniti si trouano di ogni commodità di farsene singolari, niente di meno in qual modo la pocchezza loro comporta, si conducono farlo, Quanti ne sono, i quali, non valendosi punto nè d'ingegno, nè di dottrina, scriuono pure, solamente per atta

E iii

care i suoi nomi alli stampati libri, & altri non
potendone pur anco tanto, per publicare i suoi
nomi, li fanno ritrarre per tutti i pareti, &
luoghi publichi della Città. Sonui anchora di
quelli, i quali, non potendo a nessun modo pa-
rarsi fuor della moltitudine, col far piu bene
delli altri si almanco s'ingegnano di farlo con
far piu male (come quel Herostrato il quale stu-
diandone d'esser conosciuto abbrucio il Tempio
di Diana.) i quali in quanto all'honore, mi
pare che escono fuor del uolgo, in quel modo, che
un semplicciotto ad un suo compagno stante in
prigione, disse d'hauerlo ad uscire, a cui lamen-
tandosi egli, dello continuo star rinchiuso, haueua anch'io soggiunse, un mio parente che ri
stette qui assai pure a l'ultimo se ne uscì egli, et
domandandogli il prigionere in che modo, era
disse cauato fuora per esserne appiccato, & a
questo essendo un poco riso, soggionse S. Carlo,
a punto quelli, che con far male, vogliono esser
conosciuti, cosi escono fuor della moltitudine, che
per conto del honore, gli saria stato piu utile, se
ui si fossero rimasi dentro. Ma lasciamo andar
questi, nella lor malhora, & torniamoci dritt

tamente a dir di coloro, i quali per mezo di qual
che virtu, cercano di farsi dauanti a gli altri,
& questo desiderio è tanto conforme con la eccellente natura del huomo, che esaminandoui
uoi tutte le fatiche & studii di quanti huomini, mai son stati al mondo, non ne trouarete,
(& sonne certo) altro fine che questo. Et primo riguardando all'eta passata, che diremo di
quel glorioso essempio di ambeduoi gli Decii, i
quali con uoltar in se stessi le sue arme, gli nimici loro hanno mandati in rotta? che di quel
lo di M. Sceuola, che l'assediata patria liberò,
cosi destramente con la sinistra mano? che di
quel Curtio, il qual cacciatosi drento all'arden
te grotta, ad una hora n'hebbe & rogum &
sepulchrum? Certamente quelli generosi spirti
in quell'estremo della uita, non poteuano sperar
ne altro guiderdone alli suoi meriti, di quello,
che solo fra tutte le cose al mondo, dura dopò la
morte anchora, dico l'honore. Ma lasciando
le cose passate riuogliamo gli occhi alle presenti
fra le quali che diremo delle gran imprese di tut
ti i Principi d'hoggidi? che? di quelle, che alle lor bisogne attendono facendo o della lor for-

E iiii

za o dell'ingegno proua? che? per recar le molte
parole in una, di quanti si mettono, o a far se
stessi le cose grandi, o uero a scriuer quelle d'altri,
per certo non altro, se non, che da honore accesi,
s'inducono a farlo. Ma troppo gran torto saria
a i uostri giudicii, se io mi mettessi a raccontar
ui cosi a lungo li essempii di coloro, i quali tanto al discoperto tendono a questo fine, & però fa
cendomi all'altra banda, di quelli dirò, i quali
al quanto maliciosetti, fattone sembiante d'an
dar drittamente al contrario fine, di nascosto si
riuoltano pure a questo, voglio dire per questo,
quelli ghiottoni de i Filosofi, li quali in ogni fat
to loro persuadeuano d'esser grandissimi sprez-
zatori de l'honore, ma guardateui bene di non
lasciarui gabbare a questi tristi, che per certo
costoro, con i suoi stracciati pannicelli piu uag
gheggiauano l'honore, che non faceuano gli altri
con i suoi rasi & ueluti. & come piu saui di
loro piu hanno recato ad effetto questo lor deside
rio, di sorte, che, doue la memoria di tutti gli
apparischenti cortegiani di quei tempi, è cosi
spenta, che non ne rimanga pur un minimo se
gno, la fama delle tasce, & li loro uillosi man-

toni, et altre sue pedocchierie resta anchor chia
rissima per tutto il mondo. Ben s'accorgeuan
i ghiotti, quanto il sprezzar ogni ornamento
del corpo, per esserlo a rouescio all'usanza del uol
go, piu gli facea separarsi da quello, che non ha
uria fatto l'apprezzarlo. Et questo certissima
mente è stato il fine, che hanno hauuti i filosofi
in quella lor affetata mendicità, & non sò che
altro fine ne sia possibile ad assignare, perche chi
uuole parere a gli altri di sprezzar l'honore non
uedo, perche altro il possa fare, che per esser ho
norato, il che non fuggi punto quel diuino giudicio di Platone. A chi uegnendosi, una
uolta a uisitare Diogene insieme con certi altri
filosofi, & hauendo egli la casa sua acconcia in
un bel modo, co i tapeti & altri fornimenti ho
noreuoli, non de l'uno & l'altro de i lati solamente, ma per il solaio anchora, Diogene ca-
minando sopra i tapeti, come solena, alla rusti
ca, eccoui, disse, ch'io calco la superbia di Platone, a cui Platone, che tu ti la calchi ben egli
è uero disse, ma poi con un'altra soperbia. Et
ben dicea il uero, perche manifesto è, che ogni
sprezzatura naturalmente dee hauer in se una

certa negligenza, & come vi si mette studio
nessuno, si può risolutamente pronunciare, che
quella non sia più oltre sprezzatura, ma più to
sto una estrema affettatione. Considerate già
la qualità di questi filosofi, che son certo che non
trouarete nessuno, il qual in alcuna schietta ma
niera si contentisse di sprezzar le cose del mondo, senza che egli con qualche strano modo il pa
lesasse anchora a gl'altri, come vedete che Cra
tes anchor egli volendo abandonare le ricchezze,
nõ se le disgombraua alla buona sì, come chi non
facesse caso di loro, ma le fece alla solenne portar
fin alla naue per gittarle nel mare, & similmen
te Diogene sprezzando i palazzi de i gran
Principi, non si ha preso alla ventura qualche
pouera capanna per stanza, ma con una sottil
malitia, un dolio, facendosi a quel modo, senza
costo, una casa famosa per tutto il giro del mon
do, doue altri con molti scudi a pena si sanno
procacciare, che le lor case riescano famose pur
per quella città doue ne stanno essi loro dentro.
In somma a i ben riguardanti il fatto de i filosofi, questa sua affettata sprezzatura d'hono
re, altro non si scorgerà in effetto, che un arden

tissimamente desiderarlo. Quel che ben mo
strò quel perspicace ingegno di Cicerone con un
suo argutissimo motto contra a quei libri che si
scriuono in dispregio de l'honore, i filosofi dic'egli
scribunt libros de contemnendo honore, scribunt
quidem, sed nomina sua inscribunt, assai chia
ro argomento, che i filosofi non per auuilire più
l'honore, ma per diuentarne essi loro più honorati, si mettono a questa fatica. Voi adunque si
gnori da questa ben ui potete scorgere tutte l'al
tre nostre attioni, quali sono, poi che quella
anchora che in apparenza si fa per fuggir l'honore, in effetto non sia fatta per altro, che per
acquistarlo. Et io con questo pregiuditio mi
pare di poter conchiudere giustissimamente che
l'honore, de tutte le nostre attioni, le quali col
studio ci mettiamo a fare, sia il uero & ultimo fine, aggiungendo poi questo, che a qualun
que di uoi si dà il cuore di produrne qualch'una
che ad altro fine di questo si habbia da referire
io di presente mi renderò per vinto. Rendeteui dunque disse il S. Piero, rendeteui, & non
ad altro che a quel Signor, il qual fa rendersi
ogniun, dico l'Amore, ne mi volete credo di-

re, che nessuno si conduca ad amare per il fine
del honore, anzi in questo l'amare porta il van
to di tutte quante l'attioni si fanno al mondo,
perche doue fra quelle non c'e nessuna, che non si
faccia per il fine d'una altra cosa, del Amore
non v'e altro fine, che l'Amore istesso. Eccoui dunque una attione, della quale l'honore,
non solamente non sia il fine, ma anchora doue
non ui s'habbia un minimo pensieruzod'ello co
me tutto il dì si uede all'istessi inamorati iquali
nelli amorosi lacci presi che si siano, lasciano l'ho
nore alla ventura. Allhora il S. Carlo sorriden
do, non espettiate S. Piero disse, ch'io per amor
vostro vi conceda cosa, che sia contra l'honor
mio. Non credete però d'hauermi persuaso con
questo essempio d'Amore, che sia fra le nostre
attioni qualche una, che si faccia per altro fine, che per honore, et in quanto a quella opposta
dell'Amore vi rispondo, primo che sono ben di
quelli i quali niegano di fatto, che l'Amare sia
attione nessuna, o l'essere amato passione, ma
tutto in contrario, in che dire mi paiono ancho
d'hauer ragione loro, non essendo altro l'amare
infatto che un certo spingersi ad amore, ne l'es

ser amato, altro, che un spingere altrui ad a-
mare. Pur pur per non parerui io troppo scarso
nell'amore misurandolo così al sottile ui concede
rò pure che sia a qualche modo una attione, ma
non di quelle libere gia ello, le quali procedono
della nostra volunta, ma di quelle constrette, la
quale ne facciamo sospinti da qualche altra ca
gione, la doue io hauendoui dato l'honore per i
fine delle nostre attioni, intendo delle volunta-
rie, le quale fattamente et propriatamente son
nostre, percio che so ben che nell'altre, quello che
ci sospinge ad operarle sia et la lor causa & il fi
ne, come de l'amore non vi è da dar altro fine,
che esso amore, ne però questo s'è un priuilegio
conceduto, come voi ve ne vantate, all'amer
solo, ma eccoui che così anchora auuiene egli a
tutte l'altre perturbationi dell'animo, che per
esserle sforzate, & non libere, non si fanno per
altro fine, che per se stesse, come vedemo che non
si teme per altro fine, che per temere, & chi
piange, non lo fa per altro fine, che per piange
re, & il somigliante si può dire del ira, del alle
grezza, & così di tutte l'altre, ma lo essempio
di queste attioni, che importa egli a prouare,

che l'honor non fia l'Vltimo fine di tutte l'attioni le quale della noftra libera Volunta procedono,
certo che niente, delle quale ui ridico che non Vi
è neffuna che fe referifca ad altro fine che ad ho-
nore.eccoui S. P.ch'io non mi uoglio rédere a que
fto uoftro gran Signore d'amore, il qual fecon-
do il Volgar motto non faria d'acettarfi per Vn
Signore ne ancho in terra di ciechi. E Vero rifpofe il S. Piero perche non regna egli fe non tra
li occhiati, ma lafciamo per hora andar l'amore, perche io non uoglio col replicarui nella materia di questa prima oppofta, cofi fermarmi
in questo, come se mi mancaffe altro, che opporre, che per certo infinite fono l'attioni, che ad
altro fine, che ad honore fi referifcono. Et que
fto potria anchò a buon conto dimoftrarui con
quel ifteffo effempio, del qual uoi ui fidafti cotanto arguendone il contrario, dico quello de i
Principi,i quali per certo in tante fuoi difturbe
et affanni, non s'hanno propofto per il principale lor fine l'honore, ma piu tofto il potere. Et
di questo, credo io, neffun dubitarà mai, che
confideri bene in che maniera i principi rifguar-
dano folamente al poterfi fottogiogar le città.

non mica curandofi del modo di farlo, fia l'honoreuole o pur Vituperofo, eccetto che Vogliamo
dir forfe, che l'ufar eglino frode inganno,et tra
dimento, il che ad Vn vil hominaccio ftaria
male, fia nelli Principi honoreuole. In questo
inganno, uoi Vingannate diffe il S. Carlo, del
qual, non è ad Vn modo da determinarfi ne
fatti di Principi, & quelli delli huomini pri-
uati, Vedete che nelle rotte delle armate, non fi
fminuifce punto la lode del uincitore, per hauer
fopra giunto l'inimico da dietro, doue ad un gen
til'huomo priuato, la fconfitta acquiftata in tal
guifa gli faria poco honoreuole, percioche nelle
priuate quiftioni, il Voler con Vantaggio o inganno fottentrar ad Vna proua, non faria altro che un diffidarfi della fua propria prodezza,
ma nella zuffa di due armate, doue fi uárii ac
cidenti di Fortuna tutto il di ne accaggiono, il
Voler appigliarfi al ficuro, fi puo dir che proce-
ceda del diffidarfi, della uirtù nò, ma della fortuna. Et non vi ricordate, come i Románi (i
quali a tutte le altre genti poffono effer per Vn pa
ragone d l come portarfi honoreuolmente in o-
gni lor fatto) nella fua ftendarda mettenano

l'infegna d'una uolpe & d'un Leone, infieme?
Volendo dir per questo, che di pari ne foffe hono
reuole cofa il Vincere, foffe o per ingegno, o per
forza, non è però difdiceuole ad un Principe, il
Volere cercare la fua cinanza, in quel modo se
ne fappia meglio re,fia pure o con inganno ouero
con tradimento. In quanto all'inganno, diffe
S. Piero, forfe che potria ftare cio che dicete uoi,
per moftrarci noi in quel conto fuperiori a gli nimici nel ingegno, ma questo non fo gia, come
fi proceda nel tradimento,il qual non fi puo dir
che fe deriuaffe dell' ingegno noftro, ma folamente della uiltà del traditore & fe Volete del
popolo Romano guardar altrefi all' imprefe loro nelle hiftorie, come alla imprefa nella ftendar
da loro, Vedreteui quanto n'hanno fchifati fem
pre il Vincere a quel modo, riputandolo alla lor
Valentia nell' arme meno che honoreuole. Del
che ben ne fono auueduti in quella lor guerra
contra i Falifci, doue, offerendogli un pedante di dargli a man falua quafi tutta la piu nobile giouentù de i nimici loro,i Romani non ten
nero tal'inuito, ma prefo lo pedante, il diedero
a i fuoi proprii fcolari a fcopare, fcriuendo poi al
                                      li fuoi

li fuoi nimici di piu cautamente guardarfi di
non effer traditi. Ma per Vfcirne horamai fuor
di quefti inganni, & tradimenti, poi che mi
hauete donata la Fortuna iftessa per Vincerui,
che non mi piglio questa occafione per i peli
della ciuffa,poi che della cicottola è fpelata ella.
Dunque, diffe M. Lorenzo, l'occafione, et io fia
mio fatti a rouefcio l'un all'altro, & con questo
fcoprito il capo, moftrò che dalla parte dauanti,non Vi s'hebbe pur Vn peluzzo. a che ridendo
ogniuno, il S. T. Moro,questo, diffe, facilmen
te Vi puo effere auuenuto da quello, che forfe la
noftra moglie Vi prende ogni tratto in quel mo
do, che fi Vuole prender l'occafione. cofi faceffe
diffe M. Lorenzo, & effendo a questo crefciuto
alquanto il rifo il S. Piero,poi che hebbe alquan
to efpettato, la caluezza di M. Loren.diffe, mi
fece preffo che trappaffar il cappelluzzo dell'occafione, ma non lafcierò mai fcamparmi Vna
cofi gran Ventura. Et che S. Carlo? Volete
Voi,poi che ci hauete meffa la felicità nella lode
della noftra Virtù, darci la Fortuna per gouer
natrice; per certo ch'io efpettaua che Voi,in que
fto paffo donefti Venire drittamente a contra-

                                            F

ria cōchiuſione, e che per far piu campo al uoſtro
honore, ilche dite voi, procede del merito noſtro
doureſti leuar di netto la Fortuna, come coſa fin
ta, accordandoui compiutamente a lor ſenno, i
quali dicono pure, che il ſauio fabrica a ſe ſteſſo
quella Fortuna, che egli vuole. Vorria diſſe
il S. Carlo, che egli coſi foſſe, ma che coſi ne ſia,
non voglio gia dire, percioche dato, che tutti gli
euenti ſi poteſſero da ſolo conſiglio tirarſi deſtra-
mente, ne ſeguitaria, che ſempre del miglior
conſiglio, ſi doueſſe riſultare vn miglior euento.
ma tutto il giorno ſe ne vede, et de i matti pen
ſieri, che rieſcono beniſſimo, & di ſaggii con-
ſiglii, che ſortiſcono vn diſgratiato fine. ne è di
cio marauiglia, atteſo che la noſtra conditione
non ſi regge ſecondo le noſtre attioni proprie ſolamente, ma anchora di quelle d'altri. ſecondo
che elle quadrano con le noſtre, & quantunque
il ſauio dalle ſue ben ne ſia egli ſicuro, che tutte
ne farà per lo migliore, pure che altri ne farà il
ſomigliante delle attioni loro, chi il sà? di ſorte che, a chi voleſſe ſterminar la fortuna ne i
caſi ſuoi, ſperandone con la ſola ſapienza di me
narli tutti per buona ſtrada, conuerrebbeci a

quel huomo, non pure di eſſer eſſo lui ſauio, ma
di procacciar altretanto de tutti gl'altri, che foſ
ſero ſauii anchora loro, il che chi ſi metteſſe a fa
re, ſaria credo coſi ſauio, come quel M. Paten
ſono. il qual per ſorte paſſato di là a queſte pa
role, ſentendoſi a S. Car. nominar tra i ſauii, fat
tagli una berettata molto alla ſolenne, gli diſſe,
che queſto era per la ſua gratia. a che ridendo
ogniun, S. Piero, poi che il riſo fu ceſſato, baſta
diſſe S. Carlo, che uoi c'hauete pure conſtituita
la Fortuna per vna Signora, & gouernatrice
delle coſe noſtre, & forſe che ſia vero anchora,
ma non vedolo gia, tenendo queſto per vero, come ſtia ſaldo il uoſtro honore. perche come volete, procedendo l'honore (come n'hauete gia de-
terminato) ſolamente del merito della noſtra
virtu, che ſi poſſa egli ſperar mai dalle coſe, che
prouengono da Fortuna, et queſto vedendo tut
to il di, che volendoci noi leuar ad alcuno ogni
merito di qualche ſuo bel detto o fatto, non di-
ciamo gia altro, che quel cotal douere hauerlo
ſi fatto a caſo, come ſe voleſſimo accennare,
che non foſſe da ſperar punto di lode dalle coſe,
che rieſcono da Fortuna. Vero è diſſe S. Car-
F ii

lo che le coſe, che ſono di qualità tale, che ſi poſſo
no ordinariamēte regolare col giuditio ſolo, ſi co
me ſono detti et ſcritti et tutti quelli atti, che ſi
poſſono fare compiutamente da vn huomo ſolo
non poſſono lodeuolmente procedere d'altro, che
da'l ſolo giudicio. ma nelli altri poi, doue con
la virtu, la fortuna ne tiene coſi gran ſtato,
che meritamente ſi è chiamata la conſorte della
virtu, il titolo dell'una & dell'altra ſe ne at
tribuiſce per grandiſſimo honore a ciaſcuno, chi
lo merita. donde per far della Fortuna, ſi come
della virtu, vn habito (il che neceſſariamente
ſi richiede nel honore, poi che neſſun giuſtamen-
te vien honorato di quel, che non ha) fra gl'al
tri titoli de i gran Principi vedete, che s'adiun
ga ancho quello, di fortunatiſſimo. Certamen
te, diſſe il S. Piero, che queſto incerto habito neſ
ſun dialettico vi concederebbe mai, uedendo co
me facilmente ſi perde, ne io anchora poſſo con-
ſentirui, che l'eſſer fortunato ſia d'accettarſi
per honore a neſſuno. il che cōcedendoui ne ſegui
tarebbe, che il contrario foſſe dishonore, & a
queſto modo vn huomo, benche virtuoſiſſimo,
cangiante la fortuna il ſtile tanto de l'honor ſuo

ſaria di peggio, quanto ella del fauor veniſe mā
cando, & coſi ſenza hauer cio meritato altra
mente, portarebbe vna pena la piu grauoſa, che
foſſe. & quanti ſono quelli, diſſe il S. Carlo,
che tutto il di a torto patiſcono, benche queſto
non vi doueſſe parer vn coſi gran torto, ſe ſco
ſtandoſi da qualche uno la Fortuna, ſenza mo-
uergli in altro l'honor ſuo, ne porta via ſeco quel
la parte, la quale ella ſteſſa apportandogli con
cedette in preſtanza, & non in dono. Alho
ra il S. Leonardo, e ſaria forſe da comportare,
diſſe, ſe non ci toglieſſe piu di quel, che n'è ſuo.
ma vedete, che queſta fugace Dea, partendoſi
da i gran Signori, & per lo piu ſenza dirgli a
Dio, gli ſpoglia di netto ogni honore, tirando
ſi dietro a ſi, non ſolamente il titolo del Fortunatiſſimo, ma quel del Sereniſſimo, Pruden
tiſſimo, Virtuoſiſſimo, & tutti gl'altri, an
chora. adunque, diſſe il S. Carlo, credete, che
il vero honore s'appoggia ſu li titoli ſolamente?
Et con queſto, tacendo egli, o perche penſaſſe a
cio, che gli rimaſe a dire, o uero perche non ha
ueſſe penſiero da dir piu auanti, il S. Leonardo
ſi recò a dire. ſaria ben fatto S. Carlo, che uoi
F iii

in questo termine del uero honore non ui andasti
così in sù la generalità, ma che ne chiaresti
puntalmente in questo passo, accioche noi da
quello a pieno informati, non altramente, che i
litigatori (ab editione actionis) comprendia-
mo, qual sia il nostro migliore, o contendere, o
pure sottoscriuere alli uostri domandi. Ma fin
che uoi non mi indrizzate il giudicio, facendomi a qualche contrasegno discernere il uero honore dal contrafatto, io per me in questo artico
lo non saprò mai come risoluermi, uisto sì uarie
l'opinioni intorno all'honore, riponendolo altri,
nella sola chiarezza del sangue (credendo ferma
mente che gli douesse bastar per sommo honore,
l'essere loro discesi di quelli, chi haueriano sapu
ti far valorosamente, quantunque loro stessi ne
sappiano poco) & altri, senza essere o progna-
ti di uirtuosi, o dotati di uirtù, dalle ricchezze
sole tenendosi honorati, o da trouarsi ad un luo
go honoreuole, et certi anchora senza niente altro, da questo solo sgonfiandosi, che a gran fatica si possono uestirsi da Signori, oltre a questo
tirando l'honore, chi, alli fatti d'arme solamète,
chi solamente alle cose d'ingegno, & di dottri-

na, & così ogni un abbracciando per il uero ho
nore, quello che più ne gli auuien in destro don
de potersi fornire, rifutando poi per contrafatto, tutto quel, di che si troua sfornito. Voi adun
que S. Carlo, poi che hauete allegata la felicità
ne l'honore, mostrateci a qualche indicio mani
festo, qual sia il uero. Questo, disse il S. Car.
è ben peso d'altre spalle, che non sono le mie, pure
poi che io mi troua entrato fin qui in questa impresa, anderò pur sù alli occhi chiusi, quantun
que ben sia da temere, non io per mezzo d'honore riceua uergogna. Certo è adunque, che
le cose da uoi racconte, come sono la nobiltà del
parentaggio, le ricchezze, il magistrato, & altre simili, le quali così possono auenire a gli huo
mini uilissimi, come alli uirtuosi, ben possono
elle riputarsi per grandissimi ornamenti dello
honore, ma l'istessa sostanza di quello, non è pos
sibile, che consista in qualche cosa esterna, la
qual non sia propriamente dell'huomo, ma in
quella sola, che l'huomo dentro a se stesso possiede, per mezzo o de l'animo, o ueramente del corpo, cioè la uirtù. Et per mostrar questo, ecco
ui che l'esser ad un magistrato (per proporci

F　iiii

quello per essempio) non s'è honoreuole da per se
no (come uedemo a infiniti essempii) ma l'esse
re a quello con la uirtù, sì bene. perche la uirtù è da se honoreuole, il magistrato nò, non es
sendolo certamente altro, che un chiaro indicio
atto a palesare così il nostro defetto, come la soffi
cienza, et per conseguenza a recarsi così uitupe
rio, come honore. L'honore dunque se n'è posato
solamente nella uirtù, si manifesta poi a gli segni esterni, li quali incontrandosi a i sensi nostri fannoci scorgere l'altrui uirtù. Et che que
ste cose esterne, come dir le ricchezze, gl'uffi-
cii, & altri simili, uniuersalmente si riputa
no per l'istesso honore, questo non procede d'altro,
che dall'ignoranza del uolgo, il quale tanto è
egli grosso, che non sappia, come distinguere fra
gli segni delle cose, & le cose istesse. L'honor
adunque s'è fondato unicamente nelle operatio
ni uirtuose, & quelle, o le sono dell'animo, o ueramente del corpo, & primo in quanto a quelle del corpo, benche l'huomo non ne habbia nessu
na, nella quale non sia di gran lunga auanzato
dell'altri animali, pur nò è per questo, che di quel
le non si uenga a cauare qualche honore, essendo

quello un sopra auanzare fra quei della sua spe
cie. Ma per tornare una uolta all'honore in
sopremo grado perfetto, quello è secondo me il
potere in quella istessa cosa, per la quale gli huomini passano tutti gli altri animali, andare
inanzi anchor a gli huomini istessi, cioè l'inge
gno. Et qui facendo il S. Carlo un poco di pau
sa, il S. Leonardo, non so anchora, disse, doue che mettere questo perfetto honore, & prima quanto all'ingegno dubito assai, come sara
atto a capirlo, hauendoci uoi auanti deriua
to l'honore della uirtù, & l'ingegno (sapite-
che egli si annouera fra le cose tramezzanti, non
mica più accostanti alla uirtù, che al uitio.
et di questo ben ne potria darui in essempio mol
ti, i quali ualendosi da un ingegno acutissimo
s'hanno procacciati, che per conto d'honore, saria
assai meglio per loro, se pazzi ne fossero nati.
Ma uoi S. Carlo, credo che in questo motto d'in
gegno, intendiate di quello, che con la uirtù s'è
accompagnato, ma anchora mi par, che stiamo
troppo in sù l'uniuersale, complicandosi dentro
questo termine del uirtuoso ingegno, molte spe-
tie, & quelle frase diuersissime. sapete quan-

94

to son tra se differenti l'esser faceto, & l'essere
prudente, & pur sono amendue cose d'ingegno
& di virtu. In questa difficultà, rispose il S.
Carlo, facilmente troueremo il groppo, dicendo, che gl'ingegni sieno da piu, o meno da tenersi, secondo che piu o meno s'indrizzano al'
honorato fine, cioè, secondo che, piu o meno con-
feriscono alla humana societa in questo viuer politico. Come il prudente, il cui ingegno tien piu
del giudicio, & ha per fine l'utile, si preferisce
al faceto, il qual sa piu de l'inuentione, & ha
per suo fine il diletteuole. Perche la moltitudine, della cui bocca depende l'honore, sempre am-
mira piu quelli, da quali maggior vtilità nè
sente in se stessa diriuarsi. & però essendo il gouerno, cosa sopra tutte l'altre necessaria alla humana specie, per cotenerla in questa sua vita po-
litica, astenendola da quella confusione, nella
quale al primo si trouò impacciata, menando veramente vna vita saluatica a guisa gli animali bruti, meritamente la prudenza de i gran
Principi, et altri magistrati, che sopra ciò sono,
ua inanzi a tutte quante le altre sorti d'honore.
Et essendo dopò il gouerno la secoda vtilità quel

la delle buone scienze per ammaestrar elle li huomini, come gouernarsi, il secondo honore s'è ri-
serbato a coloro, chi in quelle sono stati o sian piu
eccellenti, secondo che in cose piu importanti si
hanno affaticati. & cosi scorrendo tutti quanti i gradi di huomini, sempre trouerremo vera
questa regola, che quanto piu giouino in vniuersale, tanto piu vengono ad esser vniuersal-
mente honorati. Non si puo negar, disse il S.
Leonardo, che questa regola nò tenga del ragioneuole, pure gli essempii, mi pare, sono troppo in
contrario, in tanto che anchora questi duoi, i-
quali c'hauete produtti alla conferma di quella,
drittamente la vengono ad infirmare. Che si nò
fosse vn poco fuor di proposito, il voler adesso ragionare de i magistrati & scrittori, io con questi duo essempii ruinarci del tutto quella uostra
cotanto salda regola. conciosia che chiaro è, come ditete voi, che fra questi duoi piu giouino i
magistrati, che i scrittori non fanno: per quanto egli ne sia cosa piu gioueuole il ben fare, che
non sia il ben dire. niente di manco vedemo, che
i scrittori rimanghino con piu chiaro grido, che
non essi gli magistrati. Voi sapete di quanti cō

soli & Tribuni ne ricorda in Liuio, delli quali
la fama è offuscata & quasi che annullata, la
doue la sua resta fin qui chiarissima. & la ragione, perche cosi sia, si potrebbe assignar questa.
che i fatti non durino mai nel suo essere, senon
in quanto sono in punto di fare, doue i scrit-
ti restino sempre in quella medesima forma, la
qual gli è stata imposta dal primo suo autore.
nella quale parlandoci di continuo quelli diuini
spiriti, forza è, che si conseruino appresso di noi
in vna piu fresca memoria, che non sono quelli, di cui ne parlano. Voi fate, disse il S. Carlo,
tra il ben dire, & il ben fare vna comparatione troppo disuguale, affrontando i mezzani nel
l'uno con vn'eccellentissimo nell'altro. ma non
però haurete fatto nulla, perche l'essere i scrittori piu famosi de i magistrati, nò ui gioua punto a prouare, che sieno piu honoreuoli di quelli, et
non è da determinare cosi d'honore, che consista
nel tenersi noi in piu chiara o fresca memoria appresso gli huomini (perche a questo modo il Ne-
rone saria il piu honoreuole Imperatore quasi di
tutti gli altri) ma nel tenersi in vna piu gran
de estimatione di virtu. et non c'è credo io nessu

suno, il qual ricordandosi d'un qual si uoglia cō-
sole, che a quell'ufficio fosse sacente, non giudi-
chi quello cotal Console, douer esser stato al suo
tempo huomo di maggior virtu, che non fu T.
Liuio nel suo. Alhora il S. Paolo troppo è lungo, disse, questo discorso, di volerne intrare per
adesso, & io per ritrarui di queste strauagan-
ti questionelle per le quali gia vn pezzo mi par,
che sete trasportati, verrò drittamente incontra al uostro honore, il qual che non si douesse
accontare per la felicità, a molte conietture parmi piu che manifesto, et in prima, al modo istesso d'ottenerlo. acquistandoci noi l'honore, a guisa, che nel Nilo beuè il cane, cioè fuggendo-
lo. perche sapete, che quelli veramente si trouā-
no honorati, i quali mostrandosi schifi d'honore, facciano il bene per fine dell'istesso bene, oue
quelli chi con braccie aperte gli si facciano incontra, ne trouano cosi uote le mani, come fa il
Tatalo le sue, delle mele fugaci, di sorte che, ben
è stato comparato l'honore all'ombra. perche oltre ad essere tutte due cose senza sostanza, s'as-
somigliano anchora in questo, che fuggono a-
mendui, quello, che gli seguita, seguendo poi

quello, che gli fugge. Et però non vedo gia io,
come sia possibile di godersi a pieno quella felicità, la qual bisogna sempre fuggirla per haver-
la. Anchora che questo mi fa sospicar, non
l'honore sia pur cosa mala, non essendo mai dis-
dicevole a nessuno il perseguire il bene. Ultima
mente come volete, che l'honore si debba stimare
per la felicità, non havendolo qualche esistentia
nella persona honorata, ne manco in se stesso non
essendolo altro, che una certa comparatione, nel
la quale una cosa si preferisce ad una altra. don
de, chi fra gli huomini di più bassa conditione
ben furono honorati, fra gli altri poi, di più alto
grado, che non sono stati loro, si cacciono in die
tro, & quelli si preferiscono. a tal che la felicità
d'un honorato, si può dir, che in se stessa non sia
cosa veruna, ma che il suo essere, o non essere, di
penda del tutto di quello, a che lo vien compara
to. la qual instabilità, non conuien a nessun mo
do con la natura della felicità, la qual sempre
si volesser cosa certa da se, & chi ne vuol esser
felice, dee havern un certo habito dentro a se
stesso, ilche chi si potrebbe mai sperare dall'hono
re, non essendolo in se stesso cosa nessuna, et si ben

fosse, havendolo voi così attaccato a gli dubiosi
accidenti della fortuna, che quantunque l'huo
mo n'habbia guadagnato assai, non ne possa pe
rò mai tenerne conto, come di cosa sua, ma si co
me nel giuoco delle carte veggiamo entravenir
ci, doue in un partito di più giochi nessun se ne co
ta mai per vincitore, per haverne uinto la mag
gior parte, finche non sia compiutamente arri
uo tutto il partito, così ne più ne meno in questo
giuoco della nostra uita, a tanto che non ne sia
giunto il fine, nessun si faccia conto d'haver gua
dagnato l'honore, potendo sempre la fortuna la
qual in questo giuoco, di continuo fa le carte a
modo suo, ogni hora che le piace darti per un
Re, un Fante, & guastarti in un punto,
(si come le più delle volte si piglia spasso di fa
re) quanto tu ti haresti auanzato per lo a die
tro. L'honore dunque, il qual non torna mai per
fetto inanzi la morte, mi par che giungerà un
poco tardo per farci felici in questa uita. donde
io a quel, che voi così distesamente c'hauete ra
gionato, cioè che gli huomini desiderano l'hono
re, come l'ultimo fine, in due parole respond en-
doui, diria, che essendo l'honore di quella qua-

lità, della qual io vi l'ho dissegnata, questo fac
ciono loro, non guidati di qualche regola o giu
dicio, ma suiati d'uno vano & sfrenato appe
tito. Allhora il S. T. Moro, a queste ultime
parole di S. Paolo, disse, per quanto io n'ho com
preso, parmi, che voi S. Carlo alla difesa della
vostra felicità, poco vi sete auanzato dal dimo-
strarci, che gli huomini propostosi hanno l'honore per il fine loro, conciosia che non ui basta,
che così facciano gli huomini, ma vi conuiene
anchor instruirci, che lo facciano da huomini,
cioè usandoui la ragione. Questa non mi sia
cosa malaguole a fare, disse il S. Carlo ne mai
sara fra gli huomini, chi mi negherà, che l'honore a buona ragione sia da preporre a tutte
l'altre cose, vistone, che Iddio istesso, del suo ho
nore fassi più conto, che di altra qual si uoglia
cosa. In tanto che hauendoci egli, per i nostri
bisogni conceduto in dono questa così vaga stan
za del mondo, non ne ricerca poi altro prezzo
da, noi che l'honore solo, del qual (dice di se
stesso) è tanto geloso che a gli huomini più facil
mente perdona ogni lor fallo, che quello d'haver
gli tolto il suo honore, per darlo ad un altro, non
vero

vero Iddio. V i par dunque, che l'essempio d'un
si gran authore, non sia degno d'esser imitato
da noi altri? certo se voi negarete, io espressamente ui farò vedere, che Iddio istesso con un
suo dono grandissimo c'habbia inuitati ad imi-
tarlo. Non ui ricordate Signori, che M. Do-
menedio, fra gli altri suoi infiniti beneficii, uno
ci ha dato per il più principale, cioè una tale e
cellentia sopra a tutti quanti gli altri animali.
et l'honore, che cosa altra è egli, che un eccellere,
et preferirsi alli altri. Inuitati dunque, & del
essempio, et del dono del nostro S. Iddio, cofessia
mo l'honore per il sommo bene di questa vita.
Et ben mi par cosa giustissima il voler farlo, es
sendo l'honore quello, che in tutto ci conserua
questo nostro viver politico, senza il quale, non
dureria un fiato. Ditemi pero leuatoci l'hono
re, qual saria chi s'impacciarebbe nel gouerno
di tanta moltitudine? chi s'affaticarebbe nel
compor libri? chi (per finir in una parola) si
metterebbe a far cosa, che giouasse altrui? cer
to che io credo nessuno. Riconosceteui adunque
l'honore per la nostra felicità, se non vinti alle
sue giuste ragioni, al manco piegati alli receuu

G

ti suoi beneficii, che si ne restaste anchor duri,
eccoui che quasi in aggiunta, Vi voglio adesso
addurre vna ragione, contra alla quale, non vo
lendoui voi quasi accozzarui all'espressa uerità,
non haureste riparo, et è questa, che contentan
dosi l'anima, solamente delle cose che sono, si co
me essa, infinite, ne mai a pieno sodisfacedosi di
cosa della quale si possa scorgere il fine, non vi re
sta al mondo altro da contentarla, fuor che l'ho
nor solo, perche a chi non è manifesto, che l'ho
nor (doue tutte l'altre cose con la morte si termi
nano) non che passi di là a quel termine egli, ma
ancora, a guisa la Fenice tra le cose terrestre per
la morte, rinasce piu viuo, che mai. Et que
sto frà gl'intendenti giudici, quali ui sete voi,
parmi che douesse bastar, per conseruar all'i
stesso honore, l'honor suo, & però (non forse la
mia difesa d'honore, diuentasse cosi infinita, co
me è la sua virtù) io con questo, che la sua lode,
non habbia fine nessuno, fo fine di lodarlo. Al
lhora tacendo gl'altri, il S. T. Moro, honore
uol mente da douero, disse, difeso v'hauete il
uostro honore. pure io dubito, non questa uostra
difesa (a guisa tutte le cose honorate, che nõ con

sistono, senon nella apparenza) sia piu honora
ta, che vera. Però vegniamo a considerarne
tutte le parti a vna a vna. Et primo, Iddio
istesso, (dite voi) tanto s'è vago del honor suo
che d'infiniti suoi beneficii uerso di noi, non ricer
ca altro guiderdone, di questo solo. Eh S.C.
parui, che il nostro Signore, si faccia tanto con
to dell'honore, che noi gli sappiamo fare, per lo
istesso honore, o per punto di bene, che ne senta
di cio egli, certo voi v'ingannate di gran lun
ga, s'el credete. Per che il nostro celeste padre
non ne fastima per alcun suo comodo, ma per
hauersi a questo modo vna arra del nostro buon
amore verso di se, nel quale solo (dice egli stesso)
resta tutta la legge, & qnanto egli ne ricerca
da noi. Perche non hauendoci noi cattiuelli, al
tro, che dargli, senon l'honor solo, questo, quan
do diamoglielo volentieri, gratiosamente l'ac
cetta, non gia per l'istesso dono, ma per esserlo
vna salda testimonianza della nostra affezzio
ne verso di lui, & per dimostranza, che si
come gli doniamo quello, cosi gli daremmo cosa
di maggior neruo, se per noi si potesse dare.
Che s'il sommo Iddio si dilettasse de i nostri pic

cioli seruigii per conto del'honore, staria fresco
egli di questo suo deletto, hauendosi il mondo
da qui a picciola hora a ruinarsi tutto, & men
tre dura, non pagandogliene noi la terza par
te questo tributo, & quella ancho che gli si pa
ga, pagandol cosi malamente, et con tante uil
lanie, che non ui saria tal gentilhuomo al mon
do di si pouero cuore, che mai si terrebbe per per
sona honorata, senza vendicarsene. Ma poi, ca
so che io vi concedessi pure, che il nostro Signo
re, il qual merita ogni honore, lo desiderasse per
l'honore stesso, voletene inferir voi per questo,
che noi cattiuelli douessimo fare il medesimo an
chor noi. anzi mi par al contrario, che volen
do il nostro Signore attribuirsene a se ogni hono
re, noi non ne douessimo espettar nulla. Ma id
dio, c'inuita con vn grandissimo dono a far sti
ma del nostro honore, dandoci per vn special be
neficio, vna prerogatiua sopra a tutti gli altri
animali, & l'honore non è altro, che vn sopra
auanzar gl'altri. Vedi in questo troppo s'ingan
na il S. Carlo, mettendone l'eccellere (il che e la
istessa virtù) per l'honore, che non è, se non una
opinione di essa, et puone cosi bene stare senza la

virtù, come la virtù senza ella. Adunque
l'eccellersi noi gl'altri animali, è per il nostro
gradissimo vtile. senza la qual virtù non ci sa
ria ordine, che si alzassimo mai dalla terra per
appoggiarci fin a i cieli, ma che la opinione
di tale virtù, cioè l'honore, ci sia gia necessaria
anch'essa a questo fine, nessun il dica, chi non vo
lesse dire anchora, che il S. IESV CHRI
STO istesso sia scacciato del cielo, il qual, sa
pete, come s'è stato riputato, non che da piu del
li altri animali, ma d'assai manco anchora.
Volete adunque (poi che sete intrato in questo,
di voler all'essempio & dono di Iddio confirma
re il uostro honore,) ch'io ve ne mostri in vna
parola, qual honore Iddio c'habbia apprcuato
col suo essempto, qual ci habbia lasciato per dono,
certo non altro, che quel della Croce. Et qui
pausando il S. T. Moro, et l'altri stando atten
tissimi alle sue parole. M. Lorenzo con viso da
ridere, signori, disse, non vi dissi io al comin
cio, come questo honore del S. Carlo douesse capi
tare ad vn termine simile a quel della croce, che
vi pare hormai egli, non è stata vna profetia
la mia; Madesi, disse, il S. Moro, a punto so

migliante a quella di Pilato , il qual parlando
di Teſu Chriſto , diſſe che ad ogni modo biſognò
di morir qualch'uno per il popolo . Pur tenete-
ui vnpoco cheto M. Lorenzo , & laſciatemi ri
paſſare queſti duoi vltimi argomenti del Sig.
Carlo intorno al merito , & infinità del honore ,
nel primo di quali ci vuol dare ad intendere ,
che da honore ſi deriua a queſta noſtra vita o-
gni ſuo bene . Et ciò , chi gli concederebbe mai ?
anzi ſi vede , che la coſa và tutta in contrario ,
& che tutte le ſciagure , tutti i ruinamenti ,
che hoggidi , piu che per lo paſſato , ſi vedono per
l'uniuerſo mondo , non ſi prouengono d'altro , che
da queſto ſconcio & ingordo appetito d'honore .
Et per non partirmi io nel moſtrar queſto da i
produtti eſſempi , chi poſſa mai ſenza lagrime
ridurſi a memoria , come i Principi Chriſtiani
con vna vana maſchera d'honore , dandoſi ſem
pre ad aggrandirſi , s'hāno procacciati in tanto ,
che la Chriſtianità n'è diuenuta picciola , ſquar
ciandola eſſi con li lor proprii artigli la maggior
parte , et laſciando l'auanzo in preda al Turco ,
non potendo loro (ſia a Dio Piaccia) per l'honor
ſuo attēdere all'honor di Chriſto , del qual ſuo ho

nore , che che ne dee parer nel lor ſciocco giudicio ,
da quel giudicio , che ne farà il ſommo giudice ,
Iddio ci guardi . Il ſecōdo eſſempio , fu de i ſcrit
tori . Et qui , chi ſaprà mai dire il gran male ,
che partorì al mondo , la ſmiſurata ambitione
di coſtoro , i quali mentre che pongono ogni lor
forza nel ridurre , non le ſue opinioni alla veri
tà , ma la verità alle ſue opinioni , eccoui qual
mente nella legge diuina , & humana , contra
l'eſpreſſo comandamento delli authori dell'vna ,
et dell'altra , tante intrighe ne hanno fatte , go
riandoſi quelli nelle ſtrane opinioni , queſti nel
li ſingolari intelletti , che doue amendue le leggi , ſon fatte ſolamente per inſegnarſi , l'una del
uoler di Dio l'altra del equo et buono , horamai
mercè del buon gouerno delli eſpoſitori , ne reſtia
mo piu incerti , che mai . Et da tutto queſto ,
do la cauſa a queſto benedetto d'honore , nè mi
ſo , che altra coſa ne poſſa eſſer ſtata la cagione ,
perche dura coſa m'è a credere , che frà noi , eſſen
doci ragioneuoli , nelle coſe piu ragioneuoli di tut
te l'altre , mai ſaria apparſa tanta diſcordanza ,
quando hauremmo uoluti ſeguir la ragione piu
toſto , che tirarla . Eccoui S. Carlo , come rie

G iiii

ſcono bene l'attioni , le quali s'indrizzano a que
ſto uoſtro berſaglio dell'honore , ciò che , non ſola
mete in queſti ſopra allegat'eſſempii , ma in tut
ti gli altri ancora ſi ſcorge , di ſorte che , eſſami-
nandoui uoi tutte le piu eccellenti operationi del
l'humana vita , le trouareſte tutte quante , ſuia
te del driſto fine , per inuiarſi a queſto . donde
ben n'haueua di che ramaricarſi l'humana vita di queſto maledetto d'honore , a quel modo
che quel Carino Terentiano ſi ſciuccio col Dauo ,
cioè , quod interturbet omnia . Reſtaci ſolamente , l'ultimo uoſtro argomento , che l'honor ,
come priuilegiato ſopra tutte l'altre coſe mon-
dane , habbia forza di rinuiuerci dopo la morte ,
ilche , come ſia uero , toſto lo vederemo . Et pri
mieramente , qual ſia quella vita , ch'i morti di
qua viuono , dalla fama de i lor nomi , non m'ho
potuto mai comprendere . perche non eſſendo il
nome parte ſoſtantiale o dell'anima , o del corpo
ad alcuno , oltra a i quali non c'è di dare niente
de l'huomo , non vedo , in che conto , riſpetto a
queſta uita , ſia diſpare hora il uiuere d'Orlando
& di Giulio Ceſare , non ſentendoſi di ſue lodi
adeſſo piu piacere l'un , che l'altro . Ma noi al-

tri ſciocchi mortali , piu che le canne leggieri ,
viſtone come in queſta uita la lode per mezo del
li affetti c'arreca un gran traſtullo , laſcian
doſi ingannare a quel luſingheuole appetito , cre
diamo , che dopò la morte anchora doueſſimo
trarne qualche diletto , non auuedendoci gia ,
che per la morte habbiamo a por giu , con queſta
ſcorza tutti quelli affetti inſieme , per i quali
ſol opera l'honore ce ne porge diletto , & ſenza
i quali , tanto ci poſſa recar piacere , quanto il co
lore ad vn cieco . La quol noſtra uana imagina
tione delle coſe impoſſibili , veramente non s'è al
tro , che vn fabricare caſtelli in aria . Concioſia che la ragione non comporta a neſſun modo ,
che l'anima , hauendoſi a queſto mondo in eter
no detto a Dio , occupata gia tutta nell'eſpettar
quella importante ſentenza del ſommo Iddio ,
s'habbia a far ſtima di quello (ſe ben lo ſentiſſe)
che del fatto ſuo fauella il mondo . del quale ſcor
gendone hora mai la corruttibilità , quella cura
n'ha , che ſi ſuole hauere delle coſe viliſſime Et
qui tacendo il S. T. Moro . il S. Carlo ſtando un
poco ſopra ſe , quaſi dubbioſo , in che riſoluerſi , o
di contraſtare , o pur tacere , all'ultimo , diſſe ,

pensate dunque S. Moro, che l'honore non sia
cosa degna di tenerne conto nessuno? percerto a
questo modo voi v'auilite tutti quei doni, li qua
li i cieli piu, benigni ad vno che ad vn'altro, ci
slargano. perche toltogli questo guiderdone d'ho
nore, non sò, perche altro piu ci douessero esser
chari, non potendosi noi gia seruircene a nien
te. Anzi ad assai, disse il S. T. Mo. Et che?
non credete uoi S. Carlo, che vn'huomo virtuoso
riconoscendo la sua virtù dal vero donatore di
quella, et indrizzandola a quel solo fine di com
piacergliene, non ne espetta con maggior conten
tezza il guiderdone d'immortalita d'un così suf
ficiente pagatore, che non fa colui, il quale in
questo mondo mortale cerca di farsene immor
tale, del quale fra qui a picciola hora, che gli
durerà la vita, sarà, così diuiso che non ne sen
tirà mai piu nouella. Et ben vero, disse Sig.
Carlo, tutto quel che ne dicete. Ma questa è
vna perfettione in sopremo grado. Et noi, re
plicò il S. T. Moro, parliamo delli huomini per
fettissimi. Ma per dare qualche luogo a questi
nostri affetti, mentre che con quelli in vn mo
do inseparabile da noi si viue, ben ui concedo,

che sentendosi dotato qualchun d'ingegno & di
dottrina & altre virtù, ne senta dentro se stes
so una gran festa di contento et d'allegrezza, a
trouarsi tanto aggratiato appresso al suo creato
re, che lo degnasse d'adornar di tante sue gioie.
Ma a chi si mettesse oltre a questo a gloriarsene.
tirandole al fine del suo proprio honore, ben è peri
colo, o che il donatore cancelli a quell'huomo la
donatione per la sua ingratitudine, o che, per
il suo maggior male, preterisca di farlo. Al
lhora, standosi gli altri con grande attentione,
d'udir quello, che il S. Carlo douesse a questo ri
spondere egli con una cortesissima sommissione,
S. Moro, disse, tutto quello, che intorno all'ho
nore c'hauete ragionato, è così vero, che io all'ho
nore istesso, reputo assai piu honoreuole, lo ce
dere alla ragione, che il voler senza ragione piu
oltra contendere. Et così tacque. Quando il
S. T. Moro. uisto che l'hora era tarda, uedete
disse che questi ragionamenti, oltra che il nostro
auiso non istimaua, si son tirati in lungo, e mi
surandomi io quelli d'auenire, a ragione de gli
passati, parmi molto bene da comprendere, che
a fornir compiutamente questa essamina, sta-

remo sino alla notte. Et pero uoi, inanzi che la co
sa vada piu auanti, risoluiate di restarui sta
sera con esso me. & io dalla parte mia per risto
rarui con vna altra promessa, ui do la fede, che
inanzi che sia l'hora da cena, foremo certis
simamente la felicità, percioche a quella hora
voi stessi il rauuedrete qualmente s'incomincie
ra la miseria. A questo, tutti i gentil'huomi
ni ringratiandolo sommamente dell'inuito, ri
sposero che farebbono vie piu, che volentieri, quan
to egli ne richiedeua, ouc il lor bisogno non gli
stringesse a casa, dode non s'eran partiti la mat
tina, senon col pensiere di ritornarui la sera.
Et oltre a questo, soggionse il S. Piero, di M.
Loren. io son certissimo, che, come che uoi la fa
cesti restar quà sta notte, tutto il mondo non lo
disporrebbe a dormir quà, di cui sapete ben l'an
tico statuto, come non s'addormenta mai senon
a canto alla sua felicità, non che tre mila disco
sto. In quanto a questo rispose M. Loren. cre
do che i ricchi nel dormire, si lasciano piu facil
mente scantonarsi dalla sua felicità, che non
facciate uoi inamorati dalla nostra. Et a que
sto modo motteggiandogli vn poco insieme, a

l'ultimo il S. T. Moro, veggendo che erano pur
disposti a partire. Hor su, disse, di quanto v'ho
richiesto (per quello che mi pare) non volete sta
sera far nulla, & per certo io me ne sdirei
quando non credessi che le uostre scuse fossero giu
stissime. Ma hauendole (se come l'ho) per ue
re, per non preferire io il mio contento, al uostro
commodo, lascio per questa sera, l'andare, o
lo stare, al uostro arbitrio, si veramente, che
mi promettiate ogni modo di tornare tutti di
brigata domane a desinare. A questo, tutti
senza farsene molto pregare, rissosero che uolen
tieri, fuor che il S. Carlo solo, il qual vn poco
rispettoso, cominciò ad ordire nuoue scuse. a cui
il S. Moro piaceuolmente, & mezo sorridendo,
Charo S. Carlo disse, lasciate, di gratia, le cere
monie a coloro, chi fanno piu stima di cortesia
che d'amicitia, i quali però come si siano corte
si, nol sò, perche, essendo la cortesia vn portar
si con ogniun secondo che si conuiene, a me ne
pare tanta discortesia, il mostrarsi riguardeuoli
verso gl'intrinseci, come verso forestieri saria
il dimenarsi senza rispetto. Alhora il S. Car
lo calando della sua stranezza. S. Moro, disse,

qualmente io con voi, così in altri conti, come in
questi inuiti, sempre son stato poco rispettoso, uoi
senza che io uel ricordi, da uoi lo sapete . Vero
è, ch'io haueua a spedire domane una certa pro
cura , la quale percioche non è delle più importanti del mondo, si differirà senza danno veruno
no , & così domesticamente , risolse il S. T. Mo
ro alsì . Di che egli forte contento , basta disse , che pure all'ultimo siamo d'accordo . Ma
quantunque voi (mercè della uostra saluati-
chezza) v'hauete tenuto l'inuito , alla solenni,
nulla dimeno io ve ne farò un côuito alla schiet
ta , & come soglio fare con gl'amici . Ma se
voi disse M. Lorenzo , trattate meglio i uostri
nimici, io mi uerrò come un di questi io . Sì che
soglio, rispose il S. T. Moro , & sapete poi chi so
no i mei nimici , quelli che mi trattano a guisa
che soleua quel Eutrapile i suoi . Rise a questo il
S. Piero , & disse . con questa risposta uoi hauete fatta la pace con M. Lorenzo , stateui siguu-
ro , non uerrà mai egli da uostro nimico . A
questo poi che egli si fu alquanto riso i gentil'huomini , visto che l'intrateneuano dallo studio ,
preso dal S. T. Moro commiato , in una sua bar

chetta che a posta gli badaua , montarono , &
essendogli il viaggio si per la piaceuolezza del
fresco , si per i sollazzeuoli ragionamen
ti , molto aggradeuole , quasi pri
ma che pensassero , si furono a Lon-
dra .

IL MORO
D'HELISEO
HEIVODO
INGLESE.

∞

LIBRO SECONDO.

ORNATI il giorno
seguente secondo l'ordi-
ne posto i gentil'huomi-
ni , & dopo la conueneuo
le accoglieza arriuati da
desinare , a passo a passo,
si come il di dauanti ha-
ueuano fatto, tutti se ne
andarono al giardino , là doue , poi che spasseg-
giando l'hebbero , quasi due volte attorniato , si
ridussero dentro al pratello , & postisi a seder là
espettando gia ogniun , chi douesse primo dar
dentro

dentro alli gia tralasciati ragionamenti , stet
tero così a bada , che per un pezo non si sentiua
fra loro pur una minima parola, quando M. Lo
renzo cominciò fra se un poco a sorridere , dissi-
mulando però , & tenendo tutta uia la mano
al uiso, per farlo più copertamente, pur non lo sep
pe si fare, che il S. Pie. non sene venne accorgen
do, il quale sorridendo anchora egli un cotal poc
colin ; charo M. Lorenzo , disse , se Dio vi fac
cia ben , diteci quello , che ridete , & fatene ri
dere anchora noi , perche altramente vi terre-
mo per un troppo inuidioso , se di questo allegro
pensiero, non ci degnate la nostra parte, potendo ben farlo senza punto sminuire la uostra.
La cagione del mio riso , disse , Messer Lorenzo , poi che volete , che io ve'l dica fuor fuora , non è stato altro , ch'il pensarmi io , a i casi
uostri, et per diruilo a buona chiera, parmi fuor
d'ogni canneuolezza , che uoi habbiate a discor
rere di cosa cotanto uana, come è l'amore, mas
simamente in presenza di così contegnosi giudi
ci , & dopo sì graui ragionamenti , come sono
stati quelli d'hiersera . Vero è , rispose il S. Pie
ro , che i giudici sono molto da riuerire , et i pas

H

fati ragionamenti fono ftati grauiffimi, di for
te che, hauendomi io da produrre adeffo questo
ignudo fanciullino di Venere, meritamente du
bitarei, non lo fueniffi di vergogna, fe nō mi raf
ficuraffe, contra la uoftra prefenza, la fua cecità
et cōtra alli paffati difcorfi, il nō efferne niuno,
chi pelo pelo gli rileua nulla. In quant'alli paf
ti ragionamenti, diffe, M. Lorenzo, ben ui po
tete racconfolarui per un'altro uerfo, perche, l'a
more, per quanto alli inutili prieghi delli aman
ti n'ho comprefo io, quanto e cieco, tanto è egli
fordo, & voleffe Dio, che foffe ancora mutolo.
Se non l'udiffi gia io fteffo, diffe, il S. Piero, mai
non mi farebbe potuto capir nella tefta, che tra
gl'huomini foffe trouato qualchun si inhuma
no, che contra all'ifteffo Amore portaffe odio.
Ma a fua pofta, io non per questo rimarrommi
dall'impresa di inalzare la gran potenza d'A
more, il qual fo ben quanti nimici s'ha foggio
gato, & quelli piu poffenti che non è M. Loren
zo. Ne di lui anchora dubito, di ueder, quando
che fia, questo fuo agghiacciato cuore, cosi rifcal
dato alle amorofe fiamme, che ne lafcierà queste
fue biancheggianti montagnette d'argento, non

altramente che la neue si ftrugge al fole, confu
marsi alli raggi delli bei occhi di qualche vaga
dōna. In buona fe, diffe M.L. quād'io mi lafciaf
fi a tāta fmania trafcorrere, faria degno di pa
garne'l fio, fi come coloro: che per qualche fuo grā
fallo si condannano in una groffa quantità di cō
tanti. Ma non ui date di ciò maninconia, che
io me ne guarderò di cofi fatto capriccio, come
dal mal del capo. Et qui effendo gia il S. Pie
ro per cominciar il fuo ragionamento, M. Lo
renzo recatofi in piedi quafi fi qualche cofa di
fpeciale gratia uoleffe addomandare a gli al
tri, gli chiefe che di gratia lafciaffero a lui fo
lo il carico di combattere contra al S. Piero in
questo conflitto d'Amore, ilche fenza difficul
tà gli fu conceduto. donde affettandofi a guifa
di chi uoleffe contraftare, diffe al S. Piero, che
cominciaffe, il qual rifpoftogli, che uolentieri,
feguitò. Primieramente in questa caufa non po
co m'accrefce il coraggio, lo conofcerla libera d'o
gni pregiudicio di quelli difetti, che in contra
alle gia dette cofe fono ftati allegati, come nelle
ricchezze il defiderarfi per vn altro fine che per
fe fteffe, nell'honore, il non rimaner nella perfo

na honorata, ma nell'opinione d'altri. le quali
cofe, ch'in Amore non uadino del tutto per con
trario filo, neffun il dicagiamai. Hauendo
dunque tolta a defendere questa caufa, liberif
fima d'ogni pregiudicio, io mi terrò per vn igno
rante, fe non la faprò mantenere per buona, ma
a guifa d'un poco prattico auuocato lafciarla in
peggior termine, che non la trouai al primo. Et
maffimamente non hauendo da trattarla con
altri, che con M. Lorenzo, contra a cui s'io con
un cotale argomento da contrarii, comprobaffi
che l'Amor foffe il piu gran bene fra tutti gli
altri, per effer l'odio il piu gran male, non mi
fo, come ragioneuolmente gli uerrebbe contra
detto. Ma a Dio non piaccia, che l'Amore,
a guifa coloro i quali per la viltà delli lor nimi
ci, non per la fua propria uirtu riefcono vinci
tori, s'habbia a uincere in questa proua, & pe
rò, pofto da canto l'odio, nō farò con altro contra
M. Lorenzo, che con amore folo. Et qui reca
tofi vn poco in fe, come fogliono chi qualche lun
go ragionamento fono per cominciare, effendofi
gia le parole quafi per ufcir di bocca, fermate
ui, diffe M. Lorenzo ne fate ftima di conten

tarmi col uoler porre giu l'odio, gia che me n'ha
uete fatto il peggio che potete. Et però tor
nando a quel argomento de i contrarii, vi dico
che m'ingannate pure con l'amore, donde per nō
confondermi uoi da qui inanzi con l'ambiguità
di questo nome d'amore, uoglio prima, che fi
proceda piu oltra, con una aperta diftintione,
et chiarirmi in un tratto del termine, al quale
c'habbiamo a difputare, & incontrar infieme
all'argomento d'i contrarii. Vedete dunque,
che l'Amore due fpecie fotto fe contiene, l'vna
della bontà dell'animo, la quale, a nominarla
propriamente, amicitia fi dimanda, l'altra del
la bellezza del corpo, la quale fattamente fi può
batteggiarfi Amore. L'odio dunque, che non
è altro, che vn certo portar nimicitia in uerfo
altrui, chiaro è, che non fia il contrario d'A
more, ma d'amicitia fi bene. donde effendofi lo
odio in uero vn gran male, ne feguita che l'A
micitia fia un gran bene. Ma fe uogliamo ar
gomentare d'Amore al fuo contrario, vedere
mo tofto come la cofa buttarà tutto in cōtrario.
Perche, L'Amore, che cofa è? Vn infiāmarfi da
tropp'affezzione, verfo la perfona amata. il fuo

contrario poi, che? l'acchetarsi, & non hauer
uene piu là il pensiero? ma questo certamente è
buono, seguita però bene, che il suo contrario
sia malo. Hauete torto, soggiunse il S. Piero
a uoler con una così crudele distintione fra l'a-
micitia, et l'amore, separare come diuerse le cose, che nascono unitaméte da una medesima race. Et che diresti tenendoui a questa uostra distintione, a tutti i ragionamenti di cotanti eccellenti huomini d'hoggidi, i quali trattandosi
dell'Amore, lo congiungono in fine, non che con
l'amicitia, ma con l'. Amore diuino anchora.
Per certo, replicò, M. Lorenzo, io per rispondere a quelli ragionaméti, direi, che gli fossero tutti quanti piu sottili, che veri, & simili a quelli paradossi, ne i quali, con acutezza d'ingegno
si proua il contrario di quello, che tutto il dì si uede in esperienza. Perche oltre che la ragione non
comporti, che con uno medesimo cuore, possiamo
ad un tempo amare due cose diuerse, all'effetto
anchora si uede, qualméte questi duoi amori fra
se s'accozzano, di sorte che, l'un non sottentra
mai il petto ad alcuno, senza o menomare, o
uero smorzare, l'altro. Ma io replicò il S. Pie-

ro, per mezo & della ragione & dell'esperienza vi congiungerò insieme cotesti duoi amori,
& vedrete come s'accorderanno benissimo. Ma
desi, disse, M. L. di gratia Sig. Piero lasciate
questa sottilità alle scole, & ragionateui fra
noi alla schietta, si come habbiamo fatto noi altri. Pigliateui dunque, non uolendo partirui
dal proposito, per uostro amore, quel figliuolo di
Venere, & mostratelo, si come c'hauete detto
di fare, ignudo. Voi mi trattate, disse il S.
Piero, a guisa i piu cortesi ladri sogliono quelli,
chi gli uengono presi. a i quali leuando la miglior parte della lor robba, lasciano il rifutaio
a loro. Ma quantunque voi per questo partito
m'hauete tolto assai, non m'haurete però cotanto sualigiato, che non habbia con che uincerui
in questo cótrasto. Hor per palesarui l'alto ualo-
re d'amore, ancho della bellezza sola, considéra-
teui, che il sommo Iddio hauendoci formato questo mondo in tanta eccellente bellezza, che nella
lingua & greca, & Latina, n'habbia preso
il nome, alla conseruatione di tanta uaghezza
lasciato ci hà l'Amore, come per un suo locotenente, il cui buon gouerno nel suo officio uolendo
H iiii

ui uoi a pieno considerare, guardateui come primo fra gli animanti, quelli anchora, che uiuono dell'anima uegetatiua solamente (di qual sorte sono le piante) quanto la lor pouera conditione comporta, sentono le forze d'Amore. per
le quali approssimandosi alle cose, che con le lor
nature piu conuengano, producono nelle sue sta-
gioni i frutti frondi, et fiori, per adornarne il ua-
go mondo. Digradando poi da questi, alla piu
perfetta sorte d'animali, come sono quelli, chi
la sensitiua anima si sortiscono, scorgereteui,
(quasi di pari crescendo con l'anima l'Amore
insieme) con quanta tenerezza osseruano le sa-
cre leggi d'Amore, rileuando, generando, et
nutricando i parti loro. Ma ultimamente sa-
liendoui piu su, a quella compiuta uita dell'anima ragioneuole, guardate fra l'huomini, quante sono le sue forze, quali gli effetti, recandoci a
tanto l'amore, che in un par delli inamorati, o-
gnun habbia per la sua anima, quella dell'altro,
& ambedue insieme pur una, che le inanimi.
Ne questo ui dee parer strano, se fra gli animali, quelli, che piu participano della ragione, piu
sentono anco d'Amore. perche in uerità la ra-

gione e l'Amore (quantunque alcuni sciocchi
l'hanno tenuti per contrarii) non ad altro modo
fra se son differenti, che sia il genere da una sua
specie. Non essendo altro tutti duoi, che un comprendere il uero essere, l'una d'ogni cosa, l'altro
della bellezza. perche che altro sarà l'amare u-
na donna, che un perfettamente comprendere
quanto sia bella, che se mi direte qui, che l'amore
oltra al scorger la bellezza, sia anchora un desi-
derarla, a ciò ui rispondo, che nel bello il scorger-
lo, & il desiderarlo sia una medesima cosa, ne
mi bisogna credo prouarui questo. percioche essendo il desiderabile l'unica qualità, per la qual
sola il bello si conosce, il conoscer una cosa per bella
non è altro, che il conoscerla per desiderabile, ne
il conoscerla desiderabile, altro, che il desiderar-
la, perche se uolessimo dire, che si potesse qualchü
conoscere una cosa per desiderabile, senza desi-
derarla poi esso, ne seguitaria un inconueniente
grandissimo, cioè, che quel cotale, si persuades-
se ad un tempo di duoi contrarii, come d'esser ad
una hora desiderabile et nõ desiderabile una medesima cosa. Non è perciò altro il desiderar la
bellezza, che il conoscerla. & da questo viene

che i piu ſuegliati ſpiriti, per comprenderſi egli
no piu altamente la perfettione della bellezza,
tanto piu che altri ſe ne inuaghiſcono, la doue
i meno rileuati ingegnii, quaſi per coſa ordi-
naria la trapaſſano. A punto come a gli ri-
guardatori delle eccellenti pitture ſpeſſo vedemo
entrauenire, che gli ignoranti, ſuperficialmen-
te mirandole, preſto ſe ne ſationo, oue i piu intẽ
denti in quella arte, piu intrinſecamente con-
ſideratole, quanto piu fiſſa le riguardono, tanto
piu ne ſtupiſcono, et di piu guardarle ſi rapiſco-
no. Allhora M. Lorenzo, viſto qualmente
il S. Piero s'andaua ſempre piu diſtendendo in
queſto diſcorſo, è meglio, diſſe, che io non per-
metta al S. Piero il ſlargar piu oltra queſto ſuo
paradoſſo, non m'auenga a forſe quello, che intra
uenne a quel ſuo riguardatore della pittura, cioè
che come egli alla proportione di quella reſto ſtor
dito, coſi io alla ſproportione di queſto aſſonto,
tanto mi perda, che non mi poſſa ricouerar a ri-
ſpondergli. Veramente S. Piero, a gran fatica io mi ſon rattemperato da ridere, quando
uoi con una tanta proſopopeia ſublimaſti quel
noſtro amore, ad ufficio del locotenente di Dio,

commendandolo poi dal ſuo buon maneggio di
quel gouerno, il qual, ogni un' ne vede, come
non attende quaſi mai ad altro, che a guaſtar
le leggi diuine, naturali, & humane. Certamente che queſto cieco locotenente di Dio, nõ gli
ſerua mai ad altro, ſenon per tenerlo fuor d'o-
gni luogo, doue egli una volta poſſa ficcarui il
piede. Et ditemi per la uoſtra fe ſinceramen-
te, come credete uoi S. Piero, che penſi alle coſe da Dio quell'huomo, che s'è inamorato da do
uero in una donna? certamente io ſono in queſto
parer come ui diſſi, che non ſia mai poſſibile che
da uno medeſimo cuore, s'amino ad un tempo
due coſe diuerſe. In queſto paſſo, diſſe, il Sig.
Carlo, uoglio aiutare il S. Piero, con l'eſempio
d'una mia nipota, la quale inamorataſi in una
perſona piu vile, che la ſua conditione nol richiedeua, con gran diſpiacere di tutti quanti i
ſuoi parenti, fu una volta confortata molto da
un ſuo padre ſpirituale, che ſi rimaneſſe da queſto
amore, il qual fra li altri mezi che uſo per aſte
nerla dal ſuo propoſito, le domandò coſi, & come credete uoi di potere amare Iddio, amando
contra l'animo del noſtro padre, queſto voſtro

amante? anzi nimico, poi che vi è cagione di
tanto male, & per queſto l'amo, riſpoſe la don
zella, per compiacerne a Dio, il qual, ſapete, co
me c'ha comandato d'amare gli noſtri nimici.
A queſto, poi che fu alquanto riſo, Veramente, diſſe, ridendo M. Lorenzo, che queſta fu u-
na ſanta riſpoſta, ma io temo nõ ella gia haureb
be uolentieri guaſtato un altro di comanda-
menti, per oſſeruare compiutamente queſto, pur
lo rimettiamo a lei, & torniamo drittamente
all'ultima parte del paſſato ragionamento, doue (ſe uogliamo hauer fede alle parole del S. Pie
ro) l'Amore diuenterà una ſpecie di ragione,
ma ò Dio benedetto, quanti ne ſono i quali con
queſta ſpecie di ragione diuẽtano matti? quan
ti anchora, i quali per ſouerchio peſo di queſta
ragione s'appicano per la gola, credo (come ſono
corteſi) per tener compagnia, a quel mio ana-
ro, & non forſe egli ſolo ſenza piu, s'appicaſſe
ſenza propoſito, s'appiccano anchora loro, per a-
more come dicono, pure queſto mi par che tien
piu dell'odio. Eccoui Signori la ragione del S.
P. Che s'io uoleſſi qui contarui partitamente
l'impetuoſità d'Amore, la ſua cecità, l'incer-

tezza, la deſperatione, con tutte le ſue belle par
ti, (perche tutte n'ha a roueſcio di quelle di ragione) ſon certo, che ſubito ſareſte col S. Pie. gri
dãdogli adoſſo che ui haueſſe qui fatta queſta ra
gione, a grandiſſimo torto. Ma accio che la
mia riſpoſta, dallo precedẽte ragionamento nõ
ſi diſlunghi, uogliamo conſiderare un poco ſolamente queſto, cioè come l'Amore ſia un buono conſideratore della bellezza, perche per mezzo di queſta il S. Piero s'ha cercato di congiun-
gerlo in affinità con la ragione. Et che Signori? credete uoi, che l'Amore (come diſſe egli)
ſia un comprendere la uera perfettione della bel
lezza? certe che queſto ſaria un brutto errore
a crederlo, uedendoui uoi ſteſſi tutto il giorno
delli inamorati, i quali vagghegiano non che
le poco amoreuoli donne, ma anchora le piu diſpa
rute, & contrafatte che ſiano. Come poco fa
Checco mio ſeruidore, focoſamente s'acceſe d'u
na, la quale benche non hebbe altro che un occhio in capo, pure egli non haueua altr'occhio in
capo che lei, con cui burlando ſopra queſto ina-
moramento un ſuo compagno, eccoui, diſſe,
quanta cecità s'è nell' Amore, la donna di

Checco non ha senon un occhio, & egli mi pare
che non ha nessuno . Inamorandosi dunque gli
huomini cosi delle brutte donne , come delle bel
le , non accade credo di cercar piu chiaro me\zo
per dimostrarui , che l'Amore non sia un scor
gere la uera perfettione della belle\za , & cosi ,
che non sia da appaiarsi per questo uerso con ragione , si come il S. Pie . s'e ingegnato di persua
derci . Ma uolete hora , che io ui mostri alla
buona , che cosa sia l'Amore , certissimamente
non altro , che un morbo dell'animo , cagiona
to del souerchiante affetto . Perche come negli
humori del corpo souerchiandone qualchuno , ne
partorisce al corpo qualche malattia , cosi tra
gl'affetti dell'animo , passandone qualch'uno il
suo termine , fa nascere una perturbatione , la
quale (non altramente che faccia il morbo al
corpo) disturba l'animo , cacciandolo fuor del
suo naturale stato . Et che questa opinione in
torno all'amore (cioè che nasca dal defetto del-
l'animo nostro piu tosto , che della perfettione
della altrui bellezza) sia piu uera , che la uostra
non è , uedete che gli huomini non s'inamorino
secondo che gli uien uista qualche bellissima don

na , ma secõdo che loro stessi son piu atti ad appic
ciarsi dal fuoco , come assai ne sono i quali , forse
gia mille uolte hauendosi uista qualche donna
senza punto inamorarsene , pure all'ultimo , qua
si gia disposti ad appréndere il male , subito ne l'a
more di lei s'impaniano . Il quale Amore , ma
nifesto è , che non proceda qui della belle\za
della cosa amata , la quale è stata sempre quasi
ad un medesimo termine , ma delli affetti dell'
innamorato , li quali piu ad un tempo , che ad
un altro s'accendono , seguendo la dispositione
del corpo . Non attribuite dunque S. Piero , al
l'Amore tanta accortezza di uista , come sarebbe di comprendere ello il uero essere di qual
si uoglia cosa , ma confessatelo (come al primo
l'hauete introdutto , & come tutti l'introduco
no) per cieco . In buona fe , disse , il S. Paolo
parmi , che M. Loren\zo al scoprire la cecità d'a
more , è stato molto bene occhiato . Ne m'auue
do S. Piero , come ui sia possibile a qualche modo ragioneuole piu oltra defender quel uostro as
sonto , cioè , che l'Amore sia un perfettamen
te scorgere la belle\za , inamorandosi noi cosi
delle brutte , come delle belle , et anchora di quel-

la medesima belle\za inamorandosi piu ad un
tempo , che ad un altro , donde al mio giudicio
questa risposta di M. Lorenzo è stata saldissima
Espettate un poco , disse , il S. Piero , che sopra
di me questa cosi salda risposta , non monterà
niente . Et primo non ui cale Signori ? che dou'io
accoppiaua la ragione con l'Amore pigliando
li tutti duoi nella lor pura natura , M. Lorenzo in quell' essempio delli amatori delle brutte
donne , ui ha repplicato , con un Amore intral
ciato ne i nostri deboli , & ingänneuoli sensi .
Ma sappiateui , che io con una parità u'ho pa-
rangonati queste duoi insieme , come dire , o la
ragione pura col puro Amore , o la ragione humana con l'Amore humano . Et uedete , che
la ragione , considerata come nell'huomo (secon
do ne fece M. Lor. nell' Amore) non sarà ne an
co ella un comprendere il uero in ogni cosa , per
che non fa mai quest' effetto , ingänandosi spesso
l'humana ragione , disorte che nessun se ne sia ,
che del uero non preterisca piu , che non ne sap
pia , o chi nella maggior parte delle cose , non piglia per il uero il drittamente contrario . La
ragione dunque & l'Amore , da per se colte ,
\qquad sono

sono tutte duoi un perfetto compiendere , quella
del uero , questa della uera bellezza . Ma consi
derandoli ne gli huomini , secondo la lor dritta ,
o storta natura , chi l'adoprano , o mancano al
suo effetto , o buttano pure in contrario . Che
pensate Signori ? non credete uoi , che questa so
la distintione bastasse a leuar di netto tutta la
opposta del mio auuersario , per certo , io credo
che uoi , & M. Lorenzo istesso il crediate troppo . Pure per mostrare , che l'Amore (il qua
le aguzza l'ingegno ad ogn'un a trouer scampi
ne i suoi maggior bisogni) non sia di questi lui
stesso cosi pouero , che non ne habbia piu di una
sorte , uoglio in questo ristretto , aiutarlo in un
altro modo , & questo tanto strano , che (quä
li il piu sono tutte le sue inuentioni) parerà al
primo impossibile . Dico dunque che l'amare
qualche un , alcuna brutta donna , non proceda
da altro , che del scorgere ello perfettissimamen
te la sua belle\za . Et per farui piu chiaro que
sto , sappiate primo che fra tutti gl'huomini , o
donne , non u'è forma niuna o tanto perfetta ,
che non s'habbia qualche difetto , o tanto imperfetta , che non habbia in alcuna sua parte
\qquad I

qualche perfettione, di forte che, a chi voleffe
far un uero ritratto di foprema bruttezza, bifo
gnerebbe, (a guifa che fece quel eccellente pit
tor nel ritrarre la perfetta bellezza) d'andar
per diuerfi effempii difegnando da chi la fronte,
da chi il nafo, da un altro la bocca, et cofi, gli
altri membri. Hauendo adunque ogni donna
cofi del bello, come del brutto, di tanta forza
è il bello, che in qualunque picciola particella del
uifo comprefa dall'intendente riguardatore,
dalla rimefcolata bruttezza mai non fi lafcia of
fufcare, ma occupato a chi l'ha comprefa tutt'il
concetto nò lo lafcia riuolgere piu gl'occhi alle fpro
portionate parti, o fe per cafo le riguardi, col lu
ftro delle ben proportionate l'abbelifce, fcufando
le appreffo di fe, et formandole (quanto fia pof
fibile) a ragione di quelle. A punto come nel ri
tratto non troppo fomiglieuole all'originale, ac
cortofene qualcun di picciolifsima che fia raffem
branza, o nell'occhio, o nella bocca. che alquan
to s'accofta a quella, di cui l'è ritratto, preualen
do piu nel fuo concetto il fomigliante, per tro
uar la con che affacciarfi, forma il rimanente
di diffomiglianza a petto a cotefto, et cofi gli pa

re, che quel ritratto raffomiglia pure l'originale
cofa, che un altro, non hauendo prima fcorta
quella proportione, quantunque lo guataffe non
direbbe gia mai. Donde vedemo fpeffe volte che
uno ifteffo ritratto, paia a chi fomiglieuole, a
chino: ciò che accafa parimente nelle donne,
che la medefima apparifca a tale bella, a quale
altro non gia, perche la fomiglianza, et la bel
tade ad un modo s'apprendono, rimanendole a
mendue in una proportione corrifpondente da u
na cofa ad una altra, in quefto folo differifcono,
che il fomiglieuole fia una corrifpondenza da un
indiuiduo ad un altro, et il bello, da un indi
uiduo alla idea della fua fpecie, perche hauendo
fcambieuolmente l'huomo et la donna. impref
fa nell'animo loro, una perfetta forma di quella
fpecie, quefta forma quando gli vien trouata
nelle fattezze d'altri, gl'informa rifolutamen
te quella cotale effer bella. et cofi abbattuto gia
in quello, che andaua cercando, sbalza fuor
dalla tefta ogni altra Idea, eccetto cotefta di
quella donna, contentandofi affai del baratto da
una Idea, per una Dea. A quefto fchernen
do M. Lorenzo, gran cofa, diffe, che gl'inamo

I   ii

rati (a guifa che Gioue s'ingrauido di Pallade)
portino nella tefta una Dea, pure anch'egli mi
par probabile per che eglino fimilmente fentino
gl'affanni del partorire, et fpeffe uolte non ne
vengono a copo, fenza quel minifterio, che col
la fua fcure forni Vulcano a Gioue. Vedete, dif
fe, il S. Piero, a che modo M. Lorenzo, mi rom
pe la tefta con la fcure di Volcano. ma di gratia
foprastateui un poco per veder fe io poffo da me
fteffo partorire quello che ho pofto in animo a dir
ui. Tornando dunque al propofito vi dico, che
molto era fuor di propofito quel uoftr'Vltimo ar
gomento, cioè, che l'Amor non proceda dalla
bellezza, veggendofi noi tanto fpeffo parrecchie
bellifsime donne fenza inamorarfi però, et
anchora inamorandofi di quella medefima bel
lezza piu ad un tempo, che ad un altro. Ma
vedete M. Lorenzo, che uoi fete qui in un grof
fo errore, cogliendo per il medefimo il veder una
bella donna, cioè un corpo materiale, et il fcor
gere la fua bellezza, la qual nò è fenon una fotti
lifsima proportione, et non abbatte a gli no
ftri occhi, fenon a gran uentura. Donde a que
fta uoftra oppofta non rifpondo gia altro, fenon

quello che apunto è fimile ad un bel tratto di Ma
dama la voftra conforte S. T. Moro, il che gia
piu uolte ho hauuto in talento a diruilo. Ella
(leggendous noi alle voftre figliuole, fopra la
materia della linea, et affaticandoui molto
per chiarirle, come foffe una mera lunghezza,
fenz'ogni larghezza o profundità) dopo la lettio
ne, fattole fi chiamare nella fala, le diffe, eh come
fono intendenti le mie figliuole? e bifogna al
lor padre lembicarfi il ceruello una hora inte
ra, per dimoftrarle che cofa fia una linea. ec
coui groffe che uoi fete (et con quefto additan
dole una groffifsima trabe, che attrauerfa la fa
la) quefto diffe, è affatto una linea. A que
fto fu molto rifo di ciafchuno della brigata, et
piu fi faria anchora, fe M. L. nò foffe ftato tanto
frettolofo alla rifpofta, qual riuoltofi al S. P. i
uoftri ragionamenti, diffe, fono ftati tanto fot
tili, che a dirui il uero, io non mi ho potuto ca
pirle troppo bene, pure per quanto mi fuonano le
parole, m'auuifo, che ci vogliate accennare tan
to, che hauendo l'huomo et la dòna da un inftin
to naturale la perfetta ftampa della fua fpecie,
impreffa fcambieuolmente nelli animi loro, lo

I   iii

Amore non ſia altro, che un certo raffigurare
quella proportione, in qualchun indiuiduo. la
qual imaginatione ſi potria forſe defenderſi a
qualche modo, quando gli Amanti ad una ſo
la forma ſi teneſſero fermi, ma eccoui che di con
tinuo ſi volteggiano nel lor giudicio, approban
do hora il viſo lunghetto; hora il ritondetto, ad
un tempo le piu groſſette, ad un altro, le piu
ſcarne & ſottili, & in tal modo per tutto gi-
randoſi in ſul contrario, a tal che io non mi com
prendo bene, qual ſarebbe quella Idea, a che ſi
riportano cotanto in queſti ſuoi inamorazzi, ſe
non foſſe forſe quella della chimera. Ma tempo
è hora mai di ſlanciarſi fuor di queſta ſottilità
per ſcalzare ſciettametnte gl'effetti d'Amore, perche conoſciamo, come gli confacciono con
la felicità. Et primieramente parmi alla chie
ra iſteſſa degli amanti molto ben ſcoprire la lor
poca felicità, nè mai m'è potuto capir nella te-
ſta, in qual maniera il continuo ſoſpirare, il la
grimare, il veggiare, l'eſſere ſoletto, ſieno feli
cità pur troppo grandi, & ſe pur le ſono, vede
te, come io ſono huomo ſcempio, et ſenza ogni
rugineZza, che trouandomi la notte nella piu-

ma o il giorno nella lieta brigata, mai nõ ho por
tato inuidia a queſti felici de gl'inamorati, i
quali accompagnandoſi con gl'uccelli nel boſco o
coricandoſi la notte all'uſcio della lor Dea, tor-
ninſi doppiamente raffreddati, & della ſtagio
ne, et della fredda donna. Et qui diſtende doſ
M. LorenZo come ſe voleſſe ripaſſare il ſpatioſo
campo di ſciagure delli inamorati, il S. Piero
raffrenandolo nel mezo il corſo. M. LorenZo diſ
ſe, queſti diſagii di che patiſcono gl'amanti, co
me dire l'eſſer ſoletto, il lamentarſi, il vegghia
re & altri ſimili non ui ſeruiranno da niente.
Et come? non lo ſapete uoi horamai, qualmen
te habbia maggior garbo il dolce, aggiunto che
vi ſia vn po dell'amaro, & che ogni traſtullo
di queſta vita non ſia in effetto altro, che vn
ſucceſſiuamẽte tramutarſi dall'vno de i contra
rii all altro, come il mangiare, il bere, il ripoſar
ſi non giouino ſenza hauer inanzi ſentito le con
trarie qualità; le quali quanto ſi ſieno in voi
maggiori, tanto nel cedere loro alli ſuoi contra
rii c'arrecano maggior piacere, come il ſouuer
chio della ſete fa piu grato il bere, il troppo af
famarſi piu diletteuole il mangiare. Ne mai

I iiii

ſaria ordine dell'uno ſolo de i contrarii (foſſe pur
la dolceZza iſteſſa) ſenza che ui s'aggiunga de
l'altro, guſtarne piacere neſſuno. Eccoui che
i ſpeciali nelle lor piu perfette confettioni, non le
condiſcono col ſolo zucchero, o mele puro, ma ne
rimeſcolano a queſte, le coſe, che tengono altre
tanto della contraria qualità. quali ſono le ſcor
ze di naranci, di nuoci, frutti mal maturi,
& coſe ſimili, le quali quanto in ſe ſteſſe piu ſono acerbe tanto raddolcite poi, rieſcono piu deli
cate. Penſateui dunque, quanto ſia vn eccel
lente maeſtro, queſto noſtro ſpeciale, dico l'amore, poi che anchora le lagrime, li ſoſpiri, &
affanni, (coſe in ſe ſteſſe acerbiſſime) ſappia
confettare in modo, che (ſe vogliamo hauere fe
de a quelli, chi le prouano) rieſcono dolci ſoſpiri,
dolci affanni, & dolci lagrime. O buono, buo
no, diſſe ſogghignando quà M. L. guardate
ui di gratia, in che modo queſto procurator de
gl'inamorati (non altramente, che ſogliono
eglino ſteſſi) s'ingegna di far melate le ſue paro
le, a fin che io non poneſſi mente all'inganno fat
tomi ſotto. ma non gli uerrà fatto. percio, che
vi vale S. Piero in contra alla mia oppoſta de i

diſagii (di quali ſi patiſce ne l'Amore vn mon
do) il dirmi, che ogni noſtro piacere ne naſca da
i contrarii. Perche qual ſarà colui (ſe non ſia
forſe qualche inamorato) di ſi poco ceruello, come
di concedermi, che all'attriſtarſi, o uero al veg
ghiare, ſia il contrario l'inamorarſi? certo, qua
lunche il dica, io nol crederò giamai. perciocche
ſo ben (& forZa è, che io il ſappia, tante vol
te n'ho fatto la proua) che contra la veglia, o
la triſteZza, no c'è per dileggiarle altro contra
rio, che il ſonno, et l'allegrizza. il voſtro ſpecia
le dunque a far quella ſua delicata confettione
di contrarii, mi par che habbia fatto tutto per
contrario, a punto coſi galante ſpeciale, come
era quel fante di M. Giorgio lo ſpeciale, il qual
concio c'haueſſe per un ſemplicetto un ſeruitiale,
gli ordinò, che il mangiaſſe, poi tornando il
buon huomo, & lamentandoſi della ſpiaceuo
lezza di quella ricetta, il fante portategli la ſe
guente mattina medeſimamente certe pilule,
vedendole che anchora eſſe, ſi dauano per ageuo
lar il corpo, gli preſcriſſe di riceuerle in quel mo
do, che ſi vuol receuere un ſeruitiale. queſta prat
ſica quanto giouo a quel pouer'huomo, tanto fa

l'Amore contra a quei difagii delli mefchini
amatori, li quali non lieua mia vica come vn
contrario, ma (come un maggior male tra quel
li altri minori) fa che non gli fentiamo troppo.
Ma lafciamo da canto i contrarii per tornare
drittamente al propofito. Et primamente non
m'auuedo io (effendo l'intelletto humano cofa co
tanto diuina, come voi fogliate predicarlo) co
me non ne fia vna gran pazzia, il diftorlo da
quel fuo nobiliffimo foggetto, cioè da contempla
re le cofe altiffime, per guatar continuo nel vifo
di qualche doloroſetta femina, & queſto per
vn intento, il piu uile, & beſtiale, che vi fia.
pian M. Lorenzo, diffe a queſto il S. Piero, voi
fete hora mai tanto sbarrato dal dritto, che è
faria gran peccato di slargarui le redine piu ol
tra. chi domine a tro che voi, direbbe mai, che
l'Amore diftoglieffe l'ingegno humano d'ill'al
te imprefe. anzi fi vede, come lo vada deftando
piu tofto ad effe, & quanti fono di quelli, che
fcriuendo, non gia cofaccie, o trufferie, ma ar
gomenti profundi, dotti, & arguti, ricono-
fcono poi d'amore, quanto che ne vagliano. L'in
tento anco d'Amore (per rifponderui a quello)

non è quell'atto, che voi vi imaginate, anzi
tanto ripugnante a queſto, quanto il diletto di
animo al piacere del corpo. Hor'su bene, dif
fe M. Lorenzo, benche io in quanto all'intento
d'Amore, poteſſi preualermi de gl'eſſempii di
tutti quanti inamorati fi trouano, pure nõ m'in
tendo entrare in queſto trattato, ma ponendoci
da canto queſto, di gratia rifpondetemi ad vn
dubio, che hor hora mi è venuto nella fantafia,
cioè, come vi fia poſſibile di ſpiare a queſto cat
tiuello amante, qualche ſpatio commodo di far
lo felice, effendo la felicita vna contentezza di
animo. Perche fin a tanto che gli fia fodisfat
to dell'Amor fuo, rimane egli fempre defidero
fo, nel qual ſtato (effendolo contrario all'effer cõ
tento) non fi puo negare, che non fia mifero, ma
poi che gl'e fodisfatto li quel'amore, non fi puo
dire, che fia felice di quella cofa, della quale non
faccia piu ſtima niuna. A tal che mi pare,
che queſto pouero dell'Amante, per coglierne
la felicità fempre ne giunga per tempo troppo,
o troppo tardo a guiſa che fuole il creditore ve
nire ad un fuo infufficiente debitore, cioè, o inan
zi che s'è leuato, o dapoi che s'è partito da cafa

Vedete, diffe, il S. Piero, quanto s'è follicito al
fatto mio, M. Lorenzo, temendo credo, non mi
mancaffe tempo per cõdurre queſt'amante fino
alla felicità, hauendo egli ſteſſo compartito o-
gni fuo tempo, o al defiderio, o uero alla fatie-
tà, li quali eſtremi fon contrarii tutti duoi alla
contentezza. ma in queſto M. Loren. s'è porta
to troppo ſtremamete cõtra i pouerelli d'inamo
rati. Et non credete voi, che eglino godino con
tanta contentezza l'acquiſto del fuo amore, con
quanto ſtudio fi penauano d'acquiſtarſelo. cer
tiſſimamente che io porto fermiſſima opinione,
che quella contentezza ſopraauanzi di gran lun
ga, ogni altra di queſta uita, & uoi anchora
direte il medefimo, quando vorreſti rimebraru
di che forte nell'amore nõ ci uenga mai fentita
rincrefceuolezza niuna, la doue tutti gli altri
traſtulli preſto ne ſluccano. Ne mai vi hauete vdito chi fi confeffaffe (come del feſteggiare,
& giuocare) cofi d'Amore ancho fatio, o ſtuf
fo. Et queſto, perche l'Amore con maggior
forza, & efficacia entra gl'animi noſtri,
che gl'altri piaceri non fanno, donde fra tutti
i diletti meritamente s'è tenuto per lo maggio-

re, come fra i diſpiaceri quelli fi tengono piu gra
uofi, i quali con piu graue, o lungo martiro ci
affliggono. Allhora M. Lorenzo gnardate,
diffe, come ſtaria ben freſco chi fi fidaffe alle fem
plici parole di queſti inamorati. Mi nega o affa
to hora il S. Piero, che l'Amore fia vn conti
nuo defiderare, come fe egli ſteffo non mi haueſ
fe poco fa conceduto, che l'Amore non era in
effetto altro, che un certo comprendere la bellez
za, ne il comprenderla altro, che un defiderar
la. Che accade adunque piu chiara teſtimonian
za delle fue parole proprie a voler prouare, che
l'Amore fia un perpetuo defiderare. Che fe pur
egli (fi come fpeffo fogliuno queſti amanti) uoleffe uenire contra alle fue proprie parole, la cofa è di fe ſteffa pur troppo manifeſta. perche l'a-
mare che altro è, fe non vn bramare, appetire,
& defiderare. Chiaro è dunque, che l'huomo,
mentre che ami, fempre brami & defideri, &
in quel punto che non brami, o defideri, non fia
cofa poſſibile, che egli piu oltre ami. Et da
queſto, cioè da efferlo vn defiderare, procede,
che l'Amore mai non fatia a guiſa gli altri
piaceri, i quali per effergli vn certo fruire, fa-

tiono, la doue l'amore per esserlo vn pretto deside
rare, non satia egli mai, essendo il desiderio di
rimpetto contrario alla satica. Et qui facen
do festa M. Lorenzo, come s'hauesse vinta la
proua. Non son per anco, disse il S P. in quel
ristretto, al quale voi vi pensate d'hauerme
ne condotto, Eccoui, M. Lorenzo, ch'io non
uoglio ne negarui qualche mio detto, ne manco
concederui il vostro. Vero è, che l'Amore
sia vn continuo desiderio. ne però seguita, che
non sia una perfetta contentezza. ma qui, ui uo
glio auuertire, che il desiderio non e d'una sorte
sola, ma di due, l'una, quando desideriamo co
sa, che ci manca, et questo è propriatamente
desiderio, donde appresso i Latini il desiderare si
gnifica, anco il mancare, poi che ciò, che si desi
dera, sempre ci manchi, et questo desiderio per
esser priuo della cosa desiderata, alla contentez
za e contraria anzi che no. Ma v'e anchora
vn altro desiderio improprio, per il quale ci tro
uiamo inuogliarsi di quello, che pure posseggia
mo, il qual desiderio non solamente non s'e con
trario alla contentezza, ma anchora congiun
tissimo. Perche come volete che l'huomo si con

tenti di quello, che non apprezzi, o desideri.
Et però, come sapete in quella perfettissima con
tentezza della vita eterna l'anime beate a pie
no si contentano nel contemplar la diuina maie
stà, bramando pur tutta via di contemplarla.
Eccoui M. Lorenzo, che questo desiderio non e
punto contrario alla contentezza. Che se io ui
volessi spiegar qui a parte a parte l'inestimabil
gratia di quella donna, la quale con gli suaui
sguardi, accorte parole, dolce riso, et final
mente con debita conueneuolezza in ogni suo at
to, mostra una giustissima, corrisponden-
za, et armonia fra tutte le parti, et de l'ani
mo et del corpo, non dubito, che M. Loren
zo istesso mi concederebbe, che il sentirsi abbrac
ciare nel cuore ad una cosi fatta donna, basta
rebbe a qualunque huomo fosse, per contentarlo
in cosi fatta maniera, che altro non desideri. A
se S. P. disse allhora, M. Lorenzo, hauete tor
to, di voler con la vostra retorica abbagliare gli
occhi a i giudici nostri, pur poi che n'hauete uo
luto con tanti colori sbellettare la bellezza delle
donne (ilche chi le guardasse nel uiso, direbbe,
che non ui fusse di bisogno) io uoglio anco io ac-

comodar qui un poco la mia retorica, per scolrir
ui questa lor slisciata bellezza, et questo suoi
sforzati et solenni portamenti, perche n'ho let
to anch'io la mia parte l'ullio de inuentione,
quantunque voi nol credete. Credemo d'auan
zo, rispose il S. T. M. se ui sete studiato nella re
torica di Cicerone, che n'habbiate letto piu presto
il libro d'inuentione, che quello di Partitione.
Basta disse, M. Lorenzo, et con questo s'asset
taua, come se uolesse ordire vna solenne inuetti
ua contra le donne, quando il S. Piero rompen
dogli le parole nella bocca, M. Lorenzo, disse,
io mi comprendo assai all'incominciamento, il
fine di questo uostro discorso, et però io, senza
che v'affaticate a prouarlo, ui lo concedo, che
l'affettatione sia quello, che fa perder la gratia
ad ogni cosa, et tanto piu, quanto quello, in che
s'adopra, piu douesse procedere da natura, che da
arte, di qual sorte vuol essere la bellezza delle
donne, et per consequente che non sia punto di
accarezzar la bellezza di quelle, le quali, o cō sco
perta affettatione mostrano piu studio, che in
gegno, o con troppa depintura, piu rossore, che
vergogna. Ma ciò che rileua al uituperio di
quelle,

quelle, le quali cō modi leggiadretti, garbati, et
aggratiati, cosi in ogni lor fatto cō una destrez
za ritengono la conueneuolezza, che mostri, come
a quelle, l'istessa Natura la qual le concedeste
tanta bellezza, l'habbia anco amaestrate quel
segreto del come maneggiarla. Et questo basti
ni M. Lorenzo per una breue risposta a ciò, che
ci uoleste dire, a che quantunque il dicesti a lun
go, non risponderia mai altro. Ma hora con uoi
altri Signori ben uoglio ramaricarmi, quali in
questa disputa d'amore, m'hauete assegnato vn
ανταγωνιστα απερον, donde m'è auuenuto a pun
to, come a questi maestri del giuoco d'arma si
suole, a quali abbattendo forse qualche ignoran
te, che disauedutamente, et senza ogni arte
mena le mani, piu gli da briga, et piu gli fa
scordare i precetti dell'arte, che non faria vn'al
tro valente huomo, chi sapesse con giudicio au
uentare, et parare alle coltellate. Parimente
io con questi discorsi di M. Lor. tanto mi son
suiato dal dritto, et da quello ch'io haueua in
animo a dire, che non ne ho quasi toccato niente,
a tal che, se uoi non mi lasciate incominciar
da ricapo questo ragionamento d'Amore, io

K

n'ho poca speranza di far molto in questo giudi
cio, l'hora disse, il S. T. M. è tarda, e molti so
no quelli, ch'attendono anchor'essi per vdienza in
questa materia, di modo che, non c'è ordine per
adesso di uolere ritessere di nuouo la arriuata te
la. ma sapete che sarà? ui faremo questa corte
sia, di limitarui un termine, fra qual habbiate
d'indurre queste nuoue probationi. Questo che
mi giouerà, disse il S. Piero, uolendoui uoi sta
sera sententiar in questa controuersia, la senten
tia rispose, il S. T. Moro non sarà disinitiua,
ne anco tale, che a nessuno più faccia pregiudicio, non che a noi, in quella così giusta allega
tione delli nuoui instruméti trouati. Et però S.
Piero tornandosi questo in nessun pregiudicio uo
stro, & in gran beneficio d'altri, per mostrarui
amoreuole, Iponete da canto l'amore, et non dif
ferite più oltre il S. Alessandro, il qual mi par
che stia apparecchiato, non espettando altro per
cominciar il suo ragionamento, se non, che noi
ponessimo fine al nostro. Sicuramente (disse il
S. Alessandro) assai poco è quello, che io ho in
animo a dirui, ma pure tanto importante, che
io mi stia cò grandissimo desiderio di sentir, che

ne douete rispondere. La mia assertione era, che
la somma felicità di questa vita fosse il sapere,
et io a prouarla non vsarò altro mezzo che que
sto. Voi sapete Signori, come fra le tre sorti di
anima, la ragioneuole, sia il più nobile et più per
fetta che sia, & che l'humana vita non per al
tro rispetto trapassa o quella delle piante, o quella
de i bruti, senon per goder egli la più perfetta
anima. A chi dunq; non e egli manifesto, che
fra gli huomini istessi quelli siano i più felici, i
quali più perfettamente godono quello, per il
qual solo gl'huomini sono più felici delli altri a-
nimanti. Nò mi bisogna credo mostrarui qui
come il solo mezo di goder perfettamente l'anima ragioneuole, & la sua sola sostanza, sia
il sapere, perche questa è cosa da se stessa mani-
festissima, & però vedemo, che come nell'anima vegetatiua le piante naturalmente desiderano l'humor terreno, et come nella sensitiua gli
animali il corporale nutrimento, così ne l'anima ragionale, gli huomini naturalmente ricer-
cano il sapere in tutte le cose sino alle minutissi-
me. Essendo adunque, il sapere il vero nutri
mento de l'anima ragionale chiaro è, che co-

K ii

me l'altre due anime per mancamento, del lor
nudrimeto vengono meno, così anchora l'anima
ragionali per defetto del sapere si languisce et si
strugge, donde mi par bonissima consequenza,
il dire, che gli ignoráti, non solamente non viuo
no felici, ma che (parládo d'humana vita) non
viuons, perche, quantunque non gli manca u-
na anima in genere, pure gli manca ben l'anima in quel eccellente qualità, la qual distingue
gli huomini dalle piante, et da i bruti. Et così,
benche in quanto a l'esser animali, siano ben vi
ui, non è però, che in quáto a l'esser huomini, nò
sian pur morti. In somma la mia sentenza in
torno alla felicità è, che come di questa anima
nostra, alhora che sarà nella sua pura natura, la
sua felicità sia il contemplare in presenza l'i-
stesso Iddio, così di quella (mentre che del corpo
impedita, non arriui a tanta altezza, come di
contemplar il creatore istesso, la prossima felicità sia di considerar le sue opere, dico, questa fabrica dell'vniuerso, la mirabil opera d'un tanto
artefice. Et hauendo così detto il S. Alessan
dro, subito tacque, donde il S. T. Moro, vedendo
nessun che mostrasse di uolersi opporre, gli dis

se, ottimamente in poche parole, prouatoci ha
uete la uostra opinione, intorno al quale, quello
che io ne giudico, uoglio (con la uostra licéza) dif
ferire a dirui, fin all'ultima conchiusione di que
sta disputa. In questo mezzo allegierete il gran
desio che hauete di risposta, col diletto che sentir
te del contrasto che ha da esser fra il S. Paolo, e
il S. Leonardo, in queste sue così ripugnanti opinioni intorno alla felicità, mettendola l'un in o-
gni cosa l'altro in nessuna. In uero disse, il sig.
Leonardo ch'io son stato di questa opinione al pri
mo (ne posso anchor esser d'altra) che la felicità
non sia da restringere dentro ad alcun termine,
ma da mettere ugualmente in ogni cosa, secon
do che più ci va a grado. Et è mi pare che voi
Signori (per diruelo liberalmente) habbiate
tutti quanti gran torto, in uoler restringer la
felicità (essendola cosa generale, e quella che o-
gni bene in se contiene) ad vna sua specie sola
dicendo che la felicità sia o l'amore, o l'honore, le
quali propositioni mi paiono simili a questi. ani
mal est homo. ubi species predicatur de suo ge
nere. Allhora M. Lorenzo, caro S. Alessandro
, disse se ui cal di me gouernate così questa se

K iii

licità, che io n'habbia la mia parte anch'io , sa
pete,com'io, son poco prattico ne i termini d'A
ristotele,et uoi per quanto mi pare , con predica
menti et sillogismi ui disponete a moſtrarci la fe
licità , ma ſe uolete pur far coſì, ditemi al man
co , & io mi partirò da quà per lo mio migliore . perche io mi son certiſſimo, che con coſì fatte diſpute , riuſciria piu toſto matto , che felice .
Non habbiate paura nò , diſse, S. Leonardo per
che toſto v'auuedrete, in che modo io mi ſia per
moſtrarui la mia felicità non che ſenʒa Loica
neſſuna,ma anchora con piu ſemplice modo che
neſſun di uoi fin quì, non ha moſtrata la ſua .
Et pero riſpondami a queſto,qual fra uoi ſi tien
per il piu gran maeſtro, come ſia mai poſſibile,
che, contentandoſi gl'animi noſtri diuerſiſſima
mente, la felicità (la qual è una contentezza
dell'animo) ſia da metterſi in una coſa ſola ſenza piu. & ſe uoi mi negareſti, che foſſe nell'ani
mi noſtri una tal diuerſità intorno al contentarſi, eccoui che io per prouarlo, non mi parte-
ria fuor di queſta brigata, nella quale non v'è
fin qui trouato qualchuno,che in quanto al contentarſi, non ſi diſcordi nel ſuo parer da tutti

gl'altri . Et che dico io de gl'altri, eccoui che
intorno a queſto non c'è neſſun chi non diſcordi
da ſe ſteſſo , recandoſi hora a noia quello che poco fa gli piaceua , et appiacere, quello, che hora
fu , gl'era ſpiaceuole . donde a me ne pare, che la
noſtra vita non ſia in effetto altro, che un conti
nuo andar in cerchio, rinouando ſucceſſiuamen
te il piacere per le medeſime coſe , non altramen
te che nel Zodiaco il ſole per i medeſimi ſegni ri
noual'anno . Adunque la felicità di queſta
vita , non è (ſecondo che io ne giudico) coſa de
terminata in ſe ſteſſa , ma regolata ſecondo le
qualità delli animi noſtri, & per conſeguente
da metterſi ugualmente in ogni coſa, ſecondo
che gli animi noſtri piu ſe ne contentano . Al
lhora il S. A. tacendo gli altri , il S. Leo.diſſe,
con duo mezzi, cio è la generalità di felicità, et
la varietà delli animi noſtri c'ha voluto mo
ſtrare che la felicità non foſſe di mettere in una
coſa ſola , ma in diuerſe, i quali fondamen-
ti ſe io non m'inganno ſono tutti duoi falſi . Et
prima,chi vi cocederebbe, che la felicità foſſe un
nome generale, anʒi vedete, che è ſpecialiſſimo
perche la felicità,come ſapete,non è altro, ch'un

K iiii

ſommo bene, & l'eſſer ſommo(fra le ſpecie d'u
no medeſimo genere) non conuiene a piu che ad
una ſola ,donde queſto primo fondamento, non
che nò màtegne la noſtra aſſertione, ma ancho
ra la ruina affatto. L'altro fu della varietà del
li animi noſtri intorno al contentarſi, il qual an
chora ello s'è molto lontano dal uero, perche eſ
ſendo gl'animi noſtri ragioneuoli , & la deter
minatione di ragione cèrta , & riſoluta in ſe
ſteſſa , non credo, che ſecondo il giudicio de l'ani
mo, poſſiamo proporci piu ſorte di felicità, la
qual non è , ſenon una ſola . Che diremo dunque a quello, che il S. Leo.c'ha moſtrato per eſem
pio, come ogn'un intorno al contentarſi, diſcor
di, non che dagli altri, ma anchora da ſe ſteſſo? Certamente queſto, che il S. Leonardo in
queſto ſuo diſcorſo, per il contento d'animo s'hab
bia tolto in iſcambio, il ſodisfare all'appetito, et
coſì per la felicità, il piacere . Certiſſimamente
diſſe, il S. T. Moro, uoi hauete tocco il chiodo,
& queſto con ſì eſpreſſa verità, che neſſuno (credo io) non che il S. Leonardo ve'l nega-
rebbe giamai . In uero , riſpoſe il S. Leonar .la
riſpoſta del S. Aleſſandro, fu da ſe ſteſſa ueriſ

ſima , & gia che uoi S. M. la hauete ancora aiutata con l'autorità voſtra , rieſce piu che
piu chiara,et però, io per nò affaticarmi in u-
na impreſa impoſſibile , non dirò piu oltre, e coſì
tacque . Quando il S. Paolo , il qual ſedeua ap
preſſo , ſentendo che l'ordine il richiedeua , ſenʒa eſpettar altro inuitamento , a me tocca, diſ
ſe , il moſtrarui che queſta vita ſia priua d'ogni
felicità, intorno a che , ſi poco ſia quel , che mi
è rimaſo a douer dire,ogni un il puo vedere,ha
uendo ciaſcun di uoi, confirmato in parte,queſta
mia opinione & certo io, per prouar che non
foſſe di dare in queſta uita felicità neſſuna, non
ſo che modo , a queſto haueſſi a tener piu diritto,
che il moſtrare, che quei noſtri principali diletti non giouaſſero alla felicità . Ma queſto uoi ſteſ
ſi , la voſtra mercè, ſenza alcuna mia fatica
pienamente c'hauete conceduto . Pure non forſe, vincendo a queſto modo la parte mia, io me
ne reſtaſſi ſenʒa vittoria, anzi con vergogna
per hauerla produtta in campo, ſenʒa darle aiu
to,la accommoderò anco io di qualche argomen
ſo, in queſta ſua felice impreſa , contra la felicità . Et però Signori vi dico, che in vero io

mi marauiglio assai, che hauendoui uoi messa
la felicità nella contentezza d'animo, non ui se
te accorti al primo, quãto era impossibile di tro-
uarla in questa uita, nella quale mai non si troua ne quiete, ne contentezza alcuna, di sorte
che cercandoui uoi tutte quante le sorti d'homi-
ni che al mondo si trouano, non ne trouarete nes
suna, così ben accomodata, che non habbia qual
che suo proprio martello che di perpetuo lo tormenti, & affligi, il pouero combattuto di mil
le urgenti necessità stenta per difetto di danari, il ricco intorbidãdogli la testa, i continoi dan
ni, nimicitie, et liti, si muore di disaggio, la ro
posata uita, e priua d'honore, l'honorata di ri
poso, e così per tutto si vede in ogni stato, che per
ogni sua buona parte, habbiã con una giustissima proportione un altretanto di male. Pensa
te dunque in questa così giusta bilancia di piace
re & noia, qual si debba essere la nostra conten
tezza, essendo l'animo nostro di questa male-
detta natura, che mai nõ pensa se non a quello
solo che ci manchi. Et se bisogna mostrar questo
con essempii, eccoui, che chi ha un podere, gli di
spiace di non potere accoppiarne un'altro, & si-

milmente chi possiede un regno, ne cerca ancho
ra un'altro, & Alessandro Magno, legemo,
che pianse, per non poter all'acquisto dell'uno ag
giungere anchora un'altro mondo, a tal che i
nostri desiderii, sono in se, infiniti, & l'hauere
molto, non e, senon un altretanto raddoppiare
il desiderio. La qual sola indispositione dell'ani
mi nostri uerso la contentezza, da se stessa senza
altro, conuince la nostra poca felicità. Ma la
sciando hora gl'altri mezi, ui uoglio addurne
uno, tanto manifesto, che uoi stessi direte, che
contra di se, non admetta risposta nessuna. Voi
sapete Signori, come questa uita non sia in ef
fetto altro, che un duro esilio, & una grauosa
militia, per ricouerare, in patria. Come uolete dunque, che non sia una impietà grãdissima
il uolerne mettere felicità alcuna, il che per cer
to, non è altro, che un farsi scordare et della no
stra conditione, & del debito insieme, massimamente essendoci noi per il nostro mal'ufficio
in quella prima rotta, per un espresso comman-
damento dall'istesso Iddio, sbanditi di ogni feli
cità di questa uita, & rilegati in una valle
di miseria per stentarci là di disagio, et d'affan

ni, il uoler dunque constituire una felicità in
questa uita, che altro è, ch'un espresso cõtradi-
re alla volontà di Dio, sprezzando il suo giusto
castigamento, a guisa i desperati seruidori, i
quali, castigandogli i patroni per i lor mali por
tamenti, fin che gli doglion le spalle, pur per
gran maluagità mostrano di non curarsene.
Eccoui dunque la gran felicità di questa beata
uita, che se così sapessimo tenere giusto il conto tra il piacere, & la noia, come tra il danno
el lucro sappiamo fare, tosto ci auuedremo, come
del piacere (poi che l'hauessimo affrontato con la
noia) non solamente non soprananzaria niente, ma ci mancheria anchora, per saldar la ra
gione. Non accade qui ch'o vi chiarisca a parte
a parte questo cõto spiegãdoui la nostra imper
fetta fanciullezza, la trauagliosa giouentu, la
debole & inferma vecchiezza, o uero compar
tendo l'huomo in sue parti, mostrarui come l'a
nimo all'infiniti accidenti di Fortuna, il corpo
a continui morbi, & defetti sia sottoposto. Ma
volete che io, con una schietta dimostratione vi
chiarisca, guardate che fra i beni, non ci è
qualchuno sì forte in recar piacere che da sopra-

giungente disgratia non si conuerta in amaritu
dine, ma fra i mali, ben sono di quelli, sì possen
ti in darci noia, che di nessuno quantunque lie-
te accidenti mai si raddolciscono. A questo
mi par manifesto, che questa uita, della sua na
tura, piu tenga dello spiaccuole, che del diletteuo
le. La qual nostra così dura conditione, percerto
non piocede d'altro, che dell'abõdantissima tene
rezza del nostro celeste padre uerso di noi, il qual
temẽdo nõ forse noi, tirati dalla dolcitudine pre
sente, mettessimo in bãdo la uita d'auenir, tem
perato c'ha questa, cõ una aloe amarissima, ac
cio che non ne gustassimo troppo, non altramen
te che facciam noi stessi, con gli nostri figliuoli
in quelli frutti i quali non uolessimo che ne man
giassero troppo. Ma che mi uo io dietro a tante
proue delle sciagure di questa uita, hauendo mi
qui alle mani una, così sofficiente in suo dispreg
gio. Et con questo estendendo la mano, mostrò in
dito un anello inscritto così *MEMENTO*
MORI, et eccoui, disse, Sig. quella, la cui so
la memoria, quando fossero per altro perfettissi
mi, guastarebbe affatto tutti i nostri piaceri, et
tutta la dolcezza di questa uita. Et qui ripau

fandoſi un poco, M. Lorenʒo burlando, com'era
la ſua uſanza, S. Paolo, diſſe, ſe queſto c'ha
uete alle mani ui par come dite, coſi mala coſa,
e tanto inſoporteuole, liberateuene preſto, & là
ſciatene il carico a me, a cui piu peſa l'oro che le
parole non peſano, le quali potria anco intendere per un'altro ſtile, cioè che mi ricordaſſero
non della morte, ma di uoi S. Moro. Certamente io credo, diſſe, il S. Paolo che ſe la morte iſteſſa ueniſſe in perſona, a M. Lorenʒo pre-
ſentandoli de l'oro, li ſaria ella, la ben uenuta.
Ma quantunq; egli nella ſua eſpoſition del ME
MENTO MORI diſmetica la morte, pu
re a chi l'eſponeſſe ſecõdo il ſuo proprio ſenſo, toſto
credo la luſingheuole felicità, della preſente uita
riuſcirebbe in fumo. Et per daruene io un'eſpoſi
tione piu al propoſito, di quella di M. L. ui uoglio
addurr'in queſto caſo di morte, quella uiua ſimi
litudine che uoi ne fate S. T. Moro, in un uoſtro
libro, il qual uoleſſe Iddio, che coſi foſſe ben tra
dotta in lingua pui univerſale come s'è ben ſcrit
ta nella uolgari di queſta Iſola, Io ne uoglio per
adeſſo quella ſola comparatione, oue paragona-
ſte la noſtra conditione con quella di coſtoro, qua

li come conſapeuoli d'un medeſimo crime, tutti
a morte dannati in una ſentenʒa, & fardella
ti inſieme in un carro, ſono in uiaggio per anda
re a giuſtitia, non gia tutti ad un iſteſſo luogo,
ma, al maggior eſſempio, in diuerſiſſime bãde,
come dir, qual'alla piu uicina città, quale piu di
ſcoſto et tale un, alli eſtremi cõfini del regno. Pa
rimente noi, come conſapeuoli in quel primo fallo
d'Adamo, condennati a morte tutti da quel ſu
premo giudice, commeſſi inſieme in un carret-
to, & queſto il piu ratto di ogni altro, cioè quel
lo di tempo, tirandoſi a gran paſſo per una ſtra
da dura, & ruuida, caminiamo inuerſo la mor
te, et ſecondo al Fato, o uer alla Fortuna (quale
ogni di ne mandano ad eſecutione la ſentenʒa)
piu agrada, morimmo tutti, chi piu appreſſo, co
me ne primi anni, chi piu lontano nella meza
età, & alcuni, quali ſon pochiſſimi, nell'eſtre
mo della uita. Torniamo hora Signori alle gia
raccõte felicità, per affrontarle a una a una cõ
queſta ueriſſima ſimilitudine dello preſente ſta
to. Et che credete? che non ſia una grandiſſima
ſciochezza, o quella de i ricchi, i quali per uno
coſi corto uiaggio, fanno una coſi gran lunga

prouiſione, o quella delli honorati, & potenti
Principi, quali tanto ſi dilettano di poter diſpo
re dell'altrui uita nõ ricordandoſi gia, qualmé
te ſiamo tutti quanti ĩ un medeſimo uiaggio,
et che, forſe loro ſteſſi ſiano della prima frutta,
che s'habbia a ſpacciarſi, o uero quella di coloro: i quali nell'amore, o in qualche altro tra
ſtullo attuffano la lor felicità, eſſendogli certiſſi
mi d'arriuar toſto a quel ſegno, il quale, ogni
noſtro piacere o egli fa ceſſare, o conuertire in a-
cerbiſſimo tormento. Certamente Signori io mi
rendo ſiguro, che fra uoi, in queſto paſſo di gia
mi hauete conceduto quanto ho ragionato, ha
uendolo piu che per uero, & però, mi credo di
poter conchiudere, che la conditione di queſta ui
ta, ſia non che felice, ma anchora miſeriſſima
ella. Allhora il S. A. uiſtone come gl'altri ta
ceuano Signori, diſſe, ſariamo tutti quãti da po
co, ſi laſciaſſimo ad un ſolo, eſſendoci cinque,
torci a queſto modo, la noſtra felicità, ſenʒa far
reſiſtenza, o adoprar coſa in noſtro aiuto, et que
ſto, nõ biſognandoci qui fare cõ altro, che con pa
role, e però, poi che uoi in queſta difeſa, non mo
ſtrate di uoler far nulla io breuiſſimamente riſponderò

ſponderò a tutto quello che uoi S. Paolo alla di
feſa c'hauete ragionato, il uoſtro diſcorſo della
infelicità di queſta uita (s'io l'ho ben compre-
ſo) in tre coſe principali s'era fondato, cioè, nella
natural diſcontentezʒa dell'animo noſtro, nella
uedetta fattaci da l'iſteſſo Iddio per il noſtro pri
mo fallo, et ultimamête in quella ſpiaccuole del
la morte, il certiſſimo fine di quanti uiuono.
In quanto al primo, che non ſia di trouar in que
ſla uita, ne contento, ne ſodisfattione d'animo
non ui poſſo mai creder io, uoi m'hauete coſi m'al
ſodisfatto nel prouarlo, uolendoci moſtrar que
ſlo all'eſſempio di coloro, i quali con un inſatia-
bil deſiderio uanno dietro a queſti fumi del mõ
do, i quali in tanta ſua ingordigia, chiaro è,
che non cercano di contentar l'animo, ma l'appetito, il qual non hauendo in ſe termino alcuno, che marauiglia è, ſe mai non uengono a ca
po, di contentarlo. Ma quantunque queſti in
uano s'affaticano, i quali tenendo la ſtrada del
ſuo appetito, uanno cercando la contentezza,
non è però, che quelli, che ragioneuolmente la
cerchino, non la trouino facilmente. Et ben ui
poteſſi indur qui l'eſempii di molti ſauii, i qua-

L

li conoscendo il suo stato quanto era in se stesso
perfetto, a pieno si son contentati di quello, come di cosa vera, & certa, facendo gran riso,
poi di coloro, i quali, per il suo contento, pendono
tutti, non dal suo proprio, ma d'altrui giudicio, & fauore, & quello anchora cotale, che
non habbia in se, un giudicio stabile, ma fondato sopra l'appetito. Vedete S. Paolo, che ci
son ben di quelli che si contentano pure, in questa
vita, & si voi mi replicate, che questi, sono
in numero assai pochi, vi rispondo, che anchora il numero di quelli che si possono chiamar felici, in questa vita, non sia grande, anzi piccio-
lissimo. Resta che io mi venga a quello, oue
uoi confugiendo per aiuto a l'ira, & allo sde-
gno di Dio, affirmateci, che il nostro Signore,
per i nostri mali meriti, ci habbia rilegati in
questa valle, ripiena di miserie, per castigar-
ci, & farci stentare di disagii, & non per la-
sciarci godere nessuna felicità. In che dire, non
so come consentirui, ne mi par ragioneuole il uoler dire, che Iddio c'habbia conceduto questo cosi vaga stanza del mondo, ripieno di tutte le cose deletteuole, per farne il contrario effetto, non

hauendo egli mai fatto cosa in vano. Ben vi
voglio concedere, che la felicità preparatici in
questa vita, sia per il nostro primo fallo in gran
parte sminuita, & fatta piu difficile ad hauere, ma che sia in tutto leuata via, nessun il dica. Et non vi ricordate S. Paolo (poi che hauete voluto metter le mani, nelle cose della sacra
scrittura) quanti vi sono, i quali, seguendo i
commandamenti di Dio, da lui stesso, si confer-
mono per felici, in questo mondo, loro, e tutta la
sua posterità. Non vi souuiene anchora, quante volte, il sommo Iddio, della sua propria bocca, prometta a coloro, che osseruino i suoi sacri
precetti, di fargli benedetti, & crescergli in
figliuoli, in frumento, in vino, in oleo, & altri beni temporali, i quali se a nessun modo gio-
uassero alla felicità, non so come questa promessa, non saria vana, & senza effetto, forza è
dunque che confessiamo (per questo solo rispetto)
una felicità di questa vita, non volendo dire,
che il nostro celeste padre nel suo testamento ci
habbia fatto per utile, un lasso, di nessuna im-
portanza. Ma oltre a tutto questo, vedete S.
Paolo, che quantunque io vi concedessi pure, che,

L ij

per il nostro primo eccesso, ci fosse tolta ogni felicità di questa vita, questo che importeria alla
nostra presente conditione, essendoci gia doppo
quella sdegnosa emancipatione, receuuti di nuouo in figliuoli per una solenne adoptione cele-
brata co'l'istesso sangue del sommo Iddio. Vedete dunque S. Paolo, che il tenerci noi felici, in
questa vita, di tanti benificii, del nostro padre
verso di noi, non sarà egli come a uoi ne pare,
impietà nessuna, ne un farsi scordar la nostra
conditione o il debito ufficio verso di lui, anzi
al contrario un vero scorgersi dell'uno, & del
l'altro, hauendoci noi ad amare, et reuerir Iddio, per merito de i receuuti beneficii, come figliuoli, & non per paura del castigo, come
schiaui. Et questo bastiui, per risposta a quanto intorno alle cose di Theologia c'hauete ragionato. Ma che dirò gia io a quel uostro tanto spauenteuole discorso, sopra la morte? la cui sola
memoria, dite voi, e tanto rincresceuole &
noiosa, che se la vita nostra ben fosse per altro
dolcissima, questa sola basterebbe ad inacerbirla
tutta. In che dire mi pare, che noi habbiate
grandissimo torto, a volerci priuare della nostra

felicità, con la memoria di quella cosa, della
quale siamo tutti quanti smemoratissimi. Voi
sapete S. Paolo, quanto poco conto facciamo della morte, alla quale non habbiamo quasi mai
il pensiere, o se per sorte ne pensiamo qualche uolta, nol facciamo con alcun disturbo dell'animo
ma con quella stima, che si suol hauere nelle cose
che non importano troppo. Che si cosi non fosse, anzi se cosi fississimo ricordeuoli della morte, che quasi ogni hora ne pensassimo, non è però (non di
partendoci noi, in questo pensiere dalla ragione) che ci turbassimo punto. Et che S. P. credete voi, che la morte, sia cosa tanto spauenteuole,
come le uostre parole l'hanno rappresentata, certo v'ingannate se'l credete, che nella morte non
v'è quasi altro male, fuor che il nostro vano timore. Ne questo mi fa bisogno, credo, di prouare in casa del S. T. Moro, doue non si legge
mai altro, ch'i libri di quelli eccellentissimi huomini, i quali con suoi chiarissimi ragionamenti & essempii c'hanno fatti toccare, et uedere,
come nella morte (fuor che il suo horribil aspet-
to) non v'è altro male, la qual a guisa una spa-
uenteuol maschera, mostrando di fuori una gra-

L iii

diſſima apparenza di coſa horribiliſſima, è ue
ramente da temerſi, di dentro guardata, ſubi
toſi ſcuopre per uana, & lontaniſſima da quel
lo che appareua d'eſſere. Non penſate però, S.
Paolo con queſta maſchera, a guiſa che co i fan
ciulli ſi ſuol fare, di ſpauentarci tanto, che come
perſi non habbiamo che dire. Che proua dunque
contra la dolcezza di queſta uita, quella noſtra
ſimilitudine de i condannati? niente certo, per
che ſe la uita noſtra, non è altro in effetto, che
un uiaggio alla morte, la morte poi, che coſa
altra è, che una entrata alla uita, che hauemo dunque qui di contriſtarci della morte, della quale con ragione penſandone, potremmo eſ
ſer ſicuriſſimi, che quando che uenga ci ſia per
fare aſſai piu utile, che danno. Et però io, an
co con la morte iſteſſa, uorria combatter que
ſto, che la cõditione della preſente uita, foſſe pur
felice. Nel combatter con la morte, diſſe il Sig.
Paolo, uoi non guadagnereſti nulla, oue il me
glio che ſi puo ſperare, è il poter fugire, et con
queſto s'aſſettaua, come ſi uoleſſe cõ la fierezza
della morte, replicare contra alla riſpoſta del S.
Aleſſandro. Ma M. Lorenzo, al qual non

era troppo a grado il ſentir ſimili ragionamenti, S. Paolo, diſſe, non ui contentate di ha-
uerci gia trafitti in quella amara comparatione, ſenza che ui torniate anchora a darci la
morte una altra uolta? baſtiui di gratia che
n'habbiate una uolta guaſta la legge del S. T.
Moro, ſenza che uoi con nucue repliche, conti-
nuate il fallo, che ſe tanto ui uada a grado que
ſta ſpiaceuole della morte, tenetela per uoi, &
abbracciatela quanto ui piace ſenza inuidia, et
laſciateci goder uoi la felicità. A queſto ſorridendo gli altri, confirmando, anzi che no la
ſentenza di M. Lorenzo, il S. Paolo, poi che pu
re ui piace, diſſe, con queſte uane felicità, di-
uentar felici, a quel modo, che i fanciulli con
le lor contrafatte gioie, diuentano ricchi, &
io ui laſcierò a uoſtro modo. Ma di queſto mi
rendo ſicuro, che il S. Moro, quando le uerrà a ri
paſſare, ne ſia per fare il conto per un'altro mo
do. A che il S. T. Moro per certo S. P. diſſe,
ſe ui cerchiate quà, il mio giudicio, io non poſſo, ne con uoi, ne con coſtoro accordarmi, intor
no alla felicità, perche quantunque nelle gia det
te coſe non ſia da mettere alcuna felicità, non pe-

rò ne ſeguiterà, che non ſene poſſa trouar neſſuna. Et per moſtrarui queſto, io uoglio di nuouo addurre una felicità, tanto in ſe perfetta,
che contra a quella, uoi ſteſſi me'l concederete
che tutto il uoſtro ragionamento, non habbia
luogo neſſuno. Et con queſto recatoſi in ſe, dopo alquanto coſi cominciò. Meritamente ſaria
da dubitare, donde auerrebbe, che gli huomini
eſſendo gli fra tutti animali, ſoli ragioneuol, inõ
dimeno, ne i ſuoi deſiri piu tengono dell'irragiõ
neuole, che gli animali bruti, non fanno ne i
ſuoi, perche doue queſti, ordinatamente diſtin
guendo fra i ſuoi piaceri, perfettamente fruiſco
no, ſecondo la lor poccezza, la dolcezza della
lor uita, l'huomo in far queſto continuamente
s'inganna, o preponendo ſempre il minor diletto a i maggiori, o pure per piacere, accettando
il drittamente contrario. Queſto non fa di biſogno, che io ui moſtri hora con eſſempii, ueden
doui uoi tutto il di, come gli huomini mettono
piu felicità, nel acquiſtar le ricchezze, che non
ſano ne l'uſarle piu nella faticoſa uita che nella
ripoſata, piu nel apparer a gli altri, che nel ſen
tirſi bene in ſe ſteſſi. I quali diſegni quanto ſia

no del tutto repugnanti alla ragione, noi ſteſſi
della noſtra propria bocca il confeſſiamo, diſpreg
giando ſolennemente, quante uolte ne uien occaſione, a uiltà delle ricchezze, et il ſumo di que
ſt'honori, del qual ſumo però hauemo tutti quan
ti coſi pieni gli ecchi, che non ueggiamo il chia
ro fuoco, che dentro u'arde, & in queſto troppo è da ridere il fatto noſtro, non trouandoſi fra
noi neſſuno, il qual in queſte due coſe preteriſca
mai l'occaſione, o di diſpreggiarle, o di cercar-
le. Ma di tutto queſto, do la cauſa a quel ma
ladetto del noſtro appetito, il qual ne i noſtri pen
ſieri tanto ſoprabonda che non ci laſcia uedere a
pieno i raggi della ragione, ma a guiſa che al
cune uolte ſotto una nebbia ſi uede il ſole, con
una luce coſi ambigua che ci pare di uederlo, et
non uederlo a un tempo, coſi a punto la ragione, ſotto la folta nebbia del noſtro appetito c'ap
pare con un lume coſi debole, che con le parole la
confeſſiamo, negandolo poi ne i fatti, oue ſe la
uedeſſimo a pieno (eſſendoci ragioneuoli) la con
feſſaremo per tutto. Per uoler adunque penetra
re ſino alla felicità, ſecõdo me, nõ reſta altro che
fare, che ſapere il come giudicioſamente diſtin-

re tra la ragione, & l'appetito. Ma questo non
è mica cosa ageuole ad aspirarne, anzi piu ma-
lageuole, che nessuna altra. Percioche quantunque si combattono tra loro la ragione, & lo
appetito come contrarii, nientedimeno non ne
va tra essi, per il stilo di tutti gli altri contrarii, oue allo sminuimento dell'uno, scorgesi infal-
libilmente il soperchiamento de l'altro, & tan
to piu, in quanto ne diuenga piu straboccante
la sproportione. Hor nell'appetito, & la ragio
ne, ogni cosa passa a rouescio, oue quanto sia
maggior il mancamento della ragione, tanto
si sente meno, venendo manco in questo scemo
quella istessa cosa, per la quale sola si douesse sco
prire il defetto. Donde auuiene egli spesse volte, che tra i nostri desiri, quelli che piu si sono lon
tani da ogni ragione, piu ostinamente gli man
teniamo per ragioneuoli. Ma lasciando per ho
ra questo, torniamo a cercar della felicità, &
primamente che la residenza della felicità si con
stituisca nell'animo solo, et uoi il concedete tut
ti, & è da se stesso manifestissimo, percioche o-
gni nostro, o bene, o male che traggiamo in que
sta vita, percerto non ha altra dependenza che

dell'esso animo, in tanto che gl'istessi affanni,
o piaceri del corpo, non ci uagliono punto opera
re l'effetto loro, inanzi che l'animo ne uenga ad
accettargli per noiose, o uer piaceuole. Ilche con
l'essempio d'un metecatto, possi all'occhio dimo
strare, il quale per gagliardi ch'habbia i sensi
pur, per non possederlo il giudicio dell'animo, no
si risente alle battiture noia alcuna. Che se la fe
licità nostra, fosse posta in altro che nell'animo
solo, so che saremmo ben acconci, essendosi tut
te le altre cose, eccetto solo l'animo, sottoposte a
i continui riuolgimenti, sino a i cieli istessi. Ma
in ciò ben c'è dimostra fauoreuole alli casi nostri
la comune nostra madre Natura, la quale ha
uendo creato l'huomo di cotanta eccellenza in se
stesso, che ne meritasse quel gran titolo del Mι-
κροκοσμος, non gl'è mancata in su la cosa principali, cioè la sua felicità, ma per là saluezza
d'un tanto thesoro, gl'hà consegnato dentro a se
stesso un bastione minutissimo & inespugnabi-
le, & così fatta, che per entrar fin là, non ui è
altra cosa al mondo fuor che i suoi ministri pro
prii, dico gl'affetti, dal tradimento de i quali
guardandosi bene, per altro, si possa come si dice

dormir di buon sonno. Ben egli è uero, che que
sti suoi famigliari, & dimestichi, sono i piu
disleali, & i piu inchancheriti traditori, che
mai son stati al mondo, di modo che, di continuo si stanno quasi in orecchii, & all'erta, per
poter tradirci, rapportando poi al nostro giudi
cio per la sua instruttione, la bugia in ogn'oc-
correnza. Di sorte, che uoglio dire, è quasi im
possibile di nò allacciarsi taluolta in qualche suo
ordigno, o tradimento. Et pochissimi sono quel
li chi compiutamente n'hano saputi riguardar
si, pure ci sono bene comparsi alcuni, quali sopra questi traditori, con la guida di ragione, gli
hanno tenuto così stretta guardia adosso, che as
saliti poi essi da grauissimi lor tormenti, piu
n'hann' auanzata la felicità loro, a sentirsi uin
citori, che non l'hanno calata a uedersi in dar
no assediati. Ben sta egli dunque logata la fe
licità nell'animo dell'huomo, & però, hor che
habbiamo rimirato il modello, torniamo dritto
a considerar che cosa sia essa felicità. Et per la
sciar qui l'intrighe di coloro (i quali per non ha
uer conosciuto l'ultimo bene, con sottili discorsi
intorno a questa materia ci hanno lasciata vna

felicità piu facile a mostrare con argomenti, che
a fruire coll'effetto) io vi dico schiettamente,
che (secondo me) la felicità, non sia gia altro
(il che uoi anchora di gia n'hauete confessato
tutti) che l'istessa contentezza d'ell'animo.
Ben vi voglio qui auuertire, che il contentarsi
ad un certo termine, consista, non solamente
in non desiderare piu oltra (perche questo si puo
dir piu tosto, che sia, un non esser misero, ch'un
esser felice) ma anchora nel comprendere, qual
mente, oltre a quel termine, non ui è da desiderar piu niente. Et però gli bruti animali, quan
do da vn instinto naturale, se ne fermano ad
vn certo termine, non si dicono percio eglino, con
tentarsi di quello, del qual non possono disconten
tarsi. Ma l'huomo solo si contenta, il qual per
mezo di ragione risolue la sua volunta, del termino a che s'habbia a fermarsi, come all'ultimo fine. Quella adunque ben è d'ogni perfettio
ne compiuta felicità, qual'hora l'huomo a pie
no si contenti d'un certo bene, comprendendo per-
fettissimamente, perche il sia l'ultimo & sopremo, che si possa desiderare. Non ci bisogna
quà, credo Signori, che io parlandoui, come di

ce il prouerbio , a lettere diſcatole , ui faccia an
chora piu chiaró di quello ch'io ne vorrei per que
ſto ragguagliarui . Perche, che coſa ſarà gia
mai in tutto l'uniuerſo , di qualita per appog
giar all'altezza del ſommo & vltimo bene, ec
cetto quel ſolo , da cui proceda, & a cui s'indriz
za ogni altro bene , dico l'altiſſimo , & vnico
Iddio, qual è ogni coſa in ſe ſteſſo, et in cui ſi tro
ua perfettiſſima contentezza , & fuor di cui
non v'è di dare , ne contentezza , ne ſodisfattio
ne alcuna . Et però io me ne do grandiſſima ma
rauiglia Signori del fatto noſtro , che hauendo
ci noi fra noi , per adietro , tante uolte , & con
ſi chiari ragionamenti , conchiuſo in queſta ma
teria , qualmente non ui foſſe altra felicità del
l'huomo , che il ſolo contentarſi in Dio, come in
queſti ragionamenti , u'ha ſcappata le mani,
una coſi chiara , & eſpreſſa uerità . A queſto
tacendo gl'altri , & quaſi mezo confeſſando di
eſſer ſtati in errore , il S. Aleſſandro , anchora
oſtinato in ſu la ſua credenza , S. M. diſſe , Se
la noſtra diſputa , foſſe ſtata della felicità in ge
nere , gran traſcuraggine ſaria ſtata la noſtra
d'hauerne mai confeſſata altra , di quella che

voi ce ne hauete aſſegnata . Ma hauendoci noi
in queſta diſputa, ragionati di felicità ſolamen
te della preſente vita , non ſo anchora come
ſarà poſſibile di metterla in altro che nel ſapere
& il dirmi qui , che queſta ſia una imperfetta
felicità , oue la voſtra è perfettiſſima , non ri
lieua niente , con ciò ſia coſa che la preſente vi
ta non comporta altra felicità , ſe non quella che
ſia conforme alla ſua conditione. In oltre a que
ſto , eſſendo la felicità vn fruire , il che non è , ſe
non delle coſe preſenti , come haurà qui luogo la
voſtra felicità , la quale non è , ſe non vna ſpe
ranza delle coſe future . Vltimamente, la con
tentezza , di queſta vita , è vn riſoluere la
noſtra volontà per mezo della ragione , ma ve
dete che nella felicità da voi racconta , abon
doniamo la ragione , comprendendola per la fe
de ſola . Le coſe adunque diuine (per quanto a
me ne pare) all'hora ſaranno la noſtra felicità,
quando laſciando ſtar il crederle , verremo a ſa
perle , & in quel mentre , che l'animo noſtro nō
arriui a tanta altezza , biſogna mettere la ſua
felicità, tra le coſe piu baſſe, come ſono quelle , le
quali , per mezo di ragione , poſſono da noi com

prenderſi . Ben è vero , che queſta felicità, a ri
ſpetto quella altra , è inferma & debole , & pe
rò indegna d'eſſer da noi ſeguita , ſenon in quā
to , o giova , o vero non impediſca l'altra . A
queſto ſorridendo il S. Moro , eccoui , diſſe , che
il S. Aleſſandro , v'ha conſegnata vna felici
tà , coſi fatta , che come ne dice egli ſteſſo , non
è ſicuro di goderla troppo . Ma per certo egli è
in vn grandiſſimo errore aſſegnando all'animo
(il qual è ſempre vna coſa medeſima in ſe ſteſ
ſe ſteſſo) due coſe diuerſe per la felicità . Ilche
quanto ſia lontano della ragione ognun il puo ve
dere . Perche come ſia mai poſſibile , che l'animo
ſenza che s'inganni in vna , ſi proponga a due coſe
ſe per il ſuo vltimo bene , o che ſia d'un coſi debo
le giudicio , che mai ſi poſſa hauere per un vlti
mo bene , l'opere di Dio , ſenza accorgerſi tanto ,
che quelle cotali opere ſi deono haure hauute vn
manifattore , il qual ad ogni poſſibilità dee eſ
ſer egli coſa piu nobile , che non ſono l'iſteſſe ope
re . Vedete dunque , che l'animo ſecondo il ſuo
dritto giudicio , non haurà mai piu d'una feli
cità, ne per quella, altro buono , che l'ultimo, cioè
l'iſteſſo Iddio. Che diremo dunque a quello, che il
                                    S. Aleſ-

S. Aleſſandro , ci repplicò delle due diuerſe con
ditioni dell'animo ? certo queſto , che ſecondo le
ſue diuerſe conditioni gli conſtitueremo, non (co
me vuol egli) due diuerſe felicità, ma una ſola,
& duoi diuerſi modi di fruirla, cioè che nel ſuo
perfetto ſtato la ſua felicità ſia il godere imme
diate, la preſenza di Dio, et in queſta imperfet
ta vita, il goderlo per mezo della cognitione delle
ſue opere & delle ſue parole, et di queſti duo me
zi il piu principale e quello delle parole hauendo
ſi elle per il ſuo proprio fine l'inſegnare. Eccoui S.
A. come habbiamo acconcia la noſtra felicità,
di ſorte , che ſia non gia una felicità , ma ſola
mente un mezo ad eſſa . Non mi biſogna credo
riſponderui qui a quella oppoſta , che la conten
tezza in queſta mia felicità, ſia un riſoluerſi per
fede , & non per ragione, perche chi nō s'auue
de , come per queſto rieſca molto piu perfetta, eſ
ſendo la fede coſa piu nobile & piu perfetta, che
la ragione non è , benche ui potria anco moſtra
re , qualmente il riſoluerſi per fede , ſia un vero
riſoluerſi per la ragione . Ma laſciando per ho
ra ogni altra coſa , a quello mi verrò , che voi S.
                                    M

Aleſſandro v'affermate, che la felicità per me
racconta non ſia un fruire, ilche non è ſenon del-
le coſe preſenti, ma ſolamente un ſperare le futu-
re . Et che ? credete che il contentarſi in Dio, nõ
ſia un perfettiſſimamente fruir del bene in que-
ſta vita ? Non piaccia a Dio , che mai ci entri
in cuore un coſì fatto penſiero, che per certo, quan-
do voleſſimo col giudicio riguardare alla noſtra
conditione , ci ſia vie più che manifeſto, qual-
mente queſto ſia il ſolo bene, che poſſiamo in que-
ſta vita fruire . Et quando l'huomo mette la
ſua felicità in qualche altro bene, queſto cer-
tamente non proceda ſenon d'una grandiſſima
ſua traſcuragine , per la quale non comprende
la ſua propria dignità, ne quanto ſia egli più
nobile d'ogni altra creatura , poi che dal ſommo
Iddio ſia creato ad un coſì glorioſo fine, qual è il
contentarſi in Dio . Che ſe appreſſo di ſe eſſami-
naſſe ogniun di noi perfettamente il ſuo ſtato, cõ-
ſiderando qualmente poſſeggia dentro a ſe ſteſſo
vna eterna anima, coſa di tanto ineſtimabile
valuta, che il gouerno di quella ſola di gran
lunga gli ſia di maggiore importãzã, che nõ ſa

rebbe l'acquiſto di tutto quãto il reſto del mõdo,
certamente ogni felicità gli ſaria vana, a riſpet-
to di quella, di ſentirſi hauer logata una ſua coſì
pretioſa gioia. nelle mani di chi l'ha tãto chara,
che poco prezzo gli parſe il ſuo proprio ſangue,
a dare per lo riſcatto di quella . Il quale co-
m'è giuſtiſſimo & vero Iddio, (& con queſto
leuò gl'occhi al cielo) ſecõdo che n'ha promeſſo di
fare . quando l'huomo s'ingegna di offerirgli
queſta anima , teneramente l'abbraccia , riem-
pendola di vna coſì fatta allegrezza , & conſo-
latione, per la ſua diuina potenza, che ne riſen-
ta quell'huomo dentro a ſe una tale felicità, che
da neſſuna mortale lingua a pieno ſi poſſa eſpri-
mere . Et qui ſi tacque il S. T. Moro, laſcian-
do nelli animi di chi l'aſcoltarono vna grandiſ-
ſima ammiratione, per vedergli in che modo cõ
queſte parole, a punto corriſpõdeua la vita di chi
le proſcriuã, la qual ammiratione , nõ dopo gua-
ri , in molti doppii multiplicò la ſua veramente
chriſtiana morte , doue raſſicurandogli la ſua
nettiſſima conſcienza, alla iſteſſo colpo della ſca-
re, con lieto , & aperto uiſo , baſſo il capo, co-
　　　　　　　　　　　M ii

me quello, che per la gran fortitudine dell' ani-
mo in quel eſtremo punto, haueua più ſpe'
ranza di vita , che pau-
ra di morte.

🙰

IL　FINE.

Gli errori.

REGISTRO.

A B C D E F G H I K L M

Tutti sono quaterni, eccetto M,
ch'è duerno.

IN FIORENZA

APPRESSO LORENZO TORRENTINO

M D L V I.